What People Are Saying about *Nonprofit Board Service f*

Nonprofit governance is not easy, but Bob Wittig and Susan Schaefer have made it much more accessible. A reference for both the neophyte and the veteran, this book should be in the hands of every board member. It shows the way to an engaging and rewarding experience—in every detail. Don't miss it.

Fisher Howe
Author of *The Nonprofit Leadership Team: Building the Board-Executive Director Partnership*

Wow—really, wow! Seriously, the most understandable book I've ever seen for board members. Most are so boring, technical, and make presumptions about a newbie's knowledge. Love it, love it.

Lynn O'Connell
Nonprofit Management and Leadership Instructor at Colorado Free University

This uncomplicated, easily digestible book contains practical tools and tips for clarifying the essential building blocks of any mission-driven organization: goals, roles, processes, and relationships. And, using the guiding questions for each of the book's sections will help any board newbie or long-timer sound like a GENIUS!

Andrea Walker
Strategy/Organizational Effectiveness, National Education Association

A very practical go-to, how-to book for wannabe, rookie, and veteran board members. Kudos to Schaefer and Wittig for starting from the premise that the board/organization commitment is totally mutual—meeting the needs of the nonprofit organization can't be separated from meeting the needs of individual board members.

Hope Gleicher
Founding Board Member, Nonprofit Roundtable

Nonprofit Board Service for the GENIUS is an excellent, easy to understand, and illuminating discussion about serving on small- to medium-sized nonprofit boards. It should be required reading for every new board member orientation. I wish this resourceful handbook was available when I started serving on boards more than fifteen years ago. You'll find yourself referring to it again and again.

Suzanne Hazard
Governance Chair, InFaith Community Foundation

What People Are Saying about *Nonprofit Board Service for the GENIUS*...

There is no honor greater than being asked to serve on a nonprofit board...and no regret deeper than accepting without really knowing what you are doing. This is an easy-to-use guide that walks you through the entire experience, so whether you are a newcomer or a veteran, you will know what it takes to serve with confidence and distinction.

Greg Baldwin
President, VolunteerMatch

If you serve, or have ever thought about serving, on a board this is a book you'll always want to keep within arm's reach. It has the answers to any question you might secretly harbor in an easy-to-access, easy-to-follow format.

Terrie Temkin, PhD
Founding Principal, CoreStrategies for Nonprofits, Inc.
Editor and Contributing Author, *You and Your Nonprofit Board*

This must-read guide covers all aspects of board responsibilities and is easy and entertaining to read. It is well organized, includes sample tools and policies, and can be read cover-to-cover or by topics of interest. This insightful guide will give people confidence to take the important step of joining a nonprofit board. If you're considering board service, or are currently on, or work with, a board, this book is for you.

Suzanne B. Laporte
President, Compass

Nonprofit Board Service for the GENIUS *covers a broad range of topics and is full of helpful examples and practical tips. The authors have created a grounded and accessible resource for anyone who serves on a nonprofit board—and especially for those who are new to board service.*

Rick Moyers
Vice President, Programs and Communications, Eugene and Agnes E. Meyer Foundation; Coauthor, *Daring to Lead*

One gem among countless practical, nitty-gritty pearls of wisdom in Susan and Bob's insightful new book, **Nonprofit Board Service for the GENIUS:** *"Finding the right board is akin to finding a spouse." Their latest work is valuable reading for seasoned nonprofit veterans, diligent newcomers, and everyone in between!*

Cynthia Remec
Executive Director, BoardAssist

Nonprofit Board Service

for the GENIUS®

Susan Schaefer, CFRE
Bob Wittig, MBA

FOR THE GENIUS IN ALL OF US™

Nonprofit Board Service for the GENIUS™

One of the **For the GENIUS®** books

Published by
For the GENIUS Press, an imprint of CharityChannel LLC
424 Church Street, Suite 2000
Nashville, TN 37219 USA

ForTheGENIUS.com

Library of Congress Control Number: 2014947757
ISBN Print Book: 978-1-941050-13-2 | ISBN eBook: 978-1-941050-14-9

Printed in the United States of America
10 9 8 7 6 5 4 3 2

This and most For the GENIUS Press books are available at special quantity discounts for bulk purchases for sales promotions, premiums, fundraising, or educational use. For information, contact CharityChannel, 424 Church Street, Suite 2000, Nashville, TN 37219 USA. +1 949-589-5938

Publisher's Acknowledgments

This book was produced by a team dedicated to excellence; please send your feedback to Editors@ForTheGENIUS.com.

Members of the team who produced this book include:

Editors

Acquisitions Editor: Linda Lysakowski

Comprehensive Editor: Lisa Sihvonen-Binder

Copy Editor: Stephen Nill

Production

Book Design: Deborah Perdue

Illustrations: Kimberly O'Reilly

Layout Editor: Joy Metcalf

Administrative

For The GENIUS Press: Stephen Nill, CEO, CharityChannel LLC

Marketing and Public Relations: John Millen and Linda Lysakowski

About the Authors

Susan Schaefer

Susan is a consultant, writer, and speaker who is passionate about the nonprofit sector. Her practical approach to fundraising and board development has made her a frequent presenter at conferences and in classrooms, including a course she teaches at Johns Hopkins University.

In 2001, Susan founded Resource Partners LLC, a consulting firm that provides professional, ethical, and collaborative fundraising counsel to nonprofit organizations. In that role, she works with staff and boards to analyze their financial goals and determine how best to achieve them.

Prior to her consulting career, Susan served as national director, foundations at the United Negro College Fund. There, she helped lead the design and implementation of the historic Gates Millennium Scholars, a $1 billion program funded by the Bill and Melinda Gates Foundation.

Susan co-edited *The Nonprofit Consulting Playbook: Winning Strategies from 25 Leaders in the Field* with Linda Lysakowski, and she was a contributing author to *YOU and Your Nonprofit Board: Advice and Practical Tips from the Field's Top Practitioners, Researchers, and Provocateurs.*

She is an active volunteer, having served as president, development chair, and in multiple other leadership positions on nonprofit boards. She has held the Certified Fund Raising Executive designation since 1999, and has a master's degree in not-for-profit management and a bachelor's degree in English, both from the University of Maryland.

She lives just outside Washington, DC, with her husband and two sons.

Email: susan@ResourcePartnersOnline.com

Website: ResourcePartnersOnline.com

Bob Wittig

While pursuing his MBA, Bob took a course on nonprofit management and was hooked!

Since 2002, Bob has been executive director of the Jovid Foundation in Washington, DC. In addition to grantmaking, he has provided strategic planning, board development, and technical assistance to grantees. He has also hosted a monthly "Lunch Club" for grantee executive directors. In 2009, he founded a similar group for grantee board members.

Prior to Jovid, Bob served as the executive director at Academy of Hope, development director at Joseph's House, and the direct marketing manager at Special Olympics International. In 1992, he was part of the first group of Peace Corps volunteers to serve in Ukraine.

Bob has been a contributing editor to CharityChannel and was a contributing author to *YOU and Your Nonprofit Board: Advice and Practical Tips from the Field's Top Practitioners, Researchers, and Provocateurs.*

Bob's board service includes: founding board member of Mundo Verde Bilingual Public Charter School (treasurer); All Souls Church Unitarian (treasurer); Workforce Organizations for Regional Collaboration; and the Ross Elementary School PTA (treasurer).

Bob has a master's degree in business administration and a bachelor's degree in marketing and finance, both from the University of Wisconsin at Madison. He lives in Washington, DC, with his daughter, Kayla, and their dog, Ellington.

Email: bobwittig@gmail.com

Website: nextgenerationboards.com

Dedication

Susan

To those who prepared me well for board work: my parents, who set my values; my sister, Allison, ever in support of my mission; and my sons, Nathan and Jake, for helping me redefine my vision. And to Rob, whose support has sustained all of these things, and more.

Bob

To my mother, Margot, for always believing in me; my daughter, Kayla, for keeping me on my toes; Joan and David Maxwell for their support and guidance; and my friends and colleagues in the nonprofit sector whose commitment to making the world a better place inspires me.

Authors' Acknowledgments

We want to thank the many nonprofit organizations and leaders whose experiences, successes, and struggles helped guide us with the development and writing of this book. They generously shared information, documents, and experiences, which makes this resource rich with real-life examples.

Next, a special thank you to our nonprofit colleagues who encouraged us to take on this project. Their enthusiasm helped keep us motivated throughout the writing and editing stages. We are deeply privileged and honored to have the opportunity to work in this sector and are grateful to have such supportive peers.

We also owe deep appreciation to our publisher, Stephen Nill, for giving us the opportunity to write this book, and our editing and production team, Linda Lysakowski, Lisa Sihvonen-Binder, Joy Metcalf, and Kim O'Reilly, for supplementing our sometimes-weary eyes.

The book's content would not be as crisp or as thorough if not for the insights of three governance experts who put their all into its review: Rick Moyers, Maureen Robinson, and Fisher Howe. We could not have found a more astute team of readers.

We also relied on the following experts for their wisdom and insights: Anne Schrantz, Stephanie Gerard Cohn, Lisa Landmeier, Benjamin Takis, Marjorie Spitz Nagrotsky, Doug Harbit, and Andrea Walker.

A special thanks to our families and friends for their patience and support while we completed this project.

Finally, we want to applaud and acknowledge the many individuals who consider serving on boards and those who take the plunge. The dedication and oversight of committed board members make nonprofits more stable, sustainable, and impactful. The public depends on them as stewards of the mission and finances. It is our great hope that this book inspires committed and engaged board service.

Contents

Summary of Chapters

Chapter 5
Getting From Here to There: From Candidate to Board Member

How boards recruit new members varies from one organization to the next. Some have formal processes in place, while others will take anyone who says "yes." This chapter lays out various recruitment methods and strategies that can help ensure a thorough and thoughtful screening process both for you and for the board.

Part 2—Hit the Ground Running

This section provides a solid foundation for any new board member. We recommend where to focus your time and energy so you can get off to a great start.

Chapter 6
Ready, Set, Action! Wait, Who Does What?

One of the most debated—and debatable—topics around board service is figuring out who does what, when. This chapter delineates board versus staff roles.

Chapter 7
Board Anatomy 101

This chapter explains the typical ways boards are structured, how volunteers and staff support board activities, and state requirements imposed on nonprofit boards.

Chapter 8
Bylaws, Articles of Incorporation, 990s...Oh My!

A board's oversight roles include ensuring that the nonprofit complies with all legal requirements and submits information as required. This chapter lists those key documents, their purpose, and filing requirements. It also wades into the lively topic of term limits.

Chapter 9
Creating a Roadmap: Strategic Thinking and Planning 91

When boards get involved in planning, they are fulfilling a commitment to organizational health. In this chapter, we examine multiple ways to conduct strategic planning, the board's role in this process, and how to keep the plan alive and useful.

Part 3—Digging In 103

A diligent board member will want a basic understanding of a few key topics: financial literacy, fundraising, risk management, and organizational impact. This section lays the foundation for each.

Chapter 10
Budgets: A Financial Blueprint. 105

Financial oversight requires that every board member has basic financial literacy. This chapter focuses on the budget as the key financial planning document. It lays out a board's role in drafting and approving the budget and how best to monitor it.

Chapter 11
Other Fun Financials 119

Budgets are just the tip of the financial literacy iceberg. Here, we focus on three additional financial statements that form the basis for a board member's regular financial monitoring: cash flow statement, statement of financial position, and statement of activities. We also touch on audits and financial checks and balances.

Chapter 12
From Ambassador to Advocate. 135

Good board members spread the word about their nonprofit and are also willing to advocate to legislators and other decision-makers in support of the organization's work. This chapter provides ideas in support of these key communication roles.

Chapter 13
The "F" Word: Fundraising 147

Fundraising is a dirty word to many! But, it is an expectation
that nearly every board has of its members. This chapter will
explore how members can find ways to help raise funds in a
comfortable way that is tailored to each individual.

Chapter 14
Risk Management: Covering Your Assets 165

Risk management touches nearly all of a board's work.
The best way to manage risk is to develop—and use—solid
policies. Here, we discuss how boards can prepare themselves
for the risky business that is organizational oversight.

Chapter 15
Measuring Organizational Success: The Board's Role. 181

Board involvement in measuring and assessing
organizational impact varies from one board to the next.
Some don't do it at all. Others get too into the weeds. This
chapter lays out the importance of measuring organizational
impact and how the board can incorporate key indicators and
measures into its oversight activities.

Part 4—Behind the Curtain 197

A well-run board requires ongoing behind-the-scenes effort. The chapters in
this section cover activities that might seem mundane, but when done well,
propel board effectiveness and engagement.

Chapter 16
Board Recruitment: The Dating Game 199

For many organizations, board recruitment is done last
minute, often with little strategy. There's nothing more
directly tied to board quality than the thought that goes
into recruiting new members. In this chapter, we will

equip you with the know-how you'll need to improve and strengthen your board's recruitment process.

Chapter 17
Orientation: An Essential Beginning 213

A well-thought-out orientation for new members helps reiterate expectations and gets everyone on the same page. When done right, it can become a key ingredient in helping novices acclimate quickly. This chapter covers the topics and strategies that can help bolster this important introductory period.

Chapter 18
Make Meetings Magical. 221

Board meetings that are effective, efficient, and engaging keep members interested. This chapter focuses on ways to make your meetings meaningful, productive, and a good use of everyone's scarce time.

Part 5—The Care and Feeding of Your Leaders 241

While the executive director (ED) and board chair are two key positions, there's a need for motivated leadership on many levels. This section explores how to support those in charge, develop and sustain a leadership pipeline, and what to do when someone at the helm vacates.

Chapter 19
ED–Chair Partnership: The Dynamic Duo 243

The partnership between the executive director and board chair is an essential ingredient for organizational success and board engagement. This chapter explores what makes this relationship so important, ways the ED and chair can partner and communicate, and what to do if things sour.

Chapter 20
Forget about finance and risk management: This might be the
most complex job board members undertake! This chapter
suggests ways to support and evaluate the executive director,
without micromanaging, and while ensuring accountability.

Chapter 21
As the ultimate "boss," a board is responsible for hiring and
firing the executive director. Either task can be filled with
anxiety...and unexpected opportunity. In this chapter, we
discuss how to prepare for a change in the ED position and
ways to ensure as smooth a transition as possible.

Chapter 22
If either of your chief leaders—the executive director or board
chair—suddenly abandons ship, your organization should
have some sense of what comes next. Here, we discuss the
importance of succession planning and what a board can do
to smooth the way for what has the potential to be the most
uncertain of transitions.

Chapter 23
Boards can be influenced and impacted—for better or for
worse—if the founder is still involved with the organization.
This chapter identifies some of the pluses and minuses to
having a founder-led or -influenced organization.

Board work is a messy process largely because it involves human beings. Structure, procedures, and best practices are important but are useless if the board culture is dysfunctional. We close by exploring why board culture matters, how it impacts board experience, what influences it, and what you can do to change it for the better.

Foreword

There are approximately 1.5 million nonprofit organizations in the US and, from the smallest to the largest, the one thing they all have in common is a governing board.

The need for committed and competent board members is large and unrelenting. When nonprofit leaders are not obsessing about fundraising, they are obsessing about where to find the next great board member. Ever optimistic, nonprofit leaders frequently hope to realize both goals simultaneously and efficiently by finding a board member who checks all the boxes—passionate, generous, and well connected—the "hat trick" of board recruitment.

While this feat is possible, it is far from common. Much more often, the search for good board members involves a steady continuum of effort to identify people who will add value, interest them in joining the board, and then cultivate the knowledge and commitment that will pay dividends in many forms. And when that is done, you get to do it again, and again. Cyril O. Houle, an early and influential writer on the subject of nonprofit governance, captured this effort perfectly when he observed, "a good board is a victory not a gift." Given the effort involved, it is a good thing that the victory, when achieved, is so rewarding.

Most of the resources developed to help guide nonprofits through the board development process are intended primarily for executive directors and the valiant members of nominating committees who keep the process aloft and moving forward. Intended to help them see the process whole and guide them every step of the way, the perspective is typically that of the organization—what it needs from its board, what it should do to prepare, how it should manage the process, how new board members should ideally learn the ropes.

Susan Schaefer and Bob Wittig have done something different. Their book, *Nonprofit Board Service for the GENIUS*, has a different point of departure— the experience of the individual first invited to serve, then tasked with being effective. This book explores the experience of board service, the elements of board development, and the practices that create good governance from that singular perspective. The book covers a lot of ground but the "voice," the situations, and the good advice center on what an individual needs to do, or needs to help his or her colleagues do, to be as effective as possible.

Having spent a good part of my professional life trying to help organizations build the boards they need and deserve, I was relieved and delighted to find a resource that acknowledged from the start that a board begins with individuals who have said "yes" to the invitation to serve and have done it with their eyes and hearts open to what the work entails.

Susan and Bob respect the care and effort an organization has put into the process, even before an invitation is extended to a candidate, but they also understand that beyond the immediate honor of being asked there are many legitimate questions that an individual should ask before accepting, not to mention a little soul searching about fit, personal concerns, and commitment.

This book takes a prospective board candidate through the basics but also through the complete lifecycles of both a board and an organization. In saying "yes", an individual could join a start-up organization with a founder-led board and, with the help of the book, be an effective part of a smooth transition to the board and the organization's next stage of growth. At a different moment or in a different setting, the same individual could find herself in the middle of a leadership transition or on the cusp of a planning process and navigate both with care and confidence. Whatever the circumstances or the challenges, what this board member would always be is someone who is on the right board for the right reasons.

The book is not dogmatic; there are only a few issues on which there is only one answer or one way to go. But underpinning the span of topics the book addresses is a strong belief in the ethical dimension of board work and an equally strong belief in the fundamental goodwill that motivates people to serve. One reason board dysfunction is so demoralizing to experience and shocking to observe is the affront such behavior presents to our collective sense that the people who serve on nonprofit boards have an obligation to bring their best selves to the table.

Susan and Bob have drawn on their knowledge, beliefs, and experiences to write a comprehensive yet thoroughly accessible book that makes it clear that serving on a board is serious work but also a great privilege. In doing this, they encourage the kind of individual performances that add up to the collective power of a great board.

Maureen K. Robinson
Governance consultant and author of *Nonprofit Boards that Work: The End of One-Size-Fits-All Governance*

When you become a board member, you're no ordinary volunteer. The role can bring to light previously unimagined skill sets and networks. It can provide profound joy over the social good you help create for your community. It also comes with its own set of legal and moral responsibilities. Sound overwhelming? It can be, but for the millions of people who find themselves governing nonprofit organizations, serving on a board can be an incredible journey—professionally, personally, and civically.

Many arrive at their first board meeting—or sometimes their twenty-first—unprepared. While there are some terrific resources out there, we craved a comprehensive one that provided the basics in a user-friendly format. We wanted to highlight a board member's ups and downs honestly, in an accessible tone, sprinkled with a bit of humor. After all, those very traits define stellar boards we know: honest, accessible, fun.

Don't get us wrong, board membership is serious business. But, we have found that many resources for new members are piecemeal or academic in their approach. This reference is designed to guide you through the process of searching for a board, your first year of membership, and beyond.

The two of us have studied boards by wearing many respective hats: Bob as nonprofit staffer, executive director (ED), and grant maker; Susan as staffer and nonprofit consultant. Both of us have served on multiple boards as members and officers. What bonded us over the subject of boards was a stint at an adult literacy organization in Washington, DC, where Bob was the ED and Susan held multiple board positions, including chair. As you may know, this ED and board chair partnership is a critical one. It can be stressful at times but also rewarding. Yes, we are still talking to each other many years later!

The board we served on together was evolving, efficient, and energizing. It took a lot of work from a lot of people to create a culture that worked well for the other board members, the staff, and the adult learners served by the organization. Since then, we have longed for a resource that mimics the kind of matter-of-fact conversations that we had at the time about the array of topics that strengthen a board. As our respective careers have relied upon the sound workings of boards, we have remained steadfast in our desire to make the process of educating members as simple as possible.

Why Is It So Critical to Learn about Board Membership?

You are picking up this book at a pivotal time. While nonprofits tend to be viewed more favorably than the corporate and public sectors, there is plenty of skepticism to go around. Because of the special status bestowed on nonprofits by the government, the public tends to hold nonprofits to a higher standard: Consider the nonprofit executive who uses organizational funds to buy a fancy car for personal use rather than for providing food to homeless children. Especially in this age of new economic realities, quality boards can make or break a nonprofit organization. As scarce resources characterize nearly every institution, boards can provide human, financial, professional, and moral depth. We hope to portray a realistic view of board service, with all of the accompanying frustrations and joys.

This book is written for the millions of people who serve on boards or might want to. Along those lines, the book takes on the viewpoint of someone who is just beginning the nonprofit board adventure. We have structured it loosely from these perspectives:

- Candidate's eye view

- New board member's eye view

- Veteran or leader's eye view

If you are considering board service, we hope this book will help guide you through the process of deciding whether or not this is the best way to serve. If you've just joined a board, we hope that this book will help get you off to a great start. And if you have some experience under your belt but your service is less than satisfactory, we hope this book will help get you back on track by providing some suggestions and insights on how to improve board operations and how you as an individual member might engage differently.

Nonprofit board service is a broad topic. Deciding which elements to focus on and in what level of detail was no easy task. However, based on our collective experience of working with hundreds of nonprofits and surveys with those in the field, we believe this book covers content that many nonprofit board members need to know, and will find important and useful.

How Can You Get the Most Out of This Book?

Board service is not necessarily rocket science but it's no cakewalk either! To help you get a good grounding, we begin by helping you determine whether this is a worthy pursuit for you and move sequentially through the stages of nomination, early candidacy, and advanced topics:

- Part 1 helps you assess whether board service is right for you and how to find a personally suitable organization.

- Part 2 identifies areas that will prepare you for your first board meeting.

- Part 3 homes in on the topics that will form the basis of most of your board-level discussions.

- Part 4 takes you behind the scenes of your board meetings and shares the factors that influence the quality of your board's functioning.

- Part 5 shines a light on the many leadership factors that influence boards.

- Part 6 provides an advanced look at how to push your board to the next level.

While we would love it if everyone read this book from cover to cover, it's designed to be read in pieces. If you're a new or inquiring member, you'll likely want to focus most of your attention on the first three parts. If you're already on a board, you might be most interested in Parts 4 through 6. Or, if you are like many board members, having begun your service without much formal preparation, you might look to Parts 2 and 3 to review the basics.

As you learn or refresh your skill sets, we hope you come away with the understanding that no board is perfect. And, you don't need to be the chair to make positive change. Every member has a powerful contribution to make. You don't have to be a star in every arena, but grab an issue or two and make it happen! Throughout the book, we provide examples of inspiration or even genius from real organizations (names have been changed to protect the innocent!). We also alert you to what hasn't worked so well and what to avoid. All of these vignettes are designed to show that board work can be a messy process and that you can be creative and take measured risks.

We also provide several document templates that might benefit your board. Encourage yours to revise or adapt our samples, so you don't have to start from scratch.

A few more tips to keep in mind:

- There are many different kinds of nonprofit agencies. Our focus is primarily those that are tax-exempt, 501(c)(3) organizations.

- The information here is geared toward those who oversee small and mid-sized organizations, those that make up the majority of the nonprofit sector. That said, larger organizations could also benefit from most of the information.

- We use the term executive director (ED) to refer to the staff leader. While organizations may refer to their leaders by many different names, we have chosen to use ED because of its popularity among small and mid-sized nonprofits, which make up the bulk of organizations in this country.

No book of reasonable length could cover all of the details you need to know in depth. We have attempted to cover the most relevant and pragmatic information that comes across most board members' desks. Use the material here as a basis for questions and further reading. If your board has done little in the way of formally orienting its members, consider asking everyone to read select chapters for group discussion. That's one way of raising the bar and providing the kind of continuous improvement we advocate. There's no better way for you and your peers to bond and strengthen the organization you love.

Boards do serious work and have important responsibilities. Yet you can, and should, have fun as a board member. We hope this book's spirited tone will follow you to the boardroom.

For more information and additional resources, go to nonprofitboardgenius.com.

Susan Schaefer
Bethesda, MD
susan@resourcepartnersonline.com

Bob Wittig
Washington, DC
bobwittig@gmail.com

Board Service with Your Eyes Wide Open

We begin with what to expect as you consider nonprofit board service. Plenty of new members approach their positions with a heavy dose of emotion. We love that approach but think that the happiest board members throw in a thoughtful analysis of their own preferences and limitations as well. Our goal is to help you confirm your reasons for serving, find the best board for you, and prepare you for your first meeting. If this section causes you to decide that this experience is not for you—either now or down the road—all the better. If you decide to move forward, buckle up. You're in for what could be one of the most rewarding—and challenging—experiences of your volunteer life.

Chapter 1

Why Would Anyone Want to Serve on a Nonprofit Board?

In This Chapter...

- What motivates people to serve on a board?
- How does an organization's mission relate to board service?
- What are key areas of board oversight?
- What are the benefits of this work?

So, you're thinking about serving on a nonprofit board?

If you follow through, you will represent your peers to oversee a public organization. Yes, you will protect your fellow citizens' interests. If that thought makes you feel a combination of honor and uncertainty, then you're experiencing the normal range of emotions.

Why honor? Because you will help make judgments that are expected to contribute to the public good. You will help set the course for your organization and the dozens, hundreds, maybe even thousands of people it serves. Your experiences and values will come together in service to your community.

Why uncertainty? Because while millions of people serve on nonprofit boards, those groups are often misunderstood by the public, by many of the people who serve on them, and even by the staff of the organizations they govern. Our goal is to help you gain a solid understanding of what board service entails.

You want to ensure that you are considering this high-level volunteer work for the right reasons. After all, it *is* hard work. So before we get too far, let's spend some time making sure that you are thinking about joining—or staying—on a board for the right reasons, and what you might get out of it.

Why Serve?

Maybe you have served as a volunteer and wonder whether now is the right time for you to take your work with this nonprofit to the next level. Maybe you have a strong emotional tie to a cause and want to do all you can to advance it. Maybe a friend or colleague asked you to join a board. We asked some folks what motivated them:

- "I cared very much about the mission of the organization, and I had great respect for the two founders."

- "The commitment of the executive director inspired me."

- "I wanted to give back to my community."

- "Board membership gave me the ability to utilize my gifts and skills in a rewarding way that I don't find at work."

- "My employer is urging me to get involved in my community."

🔍 "This was a chance to engage in the community and meet new people."

🔍 "I only serve on boards whose issues clearly reflect my beliefs."

🔍 "I was asked."

These are all valid reasons. But one stands above all others: the cause, or what those in the nonprofit sector refer to as *mission*.

Should the Mission Come First?

No matter how stellar your organization, your board service will inevitably have its ups and downs. While there are many legitimate reasons to serve, nothing will get you through the tough times like a passion for the mission. And nothing will give you such pleasure during the good times as the thrill of helping to advance a cause you love.

So, yes, mission matters.

If you want to ensure that you are pursuing board service for mission-centric reasons, ask yourself:

🔍 Does the work of this nonprofit excite me?

🔍 Do I want to spend my free time making gains in this field?

🔍 Am I willing to put some of my hard-earned money toward this cause?

🔍 Am I enthusiastic about communicating the importance of this work to others?

Vision and Mission

Vision is a future-focused, aspirational goal. It often describes an idealized view of the world. For example, a literacy organization might have a vision of creating "a community in which all adults can read."

Mission gets at the fundamental purpose of an organization. It describes why a nonprofit exists and what it does to achieve its vision. The mission statement focuses on the present. For example, the nonprofit described above may have a mission of "providing adult basic education that will increase literacy in our community."

Definition

A less-cited but equally powerful motivation is *vision*—a nonprofit's long-term, ideal goal. An organization's vision might be to end childhood hunger, ensure that all adults are literate, or eradicate malaria. Along with mission, vision is one of the core elements that defines a nonprofit. While most people don't join boards with vision overtly in mind, many really are inspired by the idea of making a large-scale impact on a given field.

Values are often a less conscious but equally important criterion. No matter the good that a particular nonprofit might do in the community, it is imperative that the board—and staff, for that matter—convey a strong set of ethics. All of a board's decision making is based on a set of values, most of which are unwritten. As you interact with volunteers and staff, consider the principles that underlie their words and actions. Do those values jibe with yours?

Aside from mission, vision, and values, people cite a combination of reasons for wanting to join a board, such as building skills and networks, and giving back. What about you? Why might you want to serve on a nonprofit board?

Taking time to carefully reflect on this question is an important step on the path to board service. What motivates you to serve is what will hopefully propel you to be an engaged, thoughtful, and passionate board member.

Mission Matters

If your neighbor serves on the board of a local theater and asks you to join, should you jump in? After all, you have heard that this board is stacked with local movers and shakers. Tickets to performances are hard to come by but are available to the board. And, that annual gala is the place to be seen. What could be better? Well…what if you haven't been to the theater in years? What if you spend all of your free time walking your dog, talking to other dog lovers, and buying up every new pet gadget on the market? It sounds like the local animal shelter might be a better place for you to explore.

Inspiration

Is There More Than Mission, Vision, and Values?

Board service is a balancing act. You will need to offset your emotional connection to the mission with detached accountability and oversight. In return for being granted tax-exempt status, the government requires a board to ensure that an organization operates in accordance with its mission and does so in an ethical, transparent manner.

Boards provide oversight in these areas:

- Financial stability

- Legal compliance

- Risk management

- Organizational impact and outcomes

- Executive oversight

You can see that board service entails more than just learning about the good work an organization is doing in the community. It involves making choices about weighty topics together with a group of others. And that last bullet, executive oversight, involves managing the lead staffer. We will delve into the details of all these topics shortly, but for now, let's focus on your personal and professional reasons for pursuing this activity.

What Are the Benefits of Board Membership?

Mission is certainly not the only driver. It's worth noting that many board members' primary motivators are also among the job's biggest perks. This work really is bursting with personal and professional benefits.

Giving Back

Some people simply want to give back to the communities that have given so much to them. By serving on the board, you help your organization achieve its mission and make your community—or even society—a better place for all.

Skills

A nonprofit board is a rewarding place to put your skills to use in a setting outside your professional career. Accountants, lawyers, bankers, real estate professionals, and those with content knowledge around the nonprofit's mission are invaluable to boards. And, if you want a break from your professional specialty, this work provides a wide range of opportunities to expand your horizons. No matter what your skill set, you will inevitably learn a great deal while serving on a board.

Director, Member, or Trustee?

Board member is a common way to refer to the job, but the umbrella terms tend to be boards of directors or boards of trustees. While the terms member, trustee, and director are often used interchangeably, we use "member" throughout this book.

IMPORTANT!

Networks

You stand to expand your networks in some terrific new directions. You might meet people who can give you entree into new business or social circles. Or you might simply enjoy connecting with others who are as passionate about the mission as you.

Status

Certain boards possess an undeniable prestige. Some arts or education institutions, and national organizations of many types, fall under this umbrella. In some circles, saying that you're on a particular board gives you instant credibility. That can be quite useful if you are working your way up the corporate ladder or if you own your own business.

Leadership

This work can bolster your résumé in many ways. Some companies prioritize charitable work and love to see that their employees take volunteerism seriously.

Your board service can also highlight your leadership skills to your fellow board members and within the community. You never know when the expertise you acquire might translate into a new skill set, a leadership opportunity, or even a new career path. If you're feeling pigeonholed in your job or your life stage, the multi-faceted experience that is board work can take you in directions you never imagined.

So yes, you can emerge from board service with a wealth of new skills and networks, a more robust résumé, and the satisfaction that you are making a difference. As you reap these benefits, your most important job is to stay true to the role you have agreed to play as a steward of the nonprofit's mission.

To Summarize...

- A board is a group that provides essential organizational oversight and public stewardship.

- Mission matters. It's your primary reason for pursuing board service.

- Other reasons for joining a board include building skills and networks, and giving back.

- A good board member works hard but reaps many rewarding experiences.

Chapter 2

Board Basics

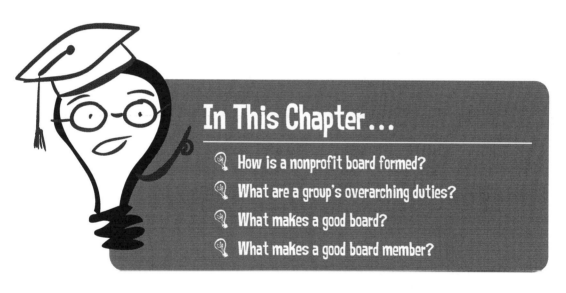

In This Chapter...

- How is a nonprofit board formed?
- What are a group's overarching duties?
- What makes a good board?
- What makes a good board member?

Once you are confident that you want to explore board service, it's time to examine this fundamental structure in our nonprofit sector. Here you will find the basics: some brief background about why boards exist, what the law requires of them, and how they relate to the other major pieces of a nonprofit's infrastructure.

How Is a Nonprofit Board Formed?

When you or your board predecessors first decided to form a nonprofit organization, the founding group likely wanted to address a societal challenge, one that—in the minds of the founders—neither the government nor the corporate sector had adequately addressed.

When the group decided to formally organize, as part of its incorporation process, the founding members sought tax-exempt status from the Internal Revenue Service (IRS). This *nonprofit* corporation, or organization, was designed to address a societal goal, or mission, rather than return a profit to owners or shareholders. Although different from its for-profit cousins, it was like them in that it was legally required to have a board of directors to serve as a legal entity overseeing its performance.

In this book, we use the terms nonprofit, organization, charity, and tax-exempt organization interchangeably. All of them refer to what the IRS deems 501(c) organizations, which are exempt from federal income taxes due to the public benefits they provide. There are many subcategories of tax-exempt organizations, some of the most common:

- Most of the organizations broadly defined as nonprofit fall under the 501(c)(3) classification, meaning that they are charitable, religious, educational, or scientific in nature. Examples include homeless shelters, schools, houses of worship, and groups that carry out scientific research in the public interest. These are the agencies to which most donations are tax deductible.

- Those designated as 501(c)(4) organizations include social welfare groups, such as AARP.

- Groups that fall under the 501(c)(6) classification are business leagues that largely include trade groups, such as chambers of commerce and professional associations.

Consult the IRS website (irs.gov) or an attorney for more detailed information.

While each state has varying regulations, all require that a nonprofit organization has a board. Yet, the method by which members come to secure their seats depends on the organization's internal rules. Some may be appointed while others are elected to the position. Elections themselves can also vary: Some rely upon the votes of current board members, while others lean on a membership body, although the latter is less common.

In any case, there are no regulations requiring a paid executive to staff the organization. That's right, the buck will stop with you and your peers. As a group, board members are responsible for the financial and ethical health of your organization.

How Does a Board Nurture Financial and Ethical Health?

When asked about their primary responsibility, most board members will say governance. A common framework used to describe a board's governance responsibilities is the "three duties" of care, loyalty, and obedience. These can come across as high-minded principles, but they really do get at the essence of board roles. In short, these are the ethical standards that members must fulfill.

Board Job Description

A board is responsible for the financial and ethical health of a nonprofit as well as its programmatic performance.

Because Americans are eligible to receive tax deductions when they contribute to many nonprofits, board members literally serve as stewards of both the donors' funds and the taxes that would otherwise be paid on those funds. They ensure that those funds are spent in support of the mission and that they are not misused.

IMPORTANT!

The Duty of Care

If you decide to join a board, you must act with diligence in all you do. After all, boards don't need another warm body that robotically approves every issue on the table. How can a member best fulfill the duty of care?

- Attend all board meetings. After all, they are the point at which the most information and viewpoints are exchanged.

- Read all materials given to you. If you do not receive timely organizational information prior to your meetings, ask for it. You simply can't make informed decisions without it.

- Ask questions. If you do not understand something, by all means, get clarity. If you vote on a measure that you don't understand, you and your fellow members risk harming the organization and those it serves.

The Duty of Loyalty

As a steward of your organization, you will be required to be loyal to that entity above all else—over other nonprofits, for-profit corporations, and even your personal interests. How?

- You, your family, and your business should disclose any contracts with the organization. The board must carefully weigh the situation to

WATCH OUT!

Can *Your* Business Do Business with Your Nonprofit?

Federal and state law typically doesn't impose a flat prohibition against board members doing business with the nonprofits they serve. In fact, such transactions might even be beneficial to the organization, especially if a board member gives favorable terms to the agency. For example, the accountant in your midst may offer to do the organization's bookkeeping at an hourly rate that is way below market, saving the organization thousands of dollars. If you as a board member wish to enter into such a transaction, you will have the burden of establishing that the contract or transaction is fair and reasonable, that you fully disclosed the potential conflict, and that the other board members approved it in good faith. Your fellow board members have the obligation, when voting on such a proposition, to do so only if it is clearly in the best interest of the organization. All of this should be spelled out in the organization's conflict of interest policy. For more information, see Chapter 14.

ensure there are no conflicts, unfair advantages, or excessive profits. Good boards establish written conflict of interest policies, which members should read and sign annually. See Chapter 14 for more on policies.

🔆 Don't accept loans from the organization. While it might not seem like you are profiting if you are merely borrowing money, loans from a nonprofit to board members are no-nos in the eyes of both the public and the law.

🔆 Keep dual board memberships straight. If you serve on two or more boards, don't bring information you learned on behalf of one nonprofit to bear for the purpose of another. If you serve on another nonprofit board and learn of an opportunity that might benefit them both, fully disclose the information to both groups. Then recuse yourself from the discussion while your peers vote on the outcome.

The Duty of Obedience

As a board member, it's important to read, understand, and adhere to the organization's governing documents—especially its articles of incorporation and bylaws. See Chapter 8 for descriptions of these documents. What makes these papers so important? Among other things, they contain the organization's mission and the basic rules that guide the nonprofit's operation:

🔆 Check all decisions against the mission. Whether your board is approving a new program, making budgeting decisions, or looking to expand, only approve those measures that directly advance the mission.

🔆 Know the rules. Take time to learn, and periodically reread, your organization's bylaws and articles of incorporation. Be familiar with major policies, particularly financial ones. These documents outline the procedures and parameters set out by your predecessors. The bylaws, in particular, include the number of annual board meetings, officer positions, number of board members, and any term limits.

Learn applicable state and federal laws. Most information is readily accessible on the website of your state's attorney general or another department that oversees charities. On the federal level, visit irs.gov and search "charity." It's the IRS that oversees all things nonprofit at the federal level.

How Do Ethics Come into Play?

You might have noticed that many aspects of the three duties remain somewhat nebulous. Few of their pieces are tied to laws, regulations, or formal policies. They rely upon your moral compass and that of your board peers. While the subject matter contained in this book—about finance, fundraising, and the like—is critical to your job, values underlie it all.

Every decision you make as a board member carries ethical weight. You will often ask yourself: Does this decision align with our mission? What will be the impact of this vote on our financial health? How will this decision impact our clients?

The nonprofit sector's consumers—its clients, patients, participants, and patrons—do not always pay for the services they receive. In many cases, donors make gifts that support a third party, so those third parties (the clients) might have little input into the way funds are spent or the quality of services. So, board members must consider the ways in which board and staff decisions impact the end users.

There are few hard rules we can lay out that get more to the point than this:

 Be candid.

 Ask questions.

 Proceed with caution.

While it might not seem so, this last point is very much aligned with the kind of calculated risk-taking that defines most successful boards. The duty of care doesn't require your group to hold back or be overcautious. But it does necessitate that each step of the way, you and your peers ask yourselves if there are any stones left unturned, any details left unresearched. What follows are a few examples of what can happen when board members don't fully extend their ethical antennae.

Ethical Foundations

Mission and outcomes underlie ethical board decisions. Ask yourself and your peers whether a particular decision will help advance your mission. Later, evaluate the effects of that decision on your organization's outcomes. See Chapter 15 for more on outcomes.

Inspiration

- An affordable housing group needed contracts signed by its board secretary, Dwayne. Staff would pile up the complex documents and present them to Dwayne after others had left board meetings, with no notice and little information. He would sign the papers, not knowing the full extent of their content and without getting input from those with direct knowledge of the issues at hand.

- Theresa chaired a museum board that required her to sign contracts over $10,000. Her friend and curator at the museum, Kathryn, decided to leave the organization and launch a business that would coincidentally sell services needed by the museum, at exceedingly high prices. When the museum began having serious financial struggles, an internal investigation uncovered several contracts signed by Theresa that directly benefited Kathryn. Theresa claimed that she had relied on the executive director to review the contracts before signing them. This internal investigation put the entire board under scrutiny.

- An affiliate of a large, national organization closed its doors. The closure—cited on financial grounds—surprised everyone. It arose when an auditor discovered that the financial reports given to the board masked a dire financial picture. When the audit team brought the issue to the attention of the chair, members realized that they had been lax about monitoring the finances. Given the severity of the situation, there was no way for the nonprofit to rebound.

You can see that sometimes it can be unclear whether board members show ill intent or make mistakes. While good intentions are certainly no excuse for incompetence, some very knowledgeable boards have been known to implode when ethical standards lapse.

There's a difference between questionable ethics and negligence, but the effect can be the same, especially for those your organization serves. It might seem obvious, but bad or indifferent board work has serious consequences.

The board must take the lead on ethical behavior. Developing a set of policies and procedures, *and using them* is key. Having frank conversations about ethics and expectations sets the tone.

If you do your homework, ask questions when necessary, and ensure that someone does the work needed to get the right answers, you will be contributing to your board's ethical health. It's a simple process that requires ongoing diligence.

What Makes a Good Board?

We know, the thought of those three duties and the complex ethics involved can seem daunting and even overwhelming. The chapters that follow will let you in on the subject matter basics. For now, let's focus on how the group must conduct itself in order to carry out those duties.

Bigger Is Not Always Better

Even small organizations can have great boards. One group with an annual budget under $500,000 has stellar board practices. Those include efficient meetings and clear board policies. How? Members take advantage of the increasing number of free or inexpensive resources: They talk to peers, research best practices via the Internet, and use limited resources to prioritize board member training.

Pure Genius!

🔍 Commitment. The best boards regularly have excellent meeting attendance, presence at events, and 100 percent record of financial giving by its members. No exceptions.

🔍 Independence. Boards must show autonomy from the executive director. And individual members must similarly think independently of each other, so that groupthink doesn't overtake deliberate decision making.

🔍 Trust. In terms of the collective character, trust trumps all else. Everyone around the table must be able to accept that opinions can be taken at face value, that there are no hidden agendas. Confidentiality is critical, and confidential topics are discussed most freely when members trust each other.

🔍 Diligence. Trust must be backed up by the knowledge that multiple people will work to understand each issue. While you may never be an expert on a particular real estate deal, it's your job to grasp the basics enough to make an informed decision about whether it should move forward.

🔍 Communication. Transparency, honesty, and even humor are among the traits that make boards great. When the chair and veteran members set the tone, new members pick up the cues. Less experienced groups can propel themselves forward when they are open about what they don't know and express their hesitation when ethical boundaries come into play.

🔍 Respect. Free-flowing opinions are the core of board work. When respect permeates meetings, people feel free to express those opinions. On the flip side, there's nothing like a judgmental environment if you want to promote inhibitions. . . and arguments.

If you and your peers collectively carry out *these* roles, then it just takes some studying to understand the financial, legal, and other logistics that will help the whole group fulfill its governance obligations.

What Makes a Good Board Member?

You now know that the board is a group that oversees the business of the nonprofit. Its members have no such power individually. Yet those members' traits are critical to the board's performance. Among the most important:

- A passion for the mission. This should be your number one reason to serve on a board.

- Willingness to dedicate time. To ensure the quorum needed for most boards to vote on issues, board members simply *must* show up to meetings. Period.

- Commitment to learning. Expect to learn about the organization's vision, mission, and financials as a start. Then move on to more general nonprofit topics covered throughout Part 2 and 3 of this book.

- Generosity. From your experience to your networks to a personal financial gift, you should be prepared to share some of the things most meaningful to you.

- Strong set of ethics. Most board-related ethics come down to doing what's right for the organization and

Modeling Good Practices

One exemplary board member is a senior officer at a local bank. He has years of business experience and a self-taught knowledge of his nonprofit's affordable housing mission. Given his extensive wisdom, he could easily dominate board discussions. Instead, he learns from those with other angles and selectively recommends resources to organizational leaders. He regularly brings those from his network to see the nonprofit at work, and he follows up with them to secure new volunteers and financial gifts. His passion for this organization is embedded in nearly everything he does.

Inspiration

playing nice with others. That includes respect for staff and fellow board members.

- Ability to follow through. Be prepared to do what you say you will do by an agreed-upon deadline. Otherwise, you stand to hinder the progress of the whole group.

If these traits make you a good board member, what does it take to be a *very* good board member? In this prolonged era of economic uncertainty, more and more consider these traits requirements:

- Access to resources. Great board members make sure the organization has the resources required to fulfill its mission. They partner with staff to raise funds or secure in-kind donations. See Chapter 13 for more details.

- Eagerness to serve as organizational ambassador. You can really make an impact if you get out into the community and speak about your nonprofit at forums, in front of potential donors, or in casual conversations with community members who might have time or money to offer.

- Willingness to lead. Effective boards need leadership. You will strengthen yours if you are willing to lead tasks, committees, and even assume board officer roles.

- Additional time commitment. In addition to board meetings, put aside time to attend events, programs, or other organizational functions. When the community sees an active board—knowing it is made of volunteers—they know this is a group that demands attention.

Let's be clear: Some boards will *require* you to engage in the above. We consider that a good thing. The higher a board sets the bar for membership, the likelier that your experience will be a good one, assuming that the leadership ensures that members follow through on their commitments.

So if you excel in nonprofit finance—a highly sought-after skill—don't expect to rest on your laurels. No matter how much your peers crave your expertise, you will be a higher-level board member if you can provide financial guidance *and* attend meetings *and* make a financial gift *and* partner with staff to raise resources *and* learn about your nonprofit's current industry challenges. Of course, there are many details that underlie each of the three duties, as well as your ethical responsibilities. Part 3 of this book will capture many of those details.

To Summarize...

- Nonprofit organizations address societal challenges.

- Nonprofits are legally required to have boards.

- Those boards are responsible for the financial and ethical health of a nonprofit.

- A board's work encompasses the duties of care, loyalty, and obedience.

- Ethics underlie all decisions that board members make.

Chapter 3

Just the Facts

In This Chapter...

- What makes me qualified to serve in this capacity?
- What kind of time commitment can I expect?
- What—if anything—will I need to contribute financially?
- Will I get paid for my board service?

We all lead busy lives these days. So it's fair to ask, before we get too far, just what kind of commitment board service entails—in terms of time, skills, and yes, money. While you can imagine that none of these elements is equal across all boards, this chapter will provide you with a springboard for your own questions as you talk to current members or the executive director.

Chapter 2 focused on high-level responsibilities. This one explores the practical side of board service, including the impact it will have on your calendar and your wallet. We will also touch on one of the most common questions budding board members ask: Am I qualified to serve?

What Makes You Qualified to Serve?

If you're asking this question, you've already met an important criterion—inquisitiveness. The best board members ask questions. They also have a short list of other traits in common, which we hinted at in the previous chapter:

- Availability. Show up for meetings, and you will begin your board service in your peers' good graces.

- Respect. Be open to different viewpoints and ideas. In essence, play nice with others. (Yes, all early life lessons apply to board membership, too.)

- Diligence. Clearly, it's a perk to work with peers who have done their homework and will not waste others' time. Read all materials given to you and be ready to lend your professional or mission-related expertise.

- Ethics. From transparency to truth-telling to just plain doing the right thing, a high set of ethics is among the most prized traits you can possess.

- Humor. We all want to have a little fun, even while we're doing serious work.

Beyond that, there are few hard-and-fast requirements for board service. If you don't already have basic knowledge of the topics below, plan to spend a good part of your first year learning about these core issues:

Understanding of Board Roles

Staff is responsible for the day-to-day running of the organization. Board members must work to stay out of those everyday operations, such as deciding the color of the lobby walls. If you want that level of involvement, apply for an executive director position! Seriously, this is a more nuanced subject than it initially appears, so be prepared to spend time understanding the expectations of your organization. You'll learn more about board member roles in Chapter 6.

Nonprofit Knowledge

It's okay to come to board service without much knowledge about the nonprofit sector, but expect to learn. Part 2 of this book covers the most important areas you will want to explore. Your corporate or government sector viewpoint—or even your life experiences—can help create more richness than a group made up exclusively of nonprofit types, so by all means, do not exclude yourself from considering board membership if you have no previous experience with tax-exempt organizations.

Nonprofit Finance

One of your primary responsibilities will be to help ensure that your organization is positioned for financial health. Does that require that you come in with accounting, investment, or audit experience? No. But it really is your job to have, or gain, some basic understanding of financial statements. Chapters 10 and 11 get at some of the information you will need to know. Learn that, and you can certainly feel free to ask questions of those on your board who know more. A good board will have at least two people with solid financial know-how capable of providing oversight on that front.

Resources

Fiduciary oversight also includes partnering with staff to secure the resources necessary for the organization to conduct its mission work. Resources most often include dollars and cents but can also encompass helping locate free space for programs, or getting food donations for the meal service. See Chapters 12 and 13 for more details.

How Much Time Will You Need to Devote?

There are many components to board service. Maybe you assumed that you'd just need to sit in a meeting a few times a year. Wrong! Board membership is a significant commitment, so let's begin by talking in years.

"Not Much" Is Not Good

Be wary of a board that doesn't ask too much of you. When you ask pointed questions about what will be expected of you and the answer boils down to "not much," stop right there. You don't want to get involved with a less-than-driven group—a prescription for eventual failure—*or* get surprised by more responsibilities than you were initially promised. So, push the envelope. Convey that you are coming to this opportunity *expecting* to give some of your time and energy: "Really? I was hoping to roll up my sleeves and really get involved." Does the tune change? If not, ask other board members about expectations and see if you get different answers.

WATCH OUT!

Terms and Term Limits

Many organizations limit members' terms to two or three years. You might have the chance to be reelected once or multiple times. It's good to know the length of your potential term so that you get a sense of your minimum time commitment.

The Daily Grind

In terms of hours per week or month, smaller and newer groups often require more of their boards. Why? Because it takes so much effort to implement new programs, formalize internal systems and structures, and engage the public. Add to that little, if any, staff assistance. Established boards can also go through periods when they require more of their boards, such as during a financial crisis, a strategic planning process, a leadership transition, or an organization's milestone anniversary celebration.

No matter what time requirements are set out for you, the bottom line is that you will get as much out of your service as you put in. Be wary of serving on a board that requires *too little* time of you: That can indicate a board that is trying to quickly fill seats.

Board Meetings

Whether monthly, bimonthly, or quarterly, don't miss board meetings. This is where the decision-making takes place, so the content determines your nonprofit's direction on the range of issues. If you can't make time for these meetings, or if their time slot is inconvenient for you, it's a deal breaker. Volunteer for the organization through other means, or join another board.

How frequently do meetings take place? Typically, the smaller the nonprofit's staff, the more frequent the meetings. This dynamic comes about because smaller organizations rely more heavily on the board to take on some roles otherwise carried out by staff. If your nonprofit is an all-volunteer group or one with minimal staff, you can expect to meet monthly. Organizations with larger budgets and more staff tend to meet quarterly or even biannually.

Committee Meetings

Many boards require that each member serve on one or more committees or task forces. These are smaller, specialized groups that address issues too detailed for the full group to tackle efficiently. Most meet monthly or bimonthly—in person, by phone, or via the Internet. If you sign up for a committee with seasonal responsibilities, such as a fundraising group that oversees a gala or an audit committee that helps with that process, plan for added time commitments during peak times of the year.

Leadership Posts

Add to the meetings above a *future* expectation of leadership positions. It's never too early to think about your potential to help lead the organization! Whether you serve as a committee chair, officer, or even chair of the full board, it's good to enter your service with the aspiration to personally move the group forward. Some of your most rewarding time as a board member is likely to come out of those leadership posts. With those commitments come more time meeting with staff, committees, and individual board members planning the future of your organization—a very gratifying way to spend your volunteer hours.

Events

Even if they are not considered a firm requirement of board membership, plan to attend major fundraising galas, ceremonies, or organizational conferences. Do you need to attend all of those? No. But if one or two larger events make up a big part of your organization's income stream, or if they attract local politicians and the socially prominent, then those dates should get on your calendar well in advance. The community will look to board member attendance as an indicator of strong internal support.

Other Volunteer Activity

Especially if you are not an end-user of your organization's services, there's no better way to understand your nonprofit's work than to interact with those it serves. Some boards may actually require you to engage in the organization's programs to help keep you connected to the mission. You will need to add these hours to your total time commitment.

Get It in Writing

If you want to get the best estimate of what a specific board expects of its members, ask whether the organization has a board job description or a commitment form. Those documents, often signed annually by members, lay out the specific responsibilities they have assigned for themselves. See Appendix A for a sample board commitment form.

Pure Genius!

What Will Be Expected of You Outside the Boardroom?

Every nonprofit has varying needs. Make yourself available. That doesn't mean that you need to be on site every day, or even regularly. But you need to be responsive to the needs of staff and your board peers.

Communication

It is simply imperative that you get back to staff—as well as fellow board members—as quickly as possible. It's rare that staff will reach out to you just for fun. Their requests are important, and sometimes urgent. When you don't respond quickly or at all, you literally take away from the work they are doing to further the mission. Ask any nonprofit staff and you will learn that one of its greatest frustrations with boards is the inability to get timely responses from members.

Contacts

Once you have served for a while and feel comfortable with your role as board member, proudly invite your family, friends, and colleagues to events and even to make financial gifts. The bridge to your personal and professional life is one that should take shape in a comfortable way. Don't surrender dozens of contacts for entry in a database, but do invite five artsy friends to the annual art auction. See if you might get your workplace to consider hosting a United Way presentation made by a staff member from your nonprofit. Make the contacts fit the occasion.

Will You Need to Contribute Financially?

Yes. While there is no legal obligation to make a donation, it is absolutely your moral obligation to do so. Why? One of the easiest ways for other donors, such as foundations, corporations, and even individuals, to judge the commitment of your board is by the percentage of members who contribute their own hard-earned funds. And yes, donors do ask what percentage of board members make personal annual gifts.

Your organization might set a baseline for board gifts, or it might leave the decision up to you. In either case, make this organization one of the top three that you give to. . . and the gift should feel like a stretch. It should be meaningful *to you*.

If your board sets a minimum gift amount, you may certainly give more than that minimum, but ask about this kind of requirement *before* you sign on so that there are no surprises.

Can You Expect to Be Paid for Your Board Service?

Likely not. The vast majority of nonprofits consider their board members volunteers. However, some will pay expenses for things like travel to regional or national meetings. Others reimburse members for approved board-related expenses.

How Many People Will Serve With You on the Board?

New, or "founding" boards tend to be small, often three people, or the minimum set out by state law. They are often made up of the founder's family members or close friends. That close-knit structure works well when early decisions reflect the personal passions of the founder.

As nonprofits increase in their sophistication, a light bulb goes off in a member's head: "Gee, we're really putting in a lot of work here. It's about time we get others involved." At that point, the founding board decides that more members bring more connections, contributions, and ideas. In most surveys, the average board size hovers around sixteen, although they can range from just a few to dozens.

There is nothing formulaic about the number of members. Long-standing nonprofits go through phases where board size ebbs and flows, depending on how efficiently the current structure works. Typically, the organization's bylaws will specify the maximum number of board members allowed and sometimes even the minimum. These numbers can be changed by amending the bylaws.

Perspiration

There Was a Nonprofit That Lived in a Shoe. . .

. . . it had so many board members it didn't know what to do! This faith-based organization was founded by a group of forty-five Episcopal churches. Each church was allowed to appoint one board member, resulting in an unwieldy board size for this otherwise small organization. Meetings were chaotic, members' skills went unknown and unused, and frustration levels were high.

A rules change replaced the existing structure with one that created a fifteen-seat executive board. It enabled all forty-five member agencies to elect board members. The change resulted in a more realistic board size given the organization's stage of development.

Closing Thoughts

More than money, connections, smarts, or skills, a good board member has to be willing to devote time. If you can't attend meetings or events, then you will quickly lose sight of an organization's latest priorities, challenges, and successes. All the smarts and skills in the world can't help if you aren't up to speed on the issues. And while money and connections never hurt, you can as easily take the role of a donor or evangelist for the cause without taking up a valuable seat on the board. If you are still reading, you're looking more and more like a board member.

To Summarize...

- Requirements differ across boards, so request board commitments or job descriptions to learn the specifics.

- Time commitments vary, but the more time you put in, the more you will likely get out of your board experience.

- Plan to make a financial contribution, ideally one that feels like a stretch.

- The board size should be sufficient to meet the needs of the organization; the number of members will ebb and flow over time.

Chapter 4

Finding the Right Match

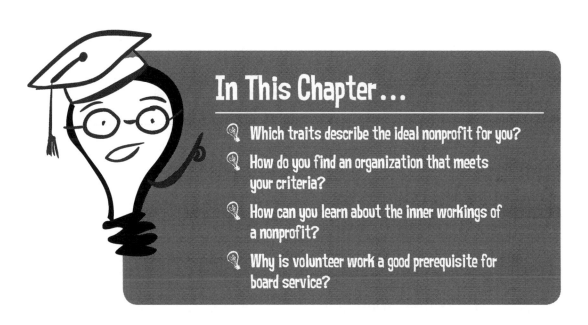

In This Chapter...

- 💡 Which traits describe the ideal nonprofit for you?
- 💡 How do you find an organization that meets your criteria?
- 💡 How can you learn about the inner workings of a nonprofit?
- 💡 Why is volunteer work a good prerequisite for board service?

Finding the right board is akin to finding a spouse: The criteria are somewhat intangible, but you often know a match when you see it. And like that dating game, no match will be perfect. So, search for a board that will provide you with the professional, social, and intellectual benefits most important to you.

Before you commit yourself to a multi-year term of high-level volunteerism, take some steps that will help you make an informed decision. Not every step you will read about here is a necessary one, but be sure that you follow through with enough of them to have a good understanding of the organization.

How Do You Find the Ideal Organization for *You?*

Let's explore how you came to consider board service. You might be part of a founding group that launched a nonprofit, finding a natural home among its first group of leaders. Or maybe you have been a longtime volunteer whose dedication and passion gets noticed by staff. Most often though, an invitation to serve comes from someone in your network; a colleague or friend may ask you to consider a leadership post at an organization where that person serves as board member. As flattering as that last offer might sound, we encourage you to pursue board service on your own terms. Not every board is a match for every person.

Create Your Own Board Candidacy

Ideally, if you are a committed volunteer, someone will take note of your dedication and invite you to become more involved, maybe even as a board member. Of course, not every organization will operate at that stage of maturity or etiquette. So, be prepared to take action on your own. Ask the board chair or executive director about the details of board service and whether there are currently any openings. A proactive board member is often the best board member!

Perspiration

Would you take a paid job because a member of your family suggested it? Maybe, but hopefully you'd give the idea a lot of thought and research other opportunities before you moved forward. The same goes for the volunteer realm. No matter how close you may be to the person who has extended the invitation, do some independent research. Even if a friend ignited the *idea* of board service in your mind, your friend's board may not be the best one for you. Let the suggestion be an inspiration to pursue the right organization *for you*.

It's also important to consider that, while there are similarities between boards, there are also striking differences.

Let's say that your passion is education. How one organization approaches education may differ markedly from another, which could impact your board experience.

If you choose to volunteer on a private school's board, you will make decisions that will directly affect a specific group of students. You might see those students regularly, and some of them might include your own children and their friends. If, instead, you choose to serve on the board of a state policy organization, your work will be more removed from individual students, but it could impact more of them. Your interest in education might similarly take you to serve on the board of a museum, an adult literacy organization, or a community-based special education program. In general, smaller organizations enable direct impact and interaction with a limited audience; larger ones have broader impact but tend to be more bureaucratic, and board members are more removed from those served.

Soul Search

Now the hard work begins: finding the right board. Start by figuring out which causes inspire you. Remember, mission matters. If a number of causes come to mind, think about an organization that might fall into one of these categories:

- One that served you, family, or friends well and that you'd like to give back to: a hospital, school, college, university, human service organization

- One that makes your community a better place to live: food bank, museum, mentoring group, theater

- One that supports your religious, spiritual, or moral beliefs: house of worship, faith-based program, philosophically-minded organization

- One that supports a demographic group that includes you or someone important to you: social welfare organization, advocacy group, business league, patient services program

One that touches your hobbies, career, or passions: animal welfare organization, professional association, activity-related group

One whose issues come into play in your daily life: neighborhood civic association, Parent Teacher Association, volunteer fire and rescue squad

Hands-On or Aerial View

Next, think about the size of the organization you want to consider. The more staff it employs, the more your board role will take you out of the nonprofit's daily grind and into the aerial view. Some people prefer that kind of board role. Others don't. So pay attention to how many staff members, if any, work at an organization.

Geography also plays into this conversation. If you get involved with a nonprofit that serves the local community, you are more likely to work alongside other board members in your area. If your organization is national in scope and you sit on that national board (as opposed to a chapter's or affiliate's board), plan to spend much of your time in the community without the presence of other board members. In other words, you will need to be more self-driven in your board work.

Naming Names

Once you have the mission and job duties in mind, it's time to talk specifics: Which nonprofit fits the bill?

It's very likely that you already have ideas. Your charitable giving or volunteer history might lead you to some promising

Find Your Ideal Board

To find the board that's best for you:

Soul search: What causes or missions make your heart flutter?

Take an aerial view: Is there an organizational size (grassroots vs. institutional, or somewhere in between) or geographic location (local vs. national vs. international) that is important to you?

Name names: Which organizations would you like to explore more?

Perspiration

prospects. Those should certainly take high priority, since you have probably spent time researching and getting to know some of the issues.

But what if your mother was recently diagnosed with diabetes, and you're suddenly moved to do all you can to advance that cause? Where can you go to learn about the many organizations that work in that field?

- You can begin by searching the issue and your geographic area on the Internet. That might give you some initial familiarity with local groups.

- Ask people you trust. Those who volunteer regularly, serve on boards, work in the sector, or are otherwise philanthropic are great resources.

- Your local United Way works with many organizations. Staff there is well equipped to point you in the right direction.

- Many regional areas now have their own community foundations or volunteer centers. Locate one in your town or nearest metropolitan region. Staff at those organizations are terrific at connecting the public with nonprofits of interest.

- See if your community has a board matching service. If you can't find one, contact your state nonprofit association or local chamber of commerce.

Where To Begin?

Before you spend too much time getting into the weeds, allow yourself to view an organization as any new donor or client would: through public information and first impressions.

The Internet

The Internet is a perfect place to begin your research. Any group that takes itself seriously has a website these days. Educate yourself about the organization's work, finances, and stakeholders. See if the agency posts its annual report, where you will find a synopsis of the organization's latest developments. Don't get bogged down in the minutiae just yet. Focus on these general areas:

The Ratings Game

You might have read about the abundance of organizations that now rate nonprofits. Charity Navigator is currently the most well known, focusing mostly on large nonprofits; none has yet emerged as a leader for smaller groups. Each service uses different methods and rating systems. Every player in this evolving field has its strong and weak points, so consider any data you find just one piece in a larger puzzle. And in any case, these services do not address the culture and effectiveness of the board. As you conduct research relevant to your own board service, the best methods are still those that take you to sources close to the organization.

Observation

Mission

Focus first on the mission, often found on the home or "about" page. Does it inspire you? How does the organization work to achieve the mission? Does that approach interest you?

Stakeholders

While you're still on the "about" page, look at the list of board members to see if it includes anyone you know, even casually. It can even help to browse donors, members, or others with a vested interest in the nonprofit. Later in this chapter, you'll find some probing questions to ask those supporters. Also look to see if the organization employs staff. Remember, that will help determine your future job description.

Financials

It can be helpful to take a peek at the financials. Guidestar.org is a terrific, free resource where you can search for a nonprofit and view its latest IRS Form 990 filing. Look to see if the organization has had net surpluses or deficits or how much money it has in the bank or investment accounts. See Chapter 8 if you're interested in exploring the Form 990 further.

Social Media

If what you've read so far piques your interest, consider following the organization on Facebook, Twitter, or another social media vehicle. Sign up to receive its eblasts. Nonprofits are all over the map when it comes to their level of social media activity. But, even if there is just an occasional channel for you to tap into, it will shed some light on the way the group presents itself to the public and its latest projects.

Why Does Volunteering Provide So Much Insight?

The best thing you can do before you jump onto a board is to volunteer for an organization. Whether you help organize one special event or spend years

Committees and Task Forces

Board committees and task forces are specialized groups that carry out the details of a board's agenda.

Definition

working with clients, you will come to the board more prepared if you have first-hand knowledge of how the organization carries out its mission. While front-line volunteerism will give you the best idea of how the programs run, committee service more closely mimics board work. Most organizations allow non-board members to serve on committees or less-permanent task forces, so ask the leadership if you can try one out. The most common options tend to fall under the umbrellas of program, finance, and fundraising.

How Else Can You Learn about the Nitty Gritty?

Talk to people. The less direct your involvement with an organization, the more you will want to spend time learning about the organization from those who know it best. Some samples follow. It's unrealistic to think that you will ask *all* of these questions of *all* of these players, but consider them a framework for the kind of thought process that will lead you to a confident decision. If you have researched and volunteered at an organization, you will likely have insights on some of these issues already.

Executive Director

One of the things that will make board service most fulfilling is the knowledge that your executive director has a vision. If a nonprofit is lucky enough to employ staff, the ED is the person who will lead the agency to new heights...or not. Ideally, you want to hear from someone with unwavering enthusiasm and passion for the organization and its mission. This is the person who will be at the center of many board meetings, organizational crises (there's bound to be at least one during your tenure!), and the primary liaison to the community.

Here are some questions you may want to ask the ED:

- What brought you to this organization? How long have you been here? Not surprisingly, you'll want to hear some passion in this answer.

- What do you perceive to be the organization's greatest achievements over the last few years? Gauge the trajectory of the nonprofit. Ensure that it is moving in the right direction.

- Can you describe the general direction that you expect the organization to take in the next few years? What will be new or strengthened? What challenges do you see ahead? These questions get at whether the board and staff are actively thinking about strategic next steps, and whether the ED has a vision for where the organization should go—a critical component to nonprofit excellence.

- How would you characterize your work with the board? Listen for nuances that get at a respectful working relationship versus one tinged with tensions.

- What would you say are this board's strengths? Its weaknesses? Do you think that the group is aware of those weaknesses? Is it actively addressing them? Ideally, you'd hope that weaknesses are openly discussed by the full board, or at least a subgroup.

- What kind of skill sets and contacts are you looking for in new board members? Describe your own and see if there are any matches there. This is just one person's opinion, but it can be fascinating to compare the ED's take on this issue with that of current board members.

- What is your long-term vision for this organization? The most thrilling leaders think big. They articulate their vision well enough to carry

Don't Let Up

If you are putting yourself out there as someone interested in board service, you stand to be formally invited to become a candidate at any point as you conduct your informational interviews. No matter when someone extends that invitation, don't let up on your due diligence. Continue your research. Ensure that this organization is suited to you, and vice versa.

Perspiration

others along with them, while conveying confidence in, and commitment to, that vision's execution.

By learning how the organization is run, you will help ensure that you can get behind both the mission *and* the management.

End Users

End users include a variety of individuals, such as those who use the organization's programs and services to acquire a skill, those who may be patrons and attend performances, or those who participate in rallies or marches to advance a cause.

You'll want to get a first-hand idea of how this organization benefits those it serves. Look into attending a *client-centered* event, that is, a run-of-the-mill program offered by the nonprofit on a very regular basis. There are few galas or other so-called special events that provide adequate insight into the mission. So, observe a class in action, a patient outreach session, an educational workshop, or a member meet-up.

Check with staff to find a participant or two who use the nonprofit's services and can shed some light on the organization's strengths and weaknesses.

Community Members

Those outside the nonprofit's inner circles can often have the most interesting opinions about an organization. Staff at other like-minded organizations, donors you know (find them in the annual report or on the website's donor lists), and even those who live in the nearby neighborhood, can all have unique takes on a nonprofit's work. Keep in mind that people's opinions may or may not be well-informed, so consider their feedback with a reporter's eye, using it as a measured part of your research effort. Ask them:

- What is your general perception of this organization?

- What do you know about this nonprofit's work?

- Have you volunteered or donated to this group? What has been your experience?

A word of caution: If you decide to contact people in funding or political circles, only contact those you know well. You can imagine that an ED likely went to great effort to cultivate some of those relationships. If, for some reason, you decide to make a cold call, we highly recommend checking in with the ED first.

Informal Interviews

One curious board candidate found a few annual reports on a nonprofit's website. Each one included a list of board members. She looked back a couple of years and found the name of a former member who happened to be her neighbor. The two spoke for hours about the pros and cons of serving on that particular board. The meeting was a terrific resource that, in this case, prompted the curious candidate to seek membership.

Pure Genius!

Board Members

If a board is wooing you, you can expect the chair or a nominating committee member to set up a meeting with you. Because those conversations are often part of the formal nominating process, we have included suitable questions in the next chapter. Of course, if you are driving this process, by all means, set up such a meeting yourself, and use the questions in Chapter 5 to guide your conversation.

How Do You Make the Final Decision?

There are so many intangibles involved in selecting the right board for you. After you have done your best to determine that those in charge are serious, visionary, and passionate about the business of running the organization, it's time to focus on those intangibles:

- How strongly do you feel about the mission?

- Does the executive director possess a visionary mindset? Does the ED come across as confident and committed?

- How well do you think you will mesh with the executive director and the general culture of the organization?

- Do you feel like you can both make a difference and be challenged as part of this group?

If your answers to these questions elicit passion and excitement, then you may well have found the organization for you. Congratulations!

Plan B

It's also possible that the research process has taught you that, while you are interested in serving on a board, this particular one might not be suited for you. If you have conducted the due diligence outlined in this chapter and come away feeling less than confident, *do not feel compelled to join this board*!

This warning is not designed to scare you from board service. But, it should confirm your need to select an organization with a mission you love, a potential for continued growth and improvement, and a community where your skills and effort will make a difference. Choose wisely. If you have spent hours

Volunteer or Board Member?

If your heart draws you to an organization, volunteer. Roll up your sleeves and serve meals, counsel patients, or organize the next special event. If your brain *also* draws you to an organization, then consider board service.

Inspiration

researching a nonprofit that seems ill suited for you, consider the fact that you just *saved* yourself many hours of unhappiness on that board.

Begin the process again with another organization in mind.

Remember, there are over a million nonprofits in this country—you don't have to take the first offer that comes your way. Do your best to ensure that the organization suits you. If it doesn't, look elsewhere. Plenty of organizations are regularly on the lookout for good board members. Bravo for making a deliberate, informed decision.

If, however, this organization seems to fit the bill, then you're ready to formalize your board candidacy. Keep reading for a preview of what you can expect next!

To Summarize...

- More than likely, someone will approach you to serve on a board. Otherwise, begin your search with organizations where you have a history of giving time or money.

- If you don't already know of a group that works on behalf of a mission you love, search the Internet and ask people in your circles.

- Conduct additional research on your organization and serve as a front-line volunteer.

- Talk to as many people as possible to get their perceptions about the organization.

- Take your time, and make an informed decision about whether to serve on a particular board. . . or not.

Chapter 5

Getting From Here to There: From Candidate to Board Member

In This Chapter...

- What are the basic steps in the recruitment process?
- How might recruitment vary by organization?
- What questions should you ask as a board candidate?
- How can you prepare for your first board meeting?

Are you ready to say "yes" to board membership?

Kudos for deciding to take on a central role in the nonprofit sector! Of course, nothing has been formalized yet. You first need to secure a nomination for candidacy. You might encounter a very methodical process, a haphazard one, or one that you will need to drive largely yourself. This chapter is designed to prepare you, the board candidate, for the range of experiences you might encounter.

And when the process is wrapped up, we present you with some homework. In the span between your formal approval and your first board meeting, you'll need to get a good understanding of this organization's history, strengths, and current challenges. Your orientation may be formal and well organized, or it may be a do-it-yourself job. (Are you seeing a pattern here?) In either case, you will do yourself and your peers a favor if you come to your first official meeting prepared.

What Can You Expect of the Recruitment Process?

Recruitment is a process of education, both for you and the people who may soon be your peers. Ideally, the board will have steps in place to facilitate this two-way exchange with its candidates. There are many variations on recruitment. The options range from formal to informal to nonexistent.

The approaches we offer here are among the most common, so a version of one of them is likely in place at your organization of choice:

Formal

Some boards have a defined recruitment process. Here are the basic steps:

- A current board member or the executive director invites you to explore your potential interest. Or, you might proactively approach an organization that you are interested in.

- You learn (or learn more) about the organization, to see if its work aligns with your interests.

- You submit a résumé and possibly a statement of interest or other biographical information.

You interview with one or more board members and/or the executive director, to learn about the board and see if your skills and personality align with those needed.

The board discusses and votes on your candidacy.

Voila.

Informal

Not all boards tackle even these basic steps. Be certain that you understand the process above so that you can fill in the gaps and request meetings with key leaders. When you skip steps, you really do yourself a disservice, since so much about the recruitment process sheds light onto the people, policies, and programs to which you may soon attach yourself.

Nonexistent

The best boards interview and orient members. But if yours does not, you must create that experience for yourself. Ask questions. Get to know as much as you can about the organization. Sit down with a few stakeholders and ask

Uninspired

Recruitment Reconnaissance

Most likely, someone you know will recruit you. That person will have approached you after a boardroom conversation that went something like this:

"We need a [fill in the blank: accountant, lawyer, woman, fundraiser, Millennial] to join our board. Anyone know someone who fits the bill?"

This is hardly the most strategic way to build a board. Many boards do not fully think through the depth of their needs—all the more reason for *you* to ensure that *you* fit the bill. Don't be afraid to ask the person who is recruiting you about how your name came up as a candidate and why.

the questions listed below and in Chapter 4. Listen to as many perspectives as you can. Then simply tell the chair or ED that you're interested in joining the board.

Just because a board doesn't formalize its nomination process doesn't mean that it's not worth your pursuit. New boards and those undergoing rapid transition might have members' attention focused away from recruitment. While we are big advocates of an ongoing, robust recruitment cycle, regular board business can certainly intervene. So, if your favored organization is slow to move, continue to remind your contact about your interest. If you don't see a fairly rapid response to your enthusiasm, unless there's a good reason given, then maybe this isn't a board worth pursuing after all.

What Might You Ask of Board Members?

You're probably wondering why we have saved your conversation with board members for last. In part, that's because organizations that recruit methodically will likely request such a meeting. This is the equivalent of your board job interview. The advantage of collecting your other data first is that you will have a much more informed perspective when you sit down to meet with those you'll want to impress the most!

Ideally, you'll want to speak with the chair or the head of the governance or nominating committee—typically the groups in charge of recruiting new members.

Spend the first part of the meeting listening, learning about the organization's work, the board's recent history, and its short-term plans. While the board member will likely have many questions for you, make sure you get in questions of your own. Some questions you might ask:

- How long have you been with this organization? Why did you get involved? What has changed during your tenure? Listen to see whether the board is on an upward trajectory in terms of its maturity and progress.

- How would you describe the board's relationship with the executive director?

Building a Leadership Pipeline

A food pantry's board members ask candidates whether they would consider a future board leadership position. While the question might make novice board members' hearts skip a beat, it is often a sign of a healthy board when its members think ahead about their next generation of leaders.

Pure Genius!

💡 Are there any likely changes in board or staff leadership on the horizon? If so, what are the plans to address them?

💡 How much time would you say you spend per month carrying out your board roles, and what are your primary activities? Are there periods during the year when more is required of you? You will want to hear this person describing activities and time commitments that sound manageable for you.

💡 How would you describe the culture of the board? Try to gauge any hesitation that might indicate a negative work environment.

💡 How would you describe the work style of the board? Here, you hope to hear messages about inclusivity, rather than hints of a clique that makes decisions without the approval of the full group.

💡 What are board meetings like? Most well-run meetings are somewhat regimented, include educational components for board members, and allow time for the group to debate important issues.

💡 What have you gained from your experience with this board? No matter whether the answer gets at the social good, networking, or a nonprofit education, listen for *passion*. Board service requires commitment.

💡 How do you think I can help your organization achieve its goals? Ideally, you'll want to hear a well-thought-out answer, one that shows that you have been invited for your skill sets and networks.

Throw in a few questions that you learned from your research, too. Ask about budget size and recent growth. Ask how the organization funds its programs. There's a reason to "test" your future peers: The more they know, the stronger the sign of a knowledgeable board.

Other questions might focus on the specifics of what this board will require of you:

- Do you have term limits? What are they?

- How often does the board conduct its meetings?

- Do you have committee requirements?

- What are your policies around members' financial gifts?

While not a deal breaker, be aware of how many of the questions you ask result in a response of "I don't know." Too many of those might raise an eyebrow.

Is There Any Stone Left Unturned?

Before you more forward, take one last opportunity to sit in on the work of the organization. . . and its board.

If you are seriously interested in a board, and its members are seriously considering you as a candidate, then ask if you can observe a meeting before final decisions are made about your candidacy. That experience will give you a first-hand feel for the interpersonal dynamics and meeting efficiencies (or lack thereof). You'll want to see a well-planned meeting that begins and ends on time. You'll want to see a group that feeds off of multiple voices and is not dominated by one or two. You'll want to see discussion of issues, rather than votes that robotically approve someone's recommendations or a rehashing of committee meeting minutes. You'll want to see a climate of respect. While you won't have enough context to understand everything on the table, go with your gut. Make sure you witness a diligent, balanced conversation.

Remember, the recruitment process is as much an opportunity for you to interview the organization as it is for the organization to interview you. You want to feel comfortable that the mission is a good fit for you, your skills will be valued, and you can commit to the requirements of board service. If not, then don't join this board!

What Can You Expect Prior to Your First Meeting?

Someone should contact you after the board has voted on your membership. Some boards will assign you a peer to help you through the transition—a "board buddy." Others will offer a formal orientation. Some groups provide both; others, nothing. These systems allow you to ask additional questions and get a baseline understanding of the current issues facing the organization.

Orientation

If your board offers a formal orientation, some combination of leaders—the executive director, board chair, or chair of the governance committee—will provide you with a history of the organization and the board's current priorities. This is your chance to get more concrete clues about the way the group works together. If you take home some timely written materials, chances are that this board is diligent in its information distribution. If the presenters offer both positive developments and recent challenges they have faced, you can assume that the group values openness.

Chapter 17 lists some of the documents you should expect to receive. Feel free to ask questions about the topics or materials that are unfamiliar to you. If you don't have a board buddy, then ask with whom you can follow up once you've had time to digest the information. You certainly shouldn't expect to be an expert on the subject matter by your first meeting. But do read up and start learning about subjects where you have holes in your knowledge.

Board Packet

Before the meeting, you'll likely receive a packet of materials, creatively referred to as a "board packet." Whether in hard copy or electronic format,

Do Your Homework

Review your board packet in advance of each meeting. If you find yourself needing a good deal of additional background on a topic, consider contacting a board member who might get you up to speed. This strategy can help keep meetings efficient if yours is a subject familiar to veteran members. If your chosen board member can't answer your question, chances are that the whole group will benefit from discussing it during the meeting, so ask the question then.

Perspiration

the documents will differ from your orientation materials in that they will be more current. They will directly tie to the meeting's agenda, or at least shed light on current organizational events.

Each board puts its packet together differently. Staff or fellow members take time away from programming to compile this information, so you do yourself and the group a great service when you take your reading responsibilities seriously. Your job is to review the packet of information *before* the board meeting and be prepared to participate in decision making around its contents.

You may not have much to say during that first meeting, or two, or even three. Many members say that it takes them a full year to feel fully up-to-speed on an organization's workings and their board responsibilities. The best way to get acclimated? Ask questions regularly: at meetings, between meetings, whenever you get a chance. The real job of a novice board member is to become a student of the organization and of the nonprofit sector. There is plenty to learn—don't be afraid to ask questions!

Once you have agreed to serve, you may find that the expectations are not always in line with those laid out to you before you signed on the proverbial dotted line. The workload may be more intense, the jargon more foreign, or the financials more complex than you expected. Yet the opportunities to learn, network, and give back may also exceed your wildest dreams.

To Summarize...

- Be prepared for a range of recruitment approaches and to fill in the gaps yourself when you don't get all the information you'd like.

- Ask questions during the recruitment process: You are interviewing the board as much as its members are interviewing you.

- Use orientation, board buddies, or self-education to learn more about the organization and its board.

- Enter the boardroom with an open mind. No two boards are alike.

- Read all materials in advance of a meeting so you come fully prepared to participate.

Hit the Ground Running

Few board members take the time to educate themselves adequately—often because they simply don't know where to go for information. The chapters in this section will get you started in a way that will give you the vocabulary and basic understanding of your roles and responsibilities. Once you master these basics, there are plenty of resources that can enhance your knowledge about each specific topic. For now, let's delve into the most critical areas you'll need to know during your first year, beginning with what in the world a board member is expected to do.

Chapter 6

Ready, Set, Action! Wait, Who Does What?

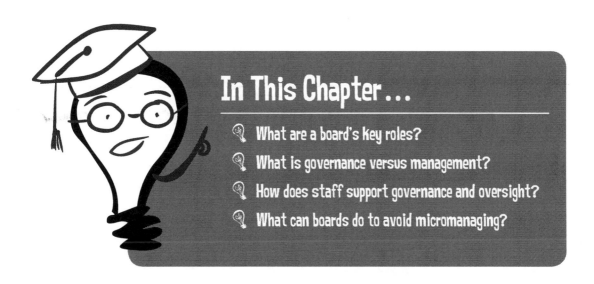

In This Chapter...

- What are a board's key roles?
- What is governance versus management?
- How does staff support governance and oversight?
- What can boards do to avoid micromanaging?

Welcome aboard!

One of the most debated—and debatable—topics around board service is figuring out who does what, when. If there's no staff, the answer is clear: The board does most everything (along with other volunteers, of course). Once staff comes into the picture, it would seem that the roles should become more obvious: The board conducts oversight and the staff is responsible for day-to-day operations. If you think this statement seems simple, you haven't served on a board before!

To be a good board member, it's important to sort out the roles played by the group, its members, the ED, and staff. Much of this chapter—and those that follow—will assume that your organization has hired at least one paid employee. This chapter will lay out board and staff responsibilities and leadership roles for each. . . at least in theory. While we will suggest that the board may be responsible for this and staff responsible for that, in reality the division of labor doesn't always divide so cleanly. The organization's age and maturity are among the factors that influence roles. Communication is the best insurance for maintaining clear boundaries for all.

What Are a Board's Key Roles?

The board has three important roles: governance, oversight, and support.

IMPORTANT!

All for One and One for All

In the context of boards, it's the group—not individual board members—that conducts governance and oversight. As a matter of fact, those actions can take place *only as a group*, during board and committee meetings. Much of that work entails learning about, discussing, debating, and voting on decisions that affect the health of the organization. So, the crux of your board service will include coming to consensus—or not—with a group of your peers.

Additionally, as an *individual* board member, you will provide support to the organization by making a financial contribution, serving as an organizational ambassador, or securing sponsors for an event.

Governance

Governance is the overarching responsibility of the board. When nonprofit status is granted to an organization, a group of peers—a board—oversees the organization to ensure fiscal stewardship and mission adherence.

Think about it this way: An airport has an air traffic tower. Sitting in this tower, high above many runways, is a group of air traffic controllers. Their job is to ensure that planes take-off and land safely. But, the actual flying of the planes and the on-board customer service is left to the pilots and flight crews. Together, all of those parties strive to provide a safe and enjoyable experience for passengers.

Likewise, boards are in the tower making sure that the organization's programs and services operate effectively, and yes, even safely. However, it's the ED and staff who act like the pilot and flight crew and manage the on-the-ground delivery of programs and services.

Oversight

Oversight puts governance into action. It helps a board break down its overarching governance responsibilities into manageable chunks.

The best boards spend their meeting time making strategic decisions that will affect their nonprofit's future. Here are some of the oversight-related topics you will most likely discuss at those meetings and the upcoming chapters where you will find more information about each.

Financial Stewardship

The board as a whole assumes fiduciary responsibility for the organization. Use those CPAs and banker-types as resources for your questions but expect to participate in budget creation and monitoring. Board members must also help secure needed resources including cash, space, and in-kind goods. See Chapters 10–13 for more information.

Legal Compliance

The nonprofit must comply with local, state, and federal laws. Depending on where your organization is located, requirements will vary. The board also needs to be mindful of its bylaws, which constitute a legal document. See Chapters 8 and 14 for more information about a board's legal obligations.

Risk Management

It's the board's job to plan for rainy days, literally. From flood or other natural disasters to computer crashes to a volunteer who falls down the stairs—these are just a few examples of the contingencies a board must plan for. Boards must even stay on top of risks to the organization's reputation, which is the foundation for donor and community confidence. One of the most common activities under this category, and one we devote a full chapter to, is how to plan for the departure of your executive director. Chapter 14 is devoted to the array of topics that fall under the risk management umbrella; Chapter 22 deals with succession planning.

Organizational Impact

An overarching responsibility of the board is to assess impact: Is the organization having its desired effect? Is it staying mission-focused? In order to assess impact, the board and staff need to identify and agree upon a set of key indicators, outcomes, and measures that will be used by the board to track success. This topic is covered in more detail in Chapter 15.

Executive Oversight

A board choreographs a delicate dance with the ED. On the one hand, it hires, fires, and evaluates its staff leader. On the other hand, it must foster a partnership with

To Have Staff or Not to Have Staff

Since boards are the only nonprofit structures mandated by law, staff is optional. If an organization has no staff, then the board will most likely perform oversight and management roles.

If your nonprofit is lucky enough to employ staff, the board partners with staff to achieve the mission.

IMPORTANT!

the ED that helps the organization thrive. Chapters 20 and 21 are devoted to executive oversight and support.

Examples of Board Oversight Activities

Oversight Category	Board Oversight Examples
Financial Stewardship	Approve final budget
	Monitor budget
	Monitor financial statements
	Approve financial policies
	Ensure adherence to financial policies
	Approve fundraising plan
Legal Compliance	Ensure that all legal filings are submitted as required
	Comply with organization's bylaws
Risk Management	Ensure adequate insurance coverage is in place
	Approve leadership succession planning documents
Organizational Impact	Approve metrics that will be used to measure impact
	Evaluate new program or service opportunities to ensure mission focus
Executive Oversight	Monitor the ongoing performance of the ED
	Conduct regular, formal performance evaluations
	Hire and fire, when necessary, the ED

Staff's Oversight Role

Effective board oversight requires staff input and support. After all, the board is a group of part-time volunteers charged with overseeing a full-time operation. There is simply no way that a board has all the pieces to the organizational puzzle. Staff provides key information, such as why a program is performing more successfully this year over last, the details that spurred a client's complaint, or the rationale for suggested changes in some budget line items. These insights inform the board's decision making.

Here are a few examples of how the ED and staff can support effective board governance and oversight. You will notice that some of them refer to committees, or working subsets of the board. See Chapter 7 for more information.

- Serve as the liaison on a board committee (e.g., a development director often serves on the fundraising committee)

- Assist the committee chair to coordinate meetings, take notes, and provide other needed support services

- Provide day-to-day insights to the board and committees that those groups would otherwise not know, given their limited on-site presence

- Provide the auditor with required information

- Generate financial statements

- Implement most of the strategic plan

Some duties are specific to the ED, such as partnering with the chair to develop the meeting agenda and identifying and recruiting new board members.

The ED delegates the remaining tasks to relevant staff. A chief financial officer or deputy director, for example, might produce financial statements for board meetings.

Support

The support role is typically not one you will find in a board job description, or even in most books. It is one of those unwritten nuances that mostly falls under the heading of etiquette, although it can be one of the best ways to nurture and cultivate a partnership between the board and ED. It's also a terrific way for you to become engaged in your organization's work. Board members can provide support in any number of ways.

If your nonprofit is small and has no fundraising staff, your grant writing experience might enable you to offer to draft grant applications. Or maybe there are not enough funds to hire a part-time bookkeeper, and you are a CPA who comes to the rescue. Perhaps you are a human resources expert who can provide valuable assistance drafting a set of personnel policies. These tasks are not requirements of the job but provide invaluable support to organizations with limited capacity.

It is possible that your organization has sufficient staff and a solid infrastructure, and therefore doesn't need the kind of support suggested above. There are still ways the board can play a supporting role (and maybe even win an Oscar!). If your organization relies on volunteers to help deliver services, then serve as a front-line volunteer. Members can cook meals, help sell tickets to performances, volunteer to teach a class, mentor a client, or contact an elected official to support an issue important to the organization.

Uninspired

A Fine Line

Pat was a board member who loved her arts education organization so much that she volunteered with its young clients frequently. When she did, she often observed things about the program that she would not have been privy to as a board member alone. What she saw while wearing her "volunteer" hat bothered her enough that she would complain about staff. She saw nothing illegal or unethical but thought that staff performance could have been stronger. While the executive director appreciated Pat's involvement, Pat had crossed the line when she brought her front-line criticisms to the board. As legitimate as those complaints might have been, the executive director thought that his authority was undermined when Pat attempted to manage the program. The solution? The executive director asked that Pat limit her volunteer time to projects that did not include staff.

An important area of board support, regardless of staff capacity, is fundraising. A strong fundraising partnership between the staff and board is essential to yielding resources sufficient to operate programs at capacity. No matter how many staff members are dedicated to garnering income, the board is one of the best messengers when it comes to cultivating donors and thanking them for their support. As a volunteer, your voice comes across as truly authentic, and your personal story of why you invest your money in this organization is one of the best ways to convince peers in the community to do so. It's hard for staff to replicate that kind of first-person passion. We devote a whole chapter to fundraising and another on how to be an effective organizational ambassador, both very important board roles.

Examples of Board Support Activities

Support Category	Support Role Example
Budget Process	Board treasurer works with staff to develop the draft budget.
Program Impact	Board member with evaluation experience works with executive director and program director to develop metrics.
Program Execution	Board member volunteers as a mentor for the organization's afterschool program.
Fundraising Event	Board member is a keynote speaker at the organization's annual gala. Board creates an events committee that takes the lead on the annual conference.
Staff Recognition	Board ensures that wages and benefits are competitive. Board hosts a thank-you lunch for staff. Board gives the ED an extra day or two of vacation.

One additional, yet very important way that members can act in a support role, is to acknowledge and thank the ED and staff for their hard work. Board members can host a "thank-you" lunch for staff, give the ED a gift certificate for a massage after a big event, or approve a holiday bonus for staff. Simple thank-you cards also do the trick. Of course, competitive salaries and benefits are always a terrific way to show the board's gratitude. More on this can be found in Chapter 20.

How Does Management Fit into the Puzzle?

Management is the front-line work of administering the organization's operations. It includes making day-to-day decisions and running the mission-related programs and services.

When the organization has no paid staff and is therefore entirely volunteer-driven, then the board most likely performs the daily operations for the organization. That includes everything from major decisions to the most mundane tasks. If, however, the organization has staff, then the day-to-day management is delegated to the executive director. In this case, the board typically has little involvement in daily operations.

This is not as simple as it sounds. Due to lack of capacity or resources, the board may, out of necessity, become more involved with the day-to-day. In these situations though, the ED is ultimately the one in charge. For example, you may be helping to fill a gap in your ED's skill sets by assisting with fundraising-related tasks. While serving in that capacity, it is not appropriate to supervise other staff or make decisions about fundraising tactics without ED input and approval. Your work will be task-oriented and is not intended in a management capacity.

This leads us to a couple of roles that board members should avoid: going rogue and becoming a micromanager.

How Can You Avoid Becoming a Rogue Member or Micromanager?

What we've covered so far spans most of your job description. The other part we'll make brief: what *not* to do! We've categorized these as "going rogue" and "micromanaging."

Most of the going rogue no-nos fall along the spectrum of going it alone. Since board membership indicates that you are part of a group, these are among the activities that you will *not* want to undertake as an individual:

- Speaking on behalf of the organization without explicit go-ahead from board leadership

- Inviting others to serve on the board without direction from those who oversee the nominating process

- Undertaking business dealings that conflict with your role as board member

In short, each of your individual dealings should support the mission and align with explicit roles assigned to you. Remember, it is only the support role that individuals execute—you will carry out the rest of your duties along with your board peers.

A whole separate category of micromanagement involves board members' interactions with staff. When possible, avoid these behaviors, which can place undue pressure on employees, especially the ED, to answer to multiple bosses. Do not:

- Request information or outputs from staff during board meetings; those typically flow from the chair to the ED, who delegates to staff

- Provide direct feedback to staff; that is the role of the executive director, or in the case of ED feedback, will be communicated by the chair

- Direct the ED to manage staff or run programs in a particular fashion

- Develop close, personal relationships with staff

How Does a Board Ensure It Is Fulfilling Its Key Roles?

An important but often underemphasized aspect of a board's work is the way it oversees its own affairs. Board self-assessment is key to effective governance, oversight, and support. Periodic self-reflection on what the board does well and where it might improve is critical to effective functioning. The ED should be an important part of this process by sharing how the board might strengthen itself. Chapter 24 goes into much more detail about how to assess the board's performance.

To Summarize...

- The board focuses on governance, oversight, and support, while staff focuses on day-to-day operations and service delivery.

- The board's formal oversight work can take place only as a group—not via individual members.

- Staff can play an important role in supporting the board by participating on committees or providing reports and information at board meetings.

- Boards should avoid going rogue and micromanaging staff and programs.

Chapter 7

Board Anatomy 101

In This Chapter...

- How are boards typically organized?
- What are advisory boards and how can they benefit an organization?
- Which committees typically support boards' work?
- How does staff interact with and support committees?

While there's a corporate trend toward "flatter" staffing structures, boards have not followed that trend. Most are quite hierarchical, with the chair filling an increasingly important leadership role.

Leadership usually consists of a group of officers who plays a crucial role in helping the group provide effective oversight of the organization and managing board functions. As the public, the media, and the government more closely scrutinize the nonprofit sector, officers must ensure that the board has fulfilled its oversight job. But officers do not act alone!

Typically the board will create any number of committees or task forces to go beyond big-picture decision making and tackle discreet tasks. In Part 3, we will address some of those assignments. But before we get there, let's get a feel for the structure.

What Is the Typical Board Structure?

While states all mandate different things of nonprofit boards, there is relatively little in the law about composition, committees, or ancillary groups. This lack of specificity accounts for the varying structures that characterize nonprofit boards, even when two organizations are similar in size and mission. Most boards are comprised of these basic parts:

- Officers

- Nonofficer members

- Committees

- Ad-hoc task forces

There's nothing terribly complicated about board structures. Common sense and creativity rule. If an organization has specific needs at a particular time in its history, there's little stopping the board from creating new structures if state laws do not preclude it. The main obstacle to restructuring is usually the bylaws, which you will read about in Chapter 8. Bylaws must be amended and voted upon by the board, and if your group keeps them simple, changes to things like committee structures can take place swiftly.

It's not uncommon for the executive director to sit on the board as an ex officio member, meaning that a seat at the board table is granted by virtue of holding that position. Your bylaws should specify whether or not this position has voting rights. We recommend that the ED be a *nonvoting* ex officio member. A strong ED already has considerable influence over the board; one without a vote helps separate the ED's influence and the board's decision making.

Two organizations we know with very similar missions and sizes have different structures. Each works well for them. Here is a general idea of their components:

Nonprofit Boards' Varying Structures

	Nonprofit One	Nonprofit Two
Maximum Number of Members Allowed in Bylaws	30	15
Current Number of Members Sitting on the Board	28	14
Committees	Finance Governance (board-related) Institutional Advancement (fundraising) Audit Strategic Planning	Finance Trustees (board-related) Resource Development (fundraising) Program Evaluation
Examples of Recent Ad Hoc Task Forces	Women's Leadership Circle; Gala	Strategic Planning; Audit

In the "Committees" row, some of those that are aligned have the same functions, just different names. You'll notice that Nonprofit One's permanent strategic planning committee finds an equivalent as an ad hoc group in Nonprofit Two. In every case, boards must do what works best for their priorities and their limited human resources.

What Are the Typical Officer Positions and Their Roles?

Officers—especially the chair—are key to the success of a board. Your state may require particular officer positions. Some do, some don't. The more typical ones and their primary duties are:

- Chair. This leader, sometimes also referred to as president, presides over full board meetings and any executive committee meetings. The chair also works in partnership with the ED to ensure that agendas reflect organizational priorities, communication flows between the staff and board, and the ED receives needed support and encouragement.

- Vice-chair. The vice-chair tends to fill in for the chair, whether due to absence, resignation, or another inability to perform duties. This officer might also serve on the executive committee and lead special efforts as requested by the chair.

- Secretary. The secretary's main duties include assuring that minutes of full board meetings are accurate and timely.

- Treasurer. This financial expert monitors and regularly reports to the board on the financial condition of the organization.

Officers who understand the responsibilities and limits of their positions enable other members to succeed. See Appendix B for more detailed officer job descriptions.

Past Leaders Can Nurture Future Success

A membership organization includes a "past chair" position as part of its board leadership. This person serves as a mentor to the leader for one year. In this organization, the past chair also heads the governance committee, which oversees recruitment and effective board operations, and performs other special roles that leverage high-level experience and expertise.

Pure Genius!

Why Have Committees?

The full board spends its time at meetings learning about internal and external trends, discussing strategic issues that require decisions, and voting on those issues. Sometimes more detailed work is necessary, and committees do that work. Some tasks that may require formation of a committee include:

- Overseeing the audit process

- Evaluating the ED

- Recruiting and orienting new board members

- Recommending revisions to bylaws

- Vetting potential merger partners

- Laying the groundwork for a strategic plan

You can see that each of these items might take significant work. And while the board would surely make decisions on each—whether to move forward and how—it would be ineffective if the full group collected information on and thoroughly analyzed every topic.

Once the board gives the go-ahead, committees might take a first stab at these items, or even work them out in detail, before making a recommendation to the full board. By having a subset of the board focus on specific issues, each member's time is used more effectively, expertise can be targeted to particular areas, and the board is more productive and effective.

Which Committees Are Most Standard?

Often, the most effective boards are those that use committees flexibly and creatively. So when the full group gets bogged down in the details of an issue or project, it's often best to enable a subset to delve into the minutiae and come back to the next full group meeting with a recommendation or set of findings. Here are some different ways to organize subgroups to help accomplish the work of the board.

Standing Committees

These committees are usually created in the bylaws and exist year after year unless bylaws are changed.

Executive

An executive committee might create the meeting agenda, discuss the overall direction of the board, or convene to make urgent decisions between meetings, within parameters approved by the full board. Traditionally, the group consists of officers and the

Beware the Program Committee

While it is not taboo to have a program committee, be careful that this group does not try to *run* projects—that is a staff function. Instead, members can assess costs, benefits, and impact for each program. Or, members might help evaluate whether a new initiative makes mission and financial sense.

WATCH OUT!

ED. The advantage of having such a committee is increased communication and coordination between officers and the ED. Some organizations prefer to function without an executive committee because they fear that this group might water down the voices from the rest of the group. Each board must do what works best within its own culture.

One nonprofit's bylaws define the role of its executive committee as follows:

> "Executive Committee: Shall consist of all officers of the Board and the Executive Director as an ex officio, nonvoting member. Unless the Directors otherwise determine, the Executive Committee shall have the power to act for the full Board of Directors on matters that require attention between meetings of the entire Board of Directors. Any decisions or actions taken by the Executive Committee on behalf of the Board must be reported to the full Board at the next scheduled board meeting. The Executive Committee may not make decisions on the following: authorize the distribution of the Corporation's assets; adopt, amend, or repeal the bylaws; fill vacancies on the Board of Directors or any Board Committee."

Finance

The finance committee analyzes the ongoing financial health of an organization. Usually, the treasurer chairs this group. At a minimum, members review the proposed budget and evaluate cash flow, statement of financial position, and the statement of financial activities. One or more members is likely to sit down with staff periodically to review the details. Sometimes, this interaction provides staff with needed expertise, and it can also provide the board with a window into details that don't always come out in the financial statements.

Governance

Governance is an increasingly popular committee that tends to focus on the overall health of the board itself. Members might work to recruit and nominate new candidates, review bylaws and recommend revisions, evaluate the strengths and weaknesses of the current group, or facilitate member self-assessments. This group also tends to take charge of creating educational opportunities or other strategies that come out of the self-assessments and are designed to strengthen the whole.

Fundraising

Fundraising committees can take on many names (development, resource, or advancement, to name a few). In any form, they work to nurture a culture of philanthropy on the board. Many people assume that committee members are the ones doing the fundraising, and therefore avoid this group like the plague. Not so. The actual task of fundraising belongs to the full board. This committee of strategists and cheerleaders supports the group in its role of giving and getting necessary resources.

While the committees listed are the most common, boards might rename, repurpose, or even remove them. Depending on the size of your organization and its current priorities, a personnel, building and grounds, or strategic planning committee might come into play. The possibilities are endless and can even be a source of excitement when your group channels its talents into a new initiative.

Many committees meet in between board meetings or on a monthly or bimonthly basis.

Ad Hoc Task Forces

Task forces are created by the board as needed, to address a specific issue facing the organization. They have very specific charges that are time limited. Once task forces have completed their assignments, they disband. They might fulfill duties like these:

- Search for and oversee hiring of a new executive director

- Conduct the executive director's evaluation

- Oversee the organization's annual audit

- Assess real estate options prior to relocation

- Oversee a major fundraising gala

- Organize the elements leading up to a strategic planning process

---

Pure Genius!

Creative Committees

A membership organization's board wanted to reach out to potential members. Thus, the Connectivity Committee was born.

When a women's rights group wanted to diversify its largely Baby Boomer volunteer demographic, it created the Junior Committee, a way for the under-forty set to forge social and philanthropic ties.

The politically-appointed trustees who govern a public library had no experience in fundraising. So they started a Community Development Council to help raise funds and conduct public relations.

Advising the Board

When a new nonprofit decided to keep its founding board small, it relied on an advisory committee to connect the burgeoning group to corporations, government entities, and even future board members. The committee was made up of well-networked community leaders who didn't have time to serve as full board members. The high-level contacts and advice offered by committee members enabled the founding board to move quickly through decisions and methodically select the profiles of its remaining members. This structure was key to propelling the fledgling organization by giving it near-instant credibility.

Example

Some task forces might form at the same time each year. For example, a group might form each May to facilitate the ED's performance evaluation and disband by the end of July, when the work is completed.

The use of task forces permits the board to be responsive to the needs of the agency as they arise, such as when the ED resigns and a search task force must be created. One caveat with increased use of task forces: The board must be clear on the goals and objectives to be met and the time frame during which the work must be completed.

Advisory Committees

Advisory committees provide additional expertise to staff and board members. Sometimes, boards add them to capture the networks or expertise of people who don't have time to serve on the governing board. They can be permanent or temporary, depending on the purpose and intent. For example, an organization might create a business advisory committee to provide access to corporate sponsorships as a nonprofit approaches its twenty-fifth anniversary. Another group might rely on a business advisory committee to gather input on how best to prepare its organization's clients for the job market.

What Dictates the Number and Type of Committees?

At its founding, a nonprofit will have little or no staff, so the entire board is like a jack-of-all-trades committee, providing essential hands-on support for the organization.

As an organization evolves and grows, committees and task forces may be required in order to conduct increasingly complex board business. When the board determines the number and types of committees, it should aim to balance the size of the board, the needs of the organization, and staff capacity. A board with ten members would be hard-pressed to have more than, say, four committees or task forces in existence at any given time.

How Does Staff Work With Committees?

Staff serves a multi-faceted role on committees. Its roles may include:

- Providing information and data needed to perform committee functions

- Serving as a valuable resource and thought partner to committee members, such as a chief financial officer who reviews financial statements with the finance committee

- Providing administrative support, such as meeting coordination and note taking

In very small nonprofits, the ED usually serves as an ex officio member of every committee. As the organization grows and adds staff, consider asking other staff members to serve as committee liaisons, since it can be difficult for the ED to attend every committee and task force meeting.

Common Staff and Board Committee Pairings

Staff	Committee Assignment
Executive Director	Executive Committee; Governance Committee
CFO or Finance Manager	Finance Committee; Audit Committee
Development Director	Fundraising Committee

You'll remember from Part 1 that the board manages only the ED, no other staff. So, board members who work with staff on a committee or task force must be very careful not to create a manager-like dynamic. Doing so can undermine the ED's management. For instance, a board committee chair should not assign work to a staff liaison who sits on that committee. Nor should the board member make any demands of the staff person. Only the ED can assign work to the staff person. Any tasks that the committee would like performed by staff should be run past the ED for review and approval.

Committees and task forces present a creative and practical opportunity for boards to dive into the details of meeting agendas. Consider your participation in them both a learning experience and a means to move the organization forward.

To Summarize...

- Boards are led by a group of officers, while the detailed work is carried out by a set of committees and task forces.

- Committees are permanent and tackle functions that are ongoing, such as financial oversight and review.

- Task forces are created as necessary, to meet a time-limited need or serve a particular function.

- The ED and staff serve as liaisons on committees and task forces, providing valuable sources of expertise.

Chapter 8

Bylaws, Articles of Incorporation, 990s...Oh My!

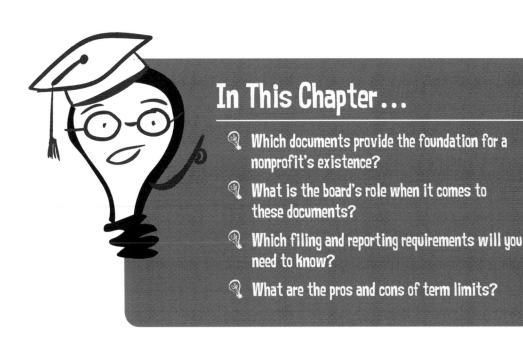

In This Chapter...

- Which documents provide the foundation for a nonprofit's existence?

- What is the board's role when it comes to these documents?

- Which filing and reporting requirements will you need to know?

- What are the pros and cons of term limits?

One of your oversight roles includes ensuring that your nonprofit stays within certain regulatory parameters. Some of those boundaries are legal ones and others are internally-created policies and procedures. The documents we discuss in this chapter are those that the board is either responsible for developing, approving, filing, or just plain ensuring they exist.

This chapter will help familiarize you with those documents—including the articles of incorporation, bylaws, the IRS Form 990, and board meeting minutes. Maybe more important than what you read here will be the time you spend reading the documents themselves. We'll attempt to steer you toward some of the more critical information in each. What you learn will give you a great foundation for your first—and hundred-and-first—board meeting.

What Are Articles of Incorporation?

The first step to becoming a tax-exempt organization is to become a legal corporate entity. To do this, an individual or group must file articles of incorporation with a state agency, often through the secretary of state's office. Each state requires varying information.

Check with your state agency for specific details, but most incorporation applications require information along these lines:

- The name of your corporation

- Your organization's principal place of business

- The name and address of your registered agent

- A statement of the nonprofit's purpose

- The corporation's duration

- The names and addresses of the incorporators, or of the initial officers or directors

- One or more incorporator signatures

As part of your application process to the IRS, your organization must have an Employer Identification Number (EIN), which becomes the organization's tax-exempt number. It is relatively easy to get and should be obtained after filing the articles of incorporation by completing IRS Form SS-4, Application for Employer Identification Number.

Once a filed or stamped copy of the articles is issued by the state agency, the organization is considered a corporate entity...but not a tax-exempt one.

With your EIN in hand, you and your colleagues are now ready to apply for tax-exempt status.

What Is an IRS Tax Determination Letter?

In order to be classified as a tax-exempt organization, the founders must submit a fee (at the time of this writing, either $400 or $850, depending on budget size) and complete IRS Form 1023 that asks questions about your organization and why it should be granted tax-exempt status. In addition, IRS Form 2848 (Power of Attorney and Declaration of Representative) is required, and Form 8821 (Tax Information Authorization) might be as well. Check irs.gov for more specific details. If approved, the IRS will issue a letter that confirms tax-exempt status. This document is often requested by institutional funders, such as foundations, corporations, and government entities. If yours is an established organization, there may be nothing to do other than know that this letter exists. Don't you just love that kind of "duty"?

Focus on the Essentials

Consider writing into your bylaws only the most essential frameworks. That way, your board gives itself some leeway. Write in the critical standing committees— such as finance, fundraising, and governance—and provide language that empowers the board to create ad hoc task forces as needed. And, consider including only a maximum number of board members in the bylaws so that you can do your work with fewer if necessary and remain in compliance.

Inspiration

What Are Bylaws?

Bylaws are akin to the organization's constitution. They are first drafted by the founding members and are normally required as part of the incorporation phase. They can be required as part of obtaining the articles of incorporation discussed above. They detail, some more than others, how the board will govern the agency.

As a new board member, take time to read through the bylaws. They will guide many of the procedures your board will follow. Look for these elements, which will be particularly useful to you:

- Board member term limits

- Maximum number of board members (most state laws dictate the minimum)

- Number of members needed for a quorum

- Committee and officer structures

- Process to remove an officer or member from service

- Number of annual meetings

- Indemnification of directors, which refers to an organization's intent to cover board members' expenses incurred during lawsuits related to their service on that board

- Process for amending the bylaws

- Agency dissolution process

Clearly, there is a lot of good information there. Many bylaws reiterate state regulations in the areas above, where applicable. This helps organizations ensure that they follow those guidelines. Most agencies add to those regulations their own internal policies. If your state requires that nonprofit boards include a chair and a treasurer, your bylaws might include those required positions. You can then add to them your board's preference to also elect a vice-chair and secretary to officer posts.

The bylaws should also state the date when they were last revised. If your current draft is as old as some of your board members, the time to revisit it

Term Limits

Whether to set term limits is a hot governance topic. If your board decides to implement them, the length of each term shouldn't be so short that the board experiences excessive turnover, but it shouldn't be so long that it scares potential board candidates away. Many organizations that adhere to term limits stipulate two-year terms that can be renewed two or three times. Officer terms often range from one to two years.

Term limit advantages:

- Makes space available to bring on new members with needed skills and energy

- Enables an easier exit for troublesome, nonperforming, or disengaged board members

- Helps with recruitment, as length of service is defined

- Encourages members to serve in leadership roles because they know they will only have to serve in those positions for a limited time

Term limit disadvantages:

- Results in a high-performing board member leaving sooner than the group would like

- Causes a strong board leader to step down when better candidates may not be on the horizon

- Results in a certain number of seats being vacated each year, which places pressure on board recruitment

- Decreases access to a member who rotates off, unless the board is diligent otherwise

- Requires the board to enforce members' term limits

Conventional wisdom and current best practices strongly encourage the use of term limits. Some of the disadvantages associated with them can be somewhat easier to overcome than the disadvantages associated with board members and officers who serve in perpetuity.

is *now*! Even if members decide not to change a thing, your board should review the document—via committee, then via the full group—every five years or so, depending on the rate of change at your organization. The full group will need to vote on any suggested revisions.

Form 990: Repercussions Beyond the IRS

An organization applied for a foundation grant. When the foundation staff asked for the Form 990, the ED of the agency realized that it had not been filed the prior year. Luckily the ED was able to get an extension from the IRS and file the 990. But the foundation board was unsure if the applicant's tax-exempt status would remain valid, so it didn't award the grant to this organization.

Uninspired

What Is a Form 990?

If the bylaws are the nonprofit's constitution, the IRS Form 990 is the State of the Union. This annual form details everything from a nonprofit's income to its board practices to its highest paid employees. The Form 990 has become the standard-bearer for interested donors, charity ratings sites, and the government.

You can view your organization's form at websites such as Guidestar. org. The forms are free to view, and they are required for most tax-exempt groups—with the exception of those with gross receipts under $25,000 and religious organizations. It is important that the 990 paints an accurate financial and programmatic picture. If an organization fails to submit the form for three consecutive years, its tax-exempt status can be automatically revoked.

The Form 990 has become a document full of juicy information. Much of the financial information, such as revenues and expenses, the amount of cash your organization has in the bank, and how much your organization owes vendors should be familiar to you by now via your orientation and early conversations with your peers. What else might interest you most as a new board member? Many of those elements will overlap with those that increasingly interest the public:

🔍 Part III of the form includes your mission and outcomes from your three largest programs. This summary is one of the few places where the public can easily align your expenses with direct program costs, so look to see whether your fresh board member eyes see those (hopefully quantifiable) program descriptions as worthy of the amount spent on them.

🔍 Part VI covers issues of governance, management, and how the organization makes its 990s and IRS tax determination letter available to the public. This section helps guide many organizations toward what is generally considered basic best practices.

🔍 Part VII contains compensation information for key staff and consultants. Because these areas are drawing increased scrutiny from the media and the public, ask questions about any figures that appear to be outliers compared to industry peers.

Typically, the Form 990 is due on the fifteenth day of the fifth month following your fiscal year end. So, if your fiscal year ends on December 31, the Form 990 is due on May 15 of the following year.

Are There Any Other Reporting Requirements?

In addition to the requirements listed above, you and your board peers must ensure that other federal, state, and local reports are filed. Here are some of the documents you will want to familiarize yourself with:

Fundraising Registration

Most states and the District of Columbia require nonprofits to be registered in order to solicit donations, or fundraise. Requirements vary by state. Look to your state's attorney general's office or secretary of state for more information.

OMB Circular A-133

As of this writing, if your organization has more than $500,000 in federal contracts and grants, you must file federal OMB (Office of Management and Budget) Circular A-133, usually in conjunction with the annual audit.

Common Nonprofit Filing Deadlines

Document	Purpose	Due Date	More Information
IRS Form 990	Reports key organization information to the IRS. Specific form required (990-EZ, etc.) depends on amount of organizational revenues	Due on the fifteenth of the fifth month following fiscal year end	irs.gov/pub/irs-pdf /i990.pdf
State Reports and Registration	May include annual financial reporting and registration	Varies by state; some require it annually, others biannually	Likely your state attorney general's office
Fundraising Registration	Permits organization to solicit funds in a state jurisdiction	Varies by state; some require it annually others biannually	Likely your state attorney general's office
Office of Management and Budget (OMB) Circular A–133	Serves as audit if amount of federal grants surpasses a set threshold	Must be completed each year the threshold is met	whitehouse.gov /omb/circulars _default

State Reports and Registration

In addition to the federal filings, states and possibly local governments might have their own requirements. Often the 990 that is filed with the IRS either satisfies reporting requirements for the state or local government or must be submitted along with other required documents. Check with your state's association for nonprofit organizations for more information.

The party responsible for filling out the above forms will depend on how much staff you have in place. While the board might not physically complete the paperwork, it is the ultimate responsibility of the board to be sure that everything is submitted as required and is accurate. Ask whether your board has a checklist of what is due when. The table above lists some of the more common documents that nonprofits must submit, along with due dates as of this writing. This list does not include things like articles of incorporation, which are filed just once. You might want to customize this list for your board and update it as forms and deadlines change.

Failure to submit documents on time could result in a loss of tax-exempt status, making your organization ineligible for all-important tax-deductible donations and sales and property tax exemptions.

Because internal and external factors can create uncertainty as to whether some of these forms are required and when, most groups consult with a lawyer who specializes in nonprofit law, a state nonprofit association, or even a nonprofit legal assistance agency that can provide you with specifics.

To Summarize...

- Take time to familiarize yourself with key organizational documents, especially the bylaws, which detail the rules of the board.

- Bylaws should convey any term limits.

- The IRS Form 990 serves as a guidepost for generally accepted best practices among donors, charity rating sites, and the government.

- Even if the board does not complete required documents and file them itself, it is responsible for ensuring that they are accurate and filed in a timely manner.

Chapter 9

Creating a Roadmap: Strategic Thinking and Planning

In This Chapter...

- Why is planning important?
- What is strategic planning?
- Why is board involvement so important to planning?
- Are there alternatives to a full-blown strategic plan?
- How do you implement a plan and keep it active?

When boards get involved in planning, they are fulfilling a commitment to organizational health. If your nonprofit has undergone this process within the last few years, request the resulting document. It can shed light on many current and upcoming initiatives. And if you remain on a board for more than a couple of years, chances are that your organization will undergo some kind of planning process during your tenure.

Good boards take time every few years to lay out a roadmap. Then they spend the interim months and years monitoring progress toward their goals and even tweaking them to ensure that they stay relevant. When a board uses its plan well, it can become a framework for nearly every decision that members make. So if your board spends the time, effort, and often money, to create a strategic plan, don't let this critical tool sit on a shelf! Used properly, it can bring the ED, board, and staff to share the same, clear vision of the future.

Why Is Planning Important?

If your organization doesn't undertake regular planning, it's likely that when the subject was last broached, a few board members moaned about one or more of these downsides:

- The length of the process

- The need for an expensive consultant

- The likelihood that the resulting document will lay on a shelf, collecting dust

And let's face it, it's hard to plan in these uncertain times. Plenty of organizations do conduct formal plans and use the results to guide their decisions and actions. When they do so, we find them to be among the strongest of nonprofits.

A plan can energize a nonprofit's many stakeholders. It can help focus limited resources—financial as well as human—where the most benefit can occur. It provides an opportunity to determine direction, set a high bar, and attempt to clear it. Together.

When done well, the planning process helps solidify the board and staff's commitment to work as a team. It can also assure stakeholders (foundations, government, clients, volunteers) that the organization knows where it wants to go and has a viable plan to get there. Often, these community members are just as interested in the process used to achieve the plan as the document itself. Why? They want to know that there is an involved group of people paying close attention to the organization's future.

Speaking of those committed people, with all the distractions that board members and staff face every day, planning ensures that the group spends some time away from the day-to-day grind and takes a long look at where the organization has been, where it is now, and where it needs to go. As we all know these days, the world often comes into sharper focus when we make time to look at the big picture.

Understand the Plan

One of the best things you can do as a new board member is request a copy of the strategic plan and ask how it is used. You will learn much about where your organization has been and where it plans to go. If you're told that one doesn't exist, suggest the creation of a plan, and make that initiative one of your first contributions to the board!

Inspiration

What Is the Board's Role in Planning?

The board's oversight role puts planning at the forefront of the group's responsibilities. While it's admittedly difficult to see too far into the future these days, a board must try to hammer out where the organization is going and how best to get there. When those plans go astray, there's nothing wrong with reexamining why and revising the plan accordingly.

Board engagement and buy-in should be authentic. A planning process that is entirely driven by the ED and staff with little to no board involvement can result in an unrealistic plan at best, and one that the board flatly rejects or ignores at worst. There are a few steps you can take, even as a new member, to encourage regular planning:

- Help ensure that your organization conducts some form of planning on a regular basis. Ideally, a task force will form to steer initial discussions and to keep subsequent activities on track.

- Offer to give some time to the process. Some elements of planning require research—about like-minded organizations, the funding environment, and more. When board members offer to assist with these tasks, it can save the organization from hiring outside help or just make a less-researched plan more robust.

💡 Attend the retreat or other meeting where planning will be the central topic. No ifs, ands, or buts about it—this is simply the most important meeting that board members will attend all year.

💡 When the resulting action plans are hammered out, volunteer to help execute activities in your areas of expertise or in other areas of interest.

What Are the Elements of a Good Plan?

Regardless of how you choose to plan, the following elements will help ensure a thoughtful and useful outcome.

💡 Mission and vision. Explore whether the mission and vision should be revised.

💡 Environment. Examine where your organization currently stands, internally and externally.

Uninspired

Mission Aborted

During its strategic planning retreat, a board's first agenda item suggested revisiting the nonprofit's mission. All involved assumed that this component would be quick and painless. Yet one board member—a very smart, dedicated businessperson— quickly slowed the process. Her idea of this school's mission was light years away from that of her peers. She meant no harm, but the discussion that followed led the board on a two-hour diversion from its agenda. Such disparities in thinking are more common than most leaders want to admit. While a few may deserve a thorough discussion, most need to be dealt with in a way that minimizes the potential to hijack the agenda.

🔦 Priorities. Identify the most pressing organizational aspirations.

🔦 Action plan. Assign responsiblities and timelines to each priority area.

What Are the Different Approaches to Planning?

Planning now goes by many different names and takes on a number of different forms. In our opinion, it's not the label or the process that necessarily matters—it's the outcome. It's the coming together of stakeholders to carefully think through the organization's future, laying out specific goals and objectives, and working methodically toward them. The nonprofit sector is moving toward more and more planning formats all the time. Below we list the most common.

Strategic Planning

Strategic planning is likely the best-known approach. Typically, the organization will hire a consultant to guide the board, staff, and other stakeholders through a prescribed process that includes revisiting the mission and vision, conducting a SWOT (strengths, weaknesses, opportunities, and threats) analysis, and developing a plan to guide the organization for about three years. It is not unusual for this process to include a daylong retreat for the board and staff. While there's not always a need to hire a consultant, we do recommend that an objective party facilitate the meeting.

Will your board end up with a binder full of information? Possibly. Results can vary from a several-page document to the aforementioned binder. Your board can scout out facilitators with varying approaches. Of course, the length of the plan is less a concern than whether or not its contents are realistic and achievable within the prescribed time period.

What does tend to scare boards is cost, time commitment, and an abundance of vague recommendations. These downsides tend to either deter organizations from embarking down the strategic planning road, or preclude future efforts. Encourage your colleauges to persevere, with a key endgame in mind: A successful plan ends with a discreet list of action steps—and a process to see them through. For example:

Goal: Bring members together to share best practices.

Strategy: Create member networking groups.

Objective: Convene two web-based cohorts before this fiscal year ends.

You can imagine that there may be multiple strategies and objectives under each goal. Create a calendar that assigns deadlines and people accountable for each objective. A committee or task force can monitor progress and report on it quarterly.

Responsive Planning

Let's suppose your ED informs the board that the organization will face serious funding cuts due to government budget reductions, a conversation familiar to many boards these days. If your organization's revenues consist of 75 percent government funding, any threat to this income stream could have a devastating impact.

The board might form a task force that is charged with assessing this situation and identifying plausible strategies to diversify funding. Since time is of the essence, the task force may well have to produce recommendations in a short timeframe. The resulting plan will be narrowly focused but incredibly important to the organization's long-term sustainability. While this kind of planning lacks the overarching vision of a more proactive, strategic plan, it allows the group to tackle pressing events efficiently.

How Does a Plan Take Shape?

It's hard to pinpoint a common set of structures that boards use to plan. It

SWOT Analysis

A SWOT analysis is a basic, and very common, way to delve into the issues that stand to impact an organization. It takes shape as a brainstorming session about a nonprofit's current strengths, weaknesses, opportunities, and threats. Its simple, methodical structure helps stakeholders identify the issues that stand to influence a nonprofit's future. It often results in some of the most important conversations during the planning process.

Definition

almost doesn't matter *who* gets the ball rolling, as long as it rolls! These are among the most common steps.

Task Force Formation

It might not be practical for every board member to be engaged in the full planning process. We recommend identifying a core group of trusted individuals to do the heavy lifting through a committee or task force. Those members can keep others in the loop and request feedback and input as needed. And of course, the draft plan will require full board discussion and approval.

Task force members should possess a diversity of views as well as in-depth knowledge of the organization. They might include board members (two or three), staff (executive director and one or two key employees), a client, and external stakeholders (some mix of foundation program officers, major individual donors, volunteers, etc.).

Timeline and Process

The task force will want to develop a timeline and process to help focus its efforts. Typically, a four- to six-month timeframe works well. Go too long, and the group can quickly lose momentum. If the process is driven by an urgent situation, the timeline might contract.

Research

Prior to developing goals and objectives, staff and board members take on various research projects. These tasks prime participants' thinking and allow everyone at the table to make educated decisions based on the current environment. A little research on topics such as these can help determine the path your planning might take:

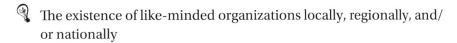 The existence of like-minded organizations locally, regionally, and/ or nationally

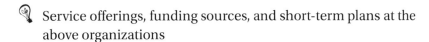 Service offerings, funding sources, and short-term plans at the above organizations

🔍 Emerging and/or unmet needs of your target client base

Your board will want to ask staff to have the following information handy so that you can assess the internal state of affairs:

🔍 Most popular and most successful programs and reasons why

🔍 Cost per unit of service or cost per client served

🔍 Overall financial health

🔍 Organizational and program data

Goals and Objectives

During the planning process, your board will want to outline ambitious but achievable goals. Some of the most impressive nonprofit growth we've seen has come from boards that set financial and programmatic goals sky high. Of course, that strategy doesn't work in every case. If your ED is newly hired

Pure Genius!

Divide and Conquer

When a healthcare organization conducted its first formal strategic plan, the board was concerned that a thorough process would eat up more time than board members could spare. So, members broke up into task forces, and each focused on one issue central to the nonprofit's work: finance, fundraising and communications, and programs. The members in each group worked with the ED to invite non-board stakeholders to participate. The resulting task forces included medical experts, practitioners, volunteers, funders, staff, current and past board members, and patients. The groups brought their recommendations back to a strategic planning committee, which compiled the recommendations for the board. The board then discussed and approved its plan. This inclusive process streamlined the time that individual members spent and created credibility within and outside of the organization.

or cash flow is a persistent problem, you want to remain realistic and avoid setting your organization up to fail.

Action Plan

Then there's implementation. Your plan will inevitably create action steps, and many of those steps will require board involvement. The list of goals and objectives created by most planning efforts is useful to big-picture thinking but doesn't assign tasks or interim deadlines. For that reason, we suggest that—no matter what type of plan your board creates—it become actionable. The simplest way to create the action plan is to ask the task force to take each goal and objective and create a table listing out the responsible parties and timelines. The full board can then review and approve the document.

Accountability

Little will get accomplished if no one oversees the plan's implementation. Some organizations keep their strategic planning task forces in place year-round to monitor the plan's progress. Others include regular reviews of the plan during board meetings, often quarterly or semiannually. Still others may assign the plan's monitoring to the executive committee. Bottom line: Someone on the board must take the lead!

How Often Should Formal Planning Take Place?

It is unrealistic and unnecessary for a full-blown

Goals Versus Objectives

Planning goals are best when they are specific enough to measure whether or not they are achieved: "Our nonprofit will diversify its funding sources."

Objectives list steps required to make progress toward a goal: "The agency will secure its first five major corporate donors—those with total giving of ten thousand dollars or more—during the next twenty-four months." Just like goals, objectives should be measurable.

Definition

Combining the Strategic Plan and ED Review

One savvy board pulls out the strategic plan as it prepares to evaluate its ED each year. Because the plan assigns discrete objectives to stakeholders, the board knows just what to include as the ED's goals for the coming year. And, if any of those items is no longer relevant or requires revision, the board has found a perfect opportunity to update its strategic plan.

Pure Genius!

process to play out annually. It's often best to write plans that span about three years. In the intervening years, a mini-review of the existing plan can ensure that everything is on track and is still relevant. You and your peers should never hesitate to revise a plan that seems off-track. That kind of retooling is exactly what continues to make boards productive, as opposed to ignoring a plan members consider outdated.

A dramatic change in events, such as the financial collapse in 2008, can render an existing plan useless or ineffective. So there can be instances when more in-depth planning might need to occur sooner rather than later.

Do You Need an Outside Facilitator?

Preferably, yes, but there are workarounds. It's ideal to have an outsider coordinate and lead the process. That way, the organization is more likely to get someone without a personal agenda. Especially if members of your board are at odds on particular issues, which you won't always know until the planning process begins, that objectivity is critical. Of course, an outside facilitator comes at a fee, so there are a few options that can sometimes reduce the cost:

- Some localities have foundations or other nonprofit support organizations that provide pro-bono planning services.

- Other foundations offer grants specifically designed to aid capacity building, often the umbrella term for planning.

🔍 Sometimes a brand new board member or other volunteer who has facilitation experience can lead group meetings.

Check with similar-sized organizations that recently completed a planning process and see who facilitated and whether services were paid for or provided pro bono.

Before your board settles on someone, ask to see that person's deliverables from previous planning efforts. If the resulting document is one of those binder-think keepsakes, and your board struggles to read its bimonthly board packets, maybe this isn't the right facilitator for you. Yet, if your board relishes delving into the details, you might have found a good match. And, don't underestimate the importance of a personality that works well with your group.

Even if your organization does hire outside help, be prepared to take on some extra workload, which can help reduce costs. Most nonprofits can't afford to pay for all of the research, writing, and thinking that goes into a thorough plan. After all, your involvement in the plan is a central reason your board will undertake it in the first place: to engage its oversight body.

To Summarize...

🔍 The planning process requires buy-in from staff, board, donors, and if possible, clients.

🔍 The planning method is less important than the full involvement of stakeholders and ongoing implementation of resulting goals and objectives.

🔍 A good plan is ambitious but achievable.

🔍 The process requires that board members dedicate time to its success.

🔍 Make every effort to secure a facilitator who can bring an objective eye during the planning process, especially if your board doesn't see eye-to-eye on the issues.

Part 3

Digging In

Now that you've poked around through the bylaws, the 990, and the latest strategic plan, you're primed to take on the details. This section sketches out the most common, ongoing elements that form the foundation of your board work. While you might not discuss fundraising at all during a particular meeting, its implications will likely frame at least one board-related discussion. And topics like risk management will surely underlie nearly every conversation. The basics are here, and when you feel comfortable with what you have read, we urge you to continue reading additional, more detailed resources. Of course, your time in the boardroom will also give you plenty of good experience.

Chapter 10

Budgets: A Financial Blueprint

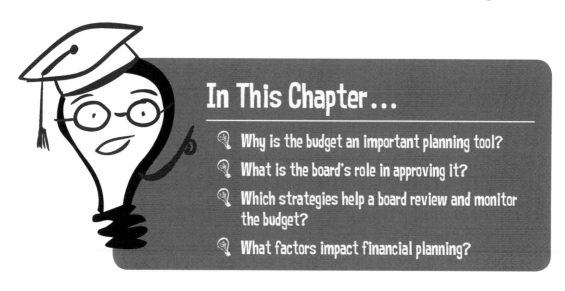

In This Chapter...

- 💡 Why is the budget an important planning tool?
- 💡 What is the board's role in approving it?
- 💡 Which strategies help a board review and monitor the budget?
- 💡 What factors impact financial planning?

One of your foremost responsibilities is to oversee money in, money out, and where it's all going. In this chapter and the next, we aim to lay out the basics. Rest assured, even corporate financiers who land at nonprofits require a learning curve. So, whether you balance the checkbook at home or have served as a corporate CFO, there are likely some new elements here for you.

Hopefully your board has one or two financial stars on it, and you can certainly rely on those people for some of the more complex matters. But their presence does not absolve you from possessing basic financial literacy. Budgeting know-how, in particular, can transform any board member into a very valuable one. So, take a deep breath and get ready to dive in—we promise you'll come out relatively unscathed.

Why Is the Budget So Important?

The *budget* is a financial map. It lays out projections of how the agency will raise and expend money to support its work. Budget basics are simple: money in (*income*) and money out (*expenses*). If it's so simple, you're likely wondering why we are devoting an entire chapter to this subject. It turns out that the numbers themselves make up just half of your board-related duties. The other half revolves around setting the philosophical parameters that lead to those numbers.

Whether you keep a budget for your household expenses or at your day job, you know that if used to its fullest, a budget can become a planning tool. It can help a board—and staff—accomplish the following:

- Establish communal goals, including how high a bar to set for the organization's growth in a given year

- Project operational plans, including which programs will grow, shrink, or cease to exist

- Demonstrate fundraising plans, by income source and amount

- Project operating surpluses or losses

A budget is a best guess of what everyone hopes will happen. Most likely it will deviate from reality a bit. Sometimes a lot. It will be your job to monitor those departures and see whether they are following predicable seasonal patterns or whether some of your collective assumptions were off.

While budgets are not public documents, funders require them when your organization applies for grants from the government, foundations, or corporations. Individual donors are also increasingly

Budget

The budget is a financial map. It lays out projections of how the agency will raise and expend money to support its work. It communicates to all stakeholders your organization's sense of realism, its commitment to diversifying income, and its spending priorities.

Definition

interested in the financial big picture. And it is quite likely that your auditor will want to see your budget, too.

What Should a Budget Contain?

Budgets outline revenues and expenses over the course of a year. Ideally, the two should equal each other, or revenues should exceed expenses. That's right, contrary to popular belief, it's okay if nonprofits make a "profit." More on that later.

Sample Organizational Budget

	FY '16 ($)	FY '15 ($)	$ Change FY '15 to FY '16	% Change FY '15 to FY '16	FY '15 YTD ($) 10 Months
Revenues					
Individual Giving	50,000	40,000	10,000	25.0	45,265
Board Giving	7,500	5,000	2,500	50.0	4,500
Foundation Grants	80,000	70,000	10,000	14.3	65,500
Government	125,000	125,000	0	0.0	100,000
Religious	15,000	10,000	5,000	50.0	9,500
United Way	3,500	3,000	500	16.7	2,950
Total Revenues	281,000	253,000	28,000	11.1	227,215
Expenses					
Salaries	165,000	155,000	10,000	6.5	129,167
Rent	60,000	55,000	5,000	9.1	45,833
Payroll Taxes	12,623	11,858	765	6.5	9,881
Client Support	15,000	12,500	2,500	20.0	13,750
Supplies	8,500	7,500	1,000	13.3	5,619
Fundraising Event	7,500	5,000	2,500	50.0	6,012
Total Expenses	268,623	246,858	21,765	8.8	210,262
Net Surplus (Loss)	12,377	6,142	6,235	101	16,953

Revenues include the various income streams for your organization. Examples of revenue categories include individual donations, grants and contracts, earned income (e.g., gift shop revenue, program fees, product sales), support from religious institutions, and United Way funding.

Expenses represent the various categories for which your organization generally pays cash. Examples include salaries and wages, payroll taxes, employee benefits, supplies, mortgage payments, rent, and insurance.

Before the start of a new fiscal year, you will want to see the projected new budget compared with last year's budget, as well as year-to-date figures for the current fiscal year to guide realistic planning. Ideally, staff will provide a document that also includes the dollar and percentage changes from last year's budget compared to the projected new figures. (See the Sample Organizational Budget on the prior page.)

Thorough budgets also include detail that shows the assumptions and figures used to calculate each category. That information can take a numeric and narrative form, each of which provides more information for board members and external supporters. For the foundation grants category used earlier, an example of detail and assumptions would be:

Foundation Grants

	FY '16 ($)	FY '15 ($)
Revenues		
Evergreen Foundation	10,000	10,000
Show Me the Money Foundation	25,000	25,000
Greenback Foundation	35,000	35,000
New Dollar Foundation	10,000	0
Total	80,000	70,000
Confirmed with all previous funders that we can expect to have our grants renewed at the same level as FY '15. In addition, thanks to Board Member Brian, we were introduced to the New Dollar Foundation and invited to submit a $10,000 request in FY '16.		

Boards are responsible for two primary tasks as they pertain to budgets: approval and monitoring.

What Does a Typical Budget Approval Process Look Like?

If yours is a large organization, the budget will obviously be complex. Newer agencies often struggle with budgeting the most because they do not yet have the experience to make realistic income and expense predictions. Some organizations begin with the end in mind. Board and staff work together to envision what they want to achieve in the coming year, and they create budgets that will take them to those goals. That might sound risky, because it means that you are establishing programmatic goals that are not necessarily aligned with financial realities. Yet, as with all things in life, this kind of aspirational strategy is often the one that tends to characterize the most ambitious nonprofits.

If your organization begins budgeting by methodically determining how much income is *possible to obtain*, and you plot your service offerings accordingly, you're not alone. This method will likely establish a less risky, albeit less driven, culture. There's nothing wrong with that, but it's important to know that these seemingly simple budget decisions have broad impact on the way your board thinks and acts.

Definition

The Fiscal Year

A fiscal year (FY) is a twelve-month period used to differentiate an organization's budget year from the calendar year. Nonprofits define a fiscal year that best matches their service cycle. An organization that receives a lot of federal funding may decide to operate on an October 1 through September 30 cycle, to mirror the federal government's fiscal year. One that works with youth might choose something closer to an academic year, say, July 1 to June 30. Refer to a particular fiscal year by its end date: A budget period of July 2015 to June 2016 is considered FY '16. A fiscal year of January 1 to December 31 can sometimes be referred to as a calendar year budget.

TBD Should Be MIA

Be wary of budget figures that do not have solid assumptions or details to back them up. These might be "plug" figures. Also, you should never see "TBD" (to be determined) as a category listed next to a budget number. TBD is a red flag indicating that the corresponding figure is likely a plug. You want to see real numbers backed up with justification for how those numbers arrived on the page.

Uninspired

While there is no one right budget process that leads to approval, these steps establish good annual protocol:

- Create a timeline. The finance committee should determine the timeline and deadlines needed to ensure that the board approves the new budget *before* the next fiscal year begins.

- Set a trajectory. The board, in partnership with the ED and staff, sets the tone for what level of growth, if any, the budget will likely undergo from the previous year. Again, at many organizations, this determination comes out of programmatic goals.

- Work the numbers. Usually, the executive director and any senior staff draft the initial budget with input from additional employees.

- Review the draft. The board's finance committee reviews the budget with relevant staff. When committee members are comfortable enough to recommend the draft to the full board, they often prepare a narrative that outlines major changes since last year and the rationale for those changes.

- Create buy-in. The draft and the narrative go to the entire board for reaction, review, and feedback. It is quite possible that other board members might identify issues not imagined by the budget drafters. This step also engenders buy-in from those who must eventually vote on the budget.

- Make any revisions or supply additional justification. Staff, in partnership with the finance committee, tweaks again, if necessary.

🔑 Final review and vote. By this point, the budget has been reviewed and vetted sufficiently, so there shouldn't be any material issues. The board votes, and the document should win approval.

This whole process can take several months; so be sure to allow enough time to draft, debate, revise, and approve the budget before the new fiscal year begins.

Budget Review Strategies

Sometimes the data in a budget can appear simplistic, especially at small organizations. But remember, the person who first drafted the document entered figures based on some combination of history, trends, assumptions, intuition, and just plain guessing. So don't let that simplicity fool you—there are many factors at work, which should prompt some thoughtful questions. Among them:

🔑 Overall, does the budget align with the organization's strategic priorities and goals?

🔑 How do the proposed figures compare with last year's actual revenues and expenses?

🔑 How does the proposed budget compare with last year's approved budget?

🔑 Which revenue and expense categories have the most significant increases or decreases? Why?

🔑 What's included in each revenue and expense category? Does it all add up and make sense?

🔑 For events, how much will the organization "net" after deducting expenses from gross revenues?

🔑 Are any proposed increases in revenues realistic and achievable?

🔑 Are revenues diversified enough that your organization is not relying too heavily on one source of funding?

🔑 Are expense increases justifiable? Affordable?

Despite this focus on what might seem like details, don't get too much in the weeds. Your job is to balance big picture budget review with appropriate in-depth analysis. So don't haggle over whether the supplies category increase of $100 is appropriate when the proposed budget shows an increase in salaries of $50,000! It is more important to understand the $50,000 increase than whether or not the organization should purchase another toner cartridge.

What Does Budget Monitoring Entail?

Once a budget is approved, the board takes on the year-round task of monitoring it. This is a core responsibility, and the finance committee should monitor the budget at least monthly and regularly report any issues or concerns to the entire board. At a minimum, those not on the finance committee should expect to see a current copy of the budget—with updated year-to-date figures—at least quarterly. Ideally, your finance chair will include a narrative that highlights any concerns or achievements that have materialized since the last meeting.

Some ongoing questions that promote sound monitoring include these:

Perspiration

Focus on the Big Money

Try to understand what's behind the significant numbers in your budget. Ask yourself questions like these:

 Which staff members are included in the salary line?

 If individual donors are projected to contribute $50,000 for the next fiscal year, what assumptions were used to arrive at that figure?

 If rent will increase 20 percent next year, has staff tried to negotiate with the landlord, or explored other space options? Is this substantial increase a regular pattern?

- If revenues are not meeting budgeted targets, should we reduce expenses, or are there new income streams that we might have overlooked?

- Are we currently in the red because we are waiting for an overdue grant payment (an increasingly common phenomenon when dealing with government agencies)?

- What is our cost per client served? Is it increasing or decreasing? Why?

The Beauty of Reserves

Even when the economy is good, your financials can take an unforeseen beating when a large grant or donation does not get renewed or when a government payment arrives late. An operating reserve can help sustain your organization during cash flow crunches. Consider maintaining at least three months of operating cash in reserve. Many organizations aim for six!

IMPORTANT!

- If we consistently experience operating surpluses, should we invest some of the excess funds?

- If the organization is having serious operating losses (expenses outpacing revenues), how might this affect our ability to deliver programs and services for the rest of the fiscal year?

How Important Is an Operating Reserve?

There seems to be a bit of an urban legend that follows if a *non*profit budgets for a surplus—a "profit"—that strategy is counter to the idea of tax-exempt organizations.

Untrue!

There are very logical and even persuasive cases that can be made to support budgeting for a surplus to build a reserve. Also called an operating reserve, it's the equivalent of having a rainy day fund. Building a reserve is an important strategy that your board might consider as part of the budgeting process. A reserve buys time in the event something unforeseen happens such as a significant loss of funding or a substantial increase in expenses.

How to show a proposed surplus in your budget:

Example #1:

Revenues	$500,000
Expenses	$485,000
Net Operating Surplus (Loss) Before Reserve Allocation	$15,000
Allocation to Reserve	$15,000
Net Operating Surplus (Loss)	$0

Example #2:

Revenues		$500,000
Expenses	$485,000	
Allocation to Reserve	$15,000	
Total Expenses		$500,000
Net Operating Surplus (Loss)		$0

As with all notable budget categories, you will want to see a narrative that helps explain the rationale for the reserve allocation. Such text can be brief, but it allows potential funders and future board members a window into why the numbers have changed since last year. Consider the following arguments for a budget surplus:

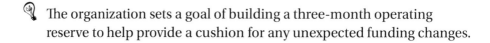 The organization sets a goal of building a three-month operating reserve to help provide a cushion for any unexpected funding changes.

💡 The organization needs to maintain a six-month operating reserve because its government contracts often come in the door weeks late. The reserve acts like an internal line of credit to help smooth out cash shortages until the government check arrives.

💡 The organization may own its building or have certain repair and maintenance responsibilities. Reserves can be used to cover any unanticipated expenses.

Reserves allow the lights to stay on, staff members to collect salaries, and programs to operate while the board and ED develop solutions to meet a cash flow crunch. You might call them a board member's best friend. They

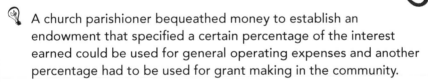

Example

Endowment vs. Reserves

An endowment is a fund that is restricted. It usually originates with a large gift made by a donor who placed stipulations on how the money may be used.

💡 A church parishioner bequeathed money to establish an endowment that specified a certain percentage of the interest earned could be used for general operating expenses and another percentage had to be used for grant making in the community.

💡 A university established a $2 million endowment through a bequest made by an alum when he died. The donor stipulated that 5 percent of the principal could be used each year to pay for a particular scholarship.

In both the above examples, the board was charged with ensuring that the stipulations were followed.

A reserve, also known as an operating reserve, usually covers unforeseen events or situations. For example, it might provide operating support when a large grant is lost. Or, its funds might replace a broken boiler. Often, boards must approve dipping into it. And, if your organization has a reserve policy, it may require that a strategy be developed to replenish the reserve to ensure that the organization has a nest egg for another emergency.

can be created through squirreling money away little by little each year or through a targeted fundraising strategy or a large bequest. It's important that board approval is obtained before tapping into a reserve.

Are Budget Deficits Always Bad?

The opposite of budgeting for a surplus is budgeting for a deficit, whereby expenses exceed revenues. You will know if your organization is running a deficit if its total expenses for the year exceed revenues. If you are unfamiliar with reading financial statements, these negative numbers show up in your budget in red, with a negative sign, or are placed in parentheses.

We are all too familiar with U.S. government deficits. But should your board approve a deficit budget? Likely, the answer is a resounding "no." But the final decision can be more nuanced.

Without any further explanation, a budget deficit communicates to external stakeholders that your organization does not have enough resources to cover its programs and services for the next fiscal year or will be eating up some reserves to subsidize the loss. This is not something to be taken lightly. Yet there are a few reasons why you may be asked to consider approving a budget that runs a deficit:

- The organization recently lost a funding source, creating a hole on the revenue side of the budget that staff is still trying to fill.

- A recent change in organizational leadership might result in some funding losses. For example, a founder or long-term ED leaves and some major donors reduce their funding because they had a close connection to that leader. The revenue side of the budget might take a hit until the new ED, along with the board, can rebuild revenues.

- There might be a sudden increase in an expense category. Maybe the organization's rent doubled. Or, the agency hired a new ED and learns that the old ED's salary was $40,000 below market rate.

- A new program is set to be launched that will not "pay" for itself until its second year.

Situations like these can result in expenses outpacing revenues. Any planned budget deficit should be considered *temporary*. Not only will it raise the eyebrows of funders, it will hinder the board's ability to move forward in positive, productive ways.

If your organization is lucky enough to have a reserve fund, give enormous pause before borrowing from it to cover the deficit. Plan to repay whatever you borrow. Many nonprofits have closed their doors in recent years because of the snowball effect associated with borrowing repeatedly from those rainy day funds without correcting the problem that caused the deficit in the first place.

If your organization has no reserves or if the proposed deficit will significantly consume the funds you have stashed away, that's a whole different story. In those instances, approving a deficit budget is akin to kicking the can down the road and highly irresponsible.

The best approach to remedy a budget deficit is to 1) determine a short timeline for its existence, and 2) develop a plan that will reduce or eliminate it without an ongoing reliance on reserves. That plan will likely include strategies to increase revenues, decrease expenses, or a combination of the two. The plan will also lessen your anxieties as a board member!

To Summarize...

- Budgets are important board planning documents and should align with organizational priorities.

- A budget is an outline of projected revenues and expenses.

- Budget creation is as much about your organization's aspirations as it is about the numbers.

- Expect to monitor revenues and expenses throughout the year.

- Attempt to budget for an operating reserve whenever possible.

Chapter 11

Other Fun Financials

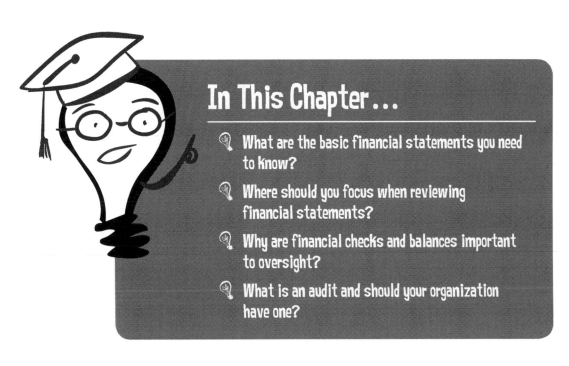

In This Chapter...

- What are the basic financial statements you need to know?

- Where should you focus when reviewing financial statements?

- Why are financial checks and balances important to oversight?

- What is an audit and should your organization have one?

You didn't think that budgets were *it* when it comes to good financial health, did you? The good news is that, while financial statements can go into minute detail, there should be at least one person on the board who is well-versed in that detail. Hopefully your board has a crackerjack treasurer (maybe it's you!) who carefully reviews financial information and raises any issues or concerns to the board. But, that does not excuse the rest of the group from reviewing financial statements.

As a new board member, you should—at a minimum—be comfortable with the three basic financial statements in this chapter: cash flow projection, statement of financial position (a.k.a. balance sheet in the corporate world), and statement of activities (a.k.a. income statement in the corporate world). Entire books are available on these statements, but if you have little or no nonprofit finance experience, use this chapter as a foundation for your financial literacy.

What Is a Cash Flow Projection?

Cash is an organization's most *liquid* asset. That is, it's readily available to pay bills or unexpected expenses. An organization rich in real estate or even an endowment might still have a hard time paying salaries if funds are tied up in those illiquid assets and there is little money in the bank to meet payroll. It's a board's job to monitor, and even project, that there will be adequate cash available each month of the year to pay for both planned and unplanned expenses.

Definition

Statement of Cash Flows vs. Cash Flow Projection

A statement of cash flows (a.k.a. cash flow statement) is an accounting document that shows the sources and uses of cash over a period of time. This financial resource is usually part of an audit and can also be produced using accounting software such as QuickBooks. This document shows cash sources and uses for a past period of time.

A cash flow projection is an internal document that projects the inflows and outflows of cash over a period of time, usually a fiscal year. Depending on the time of year, it might show past, present, and future expected activity. A cash flow projection is useful to staff and board members, as it shows anticipated monthly cash surpluses or shortfalls.

That reality makes the *cash flow projection* one of the most useful financial statements for a board member. It illustrates months when cash will be tight and months where the board can rest easy. So, pay close attention to the data. It is the best tool to spot short-term financial problems before they happen.

Below you will see a simple cash flow projection, which you can assume was prepared at the end of January. Notice that it projects anticipated monthly revenues and expenses, and a projected cash balance at the beginning and end of each month.

Sample Cash Flow Projection

ABC Organization Cash Flow Projection for January 1—March 30			
	January Actuals ($)	February Projected ($)	March Projected ($)
Revenues			
Individuals	10,295	5,000	7,500
Foundations	7,500	0	15,000
Government	0	0	50,000
Total Revenues	17,795	5,000	72,500
Expenses			
Salaries	7,500	7,500	7,500
Employee Benefits	1,500	1,500	1,500
Rent	5,000	5,000	5,000
Insurance	0	9,500	0
Total Expenses	14,000	23,500	14,000
Net Surplus (Loss)	3,795	(18,500)	58,500
Beginning Cash	4,100	7,895	(10,605)
Ending Cash	7,895	(10,605)	47,895

You can see that February will be a tough month, as shown by the negative "Ending Cash" column. The agency will not have enough cash to pay its bills until March.

When you receive this statement, it can inspire some probing questions about the current state of financial affairs. If you sat on a board that received the cash flow projection on the previous page, you might consider asking some of these questions of yourself, your treasurer, your ED, or your CFO:

- Can some invoices or payments be deferred until March, such as insurance?

- Can the government funding be received in February?

- Does the agency need a line of credit?

- Can a large, seasonal payment such as insurance be paid in installments, or can the entire payment be rescheduled to a month when revenues are sufficient?

- Going forward, how many months of operating reserves should we aim to save so that we have sufficient cash during months with shortfalls?

- Did some revenue categories come in under budget recently, exacerbating the cash flow crunch? Do we need to readjust the budget for the remainder of the year to account for these new decreases?

Save the Salaries!

Salary is typically a nonprofit's largest expense —and it must be paid on schedule. Managing cash flow helps ensure that your staff will receive their paychecks. Missing payroll can be disastrous for morale and for your organization's reputation.

IMPORTANT!

Unlike the example, which just shows a few months, the cash flow projection should lay out cash sources and uses for the entire fiscal year. Ideally, the projection will be a rolling twelve-month statement that is continually generated, regardless of a fiscal year beginning or end. Once a month has passed, staff will update the statement to show the actual amounts for each category for that particular month.

Many nonprofits run into seasonal cash flow surges and dry spells. That tends to happen because most organizations' income is not spread evenly throughout the year, and most groups do not have sufficient reserves. You and your peers can plan for this common occurrence by recognizing patterns in your annual spending and revenue—saving in the good months so that you can pay your bills when income slows.

Even if your organization's expenses remain fairly steady throughout the year, income is rarely steady: Most notably, the holiday season brings in about 40 percent of many organizations' annual revenue. And summers are notoriously quiet on the revenue front. Some nonprofit staff takes great pains to secure additional funds prior to predictable seasonal lags. But throw in a government grant that arrives late or a major donor who loses a job, and the best-laid plans can go astray.

And we haven't even talked about unexpected large bills that can throw off your cash on the expense side: that huge bill to fix a leaky roof, for example. So, make sure you've got plenty of cash on hand to pay your bills, and

---

Pure Genius!

Avoiding Cash Flow Chaos

A home health agency relies heavily on government reimbursements to pay its 200+ home care aides. In the past, this nonprofit did not have sufficient reserves or a line of credit. When government payments were late (which happened with some regularity), the agency was thrown into a cash flow crisis.

After enduring this painful cycle for too long, the board, working with the executive director, raised six months of operating reserves. Now when government payments are delayed, cash flow chaos does not ensue.

The ABCs of Financial Literacy

These key terms will aid your understanding of all things financial.

- *Assets* are what your organization owns. Examples include cash, equipment (net of depreciation), and accounts receivable. Short-term assets typically can be converted to cash in less than one year and long-term assets in more than one year.

- *Liabilities* are what your organization owes. Examples include accounts payable, rent payable, and mortgage. Similar to assets, liabilities are often defined as short-term and long-term.

- *Net assets* are the difference between the organization's assets and liabilities. Remember this equation: Assets – Liabilities = Net Assets. If your net assets are negative, then what's owed is greater than what's owned. Not good!

- *Accounts receivable* are amounts of money that an individual, foundation, or government owes your organization.

- *Accounts payable* represent amounts of money that your organization owes others such as vendors, consultants, and employees.

- *Revenues* show the income streams for your organization. Examples include individual donations, grants, earned income, and the United Way.

- *Expenses* represent categories for which your organization generally pays cash or cuts checks. Examples include salaries, payroll taxes, benefits, supplies, rent, and insurance.

- *Net surplus (loss)* is calculated by subtracting expenses from revenues. An agency with a net surplus is generally in good financial health.

- *Unrestricted revenues/funds* can be used however needed within the organization. They are also known as general operating support.

- *Restricted revenues/funds* are designated for a particular program or purpose. For example, a grant designated to purchase computers may only be used for this purpose. The board must ensure that computers are in fact purchased!

- *Depreciation* refers to a reduction in asset value over time due to usage, wear, and tear. The asset's original value is depreciated each year, resulting in a net value for the asset.

encourage your organization to maintain a healthy reserve. Those are simply two of the best financial oversight steps you can take—and they don't require you to be a CPA!

What Is a Statement of Financial Position?

The *statement of financial position* (SFP), also commonly called a balance sheet, provides a snapshot of the agency on any given day and together with the cash flow projection, these documents become a financial dynamic duo! This document shows the organization's assets, liabilities, and net assets, or net equity. Most people think of this document in terms of its corporate nomenclature, the balance sheet. It is the organizational equivalent of personal net worth. No matter the context, this formula encapsulates the SFP's contents:

Assets = Liabilities + Net Assets (or Equity)

OR

What you have or own = What you owe + What's left over

As you can see, the equation balances. How it balances is important. To illustrate, we will use a familiar example: a home mortgage. Let's say that you purchase a home (asset) worth $350,000, with a mortgage (liability) of $275,000. Your net assets (equity) in the home equal $75,000. What happens if your home value plummets to $250,000? Now your mortgage exceeds your home value by $25,000, resulting in negative equity. This is obviously an undesirable situation. If you were to try to sell your home, there wouldn't be enough cash from the sale to cover your mortgage. Similarly, nonprofits can have balance sheets with either positive or negative net assets. As a board member, when you monitor the relationship between the variables in this simple equation, you can see your organization's cumulative financial position at a particular point in time.

The above equation takes on this format in an SFP:

Sample Statement of Financial Position

ABC Organization Statement of Financial Position for September 30, 2016				
	Sept. 30, 2016 ($)		Sept. 30, 2015 ($)	
Assets				
Short-term Assets				
Bank Checking Account	15,000		25,000	
Bank CD	7,500		2,500	
Investment Accounts	45,895		52,250	
Accounts Receivable	20,000		3,750	
Total Short-term Assets		88,395		83,500
Long-term Assets				
Computer Equipment	15,000		15,000	
Less Accumulated Depreciation	10,000		7,500	
Net Computer Equipment	5,000		7,500	
Operating Reserve	15,125		25,275	
Total Long-term Assets		20,125		32,775
Total Assets		108,520		116,275
Liabilities				
Short-term Liabilities				
Payroll Taxes Payable	3,257		2,895	
Accounts Payable	4,596		7,895	
Credit Card Balances	795		0	
Total Short-term Liabilities		8,648		10,790
Long-term Liabilities				
Mortgage	75,253		78,025	
Total Long-term Liabilities		75,253		78,025
Total Liabilities		83,901		88,815
Net Assets		24,619		27,460
Total Liabilities & Net Assets		108,520		116,275

Below are some of the questions this document might prompt you to ask:

- Cash in bank. Is there enough cash in the bank to make the next two payrolls and to meet the month's expenses? Is the cash in the bank for the current year far above or below last year's figure at this time? Why?

- Accounts receivable. If cash is low, is there any money owed that has not yet been paid? Are receivables higher this year than last, or lower? Why? Are there any receivables that are past due more than, say, sixty days? If so, who owes the money and why hasn't payment been collected?

- Investment accounts. If your agency is fortunate enough to have an operating reserve that is invested, is the investment growing or shrinking? If the latter, is the cause a bear stock market? Poor financial decisions or advice?

- Equipment. Typically equipment, technology, and buildings (just to list a few) are shown at their purchase price and then are depreciated over time. Have computers been fully depreciated? This could, for example, be an indication that the computer lab might need upgrading.

- Accounts payable. How much does your organization owe others? In general, accounts payable are short term, with payment usually due within thirty days (think credit card!). Is the accounts payable line increasing? Why? Is there enough cash on hand to pay bills on time?

- Net assets. Are net assets positive or negative? If they are negative, your organization has more liabilities (money owed) than assets (cash on hand, accounts receivable, equipment, etc.). This is not good news.

It is very helpful if the financial statements you review are comparative, meaning that they show the financial state for a similar period last fiscal year. This can help you identify areas of material difference, since many organizations' financials take on seasonal patterns. So, if your October cash flow statement shows remarkably little cash on hand, a comparative statement might show that the same was true last year, until the fall gala and holiday giving filled your coffers. If your organization's statements are not comparative, make that request during a board meeting. Ensuring that you have the tools to evaluate financials is a central part of your job.

What Is a Statement of Activities?

You might hear a *statement of activities* (SOA) called an income statement, a profit/loss statement, or a revenue and expense statement. The latter is most fitting, since this document outlines. . . none other than. . . revenues and expenses over a period of time. It is most useful when it compares current year figures to the same period last year and includes a column that shows the current year's budget goals for each category. The SOA is a yardstick that helps measure the progress made toward its financial plan, the budget. The formula that this document illustrates is this:

Revenues – Expenses = Net Income or (Net Loss)

Sample Statement of Activities

ABC Organization Statement of Activities for January 1–September 30, 2016					
	01/01/16 to 09/30/16 ($)	01/01/15 to 09/30/15 ($)	$ Change 2015 to 2016	% Change 2015 to 2016	2016 Budget
Revenues					
Individual Giving	25,000	45,000	(20,000)	(44.4)	50,000
Board Giving	5,000	3,000	2,000	66.7	7,500
Foundation Grants	85,000	75,000	10,000	13.3	80,000
Government	95,000	115,000	(20,000)	(17.4)	125,000
Religious Support	12,500	9,750	2,750	28.2	15,000
United Way	3,500	2,500	1,000	40.0	3,500
Totals	226,000	250,250	(24,250)	(9.7)	281,000
Expenses					
Salaries	123,750	125,000	(1,250)	(1.0)	165,000
Rent	50,000	45,000	5,000	11.1	60,000
Payroll Taxes	9,467	9,563	(96)	(1.0)	12,623
Client Support	5,000	12,500	(7,500)	(60.0)	15,000
Supplies	4,750	7,500	(2,750)	(36.7)	8,500
Fundraising Event	5,000	4,950	50	1.0	7,500
Total Expenses	197,967	204,513	(6,546)	(3.2)	268,623
Net Surplus (Loss)	28,033	45,737	(17,704)	(38.7)	12,377

If net income is positive, the organization is running a surplus. If it is negative, there is a deficit. Focus on the items below as you look at the SOA:

- Material differences. Some boards require explanations from staff if an actual revenue or expense item is plus or minus, say, 10 percent of the budget projection.

- Budget goals. Are there revenue categories that are way off the budget targets and likely will not be reached? Are there expense categories that are over budget or appear to be on track to exceed projections? Why? It's important to note that any divergences become particularly important during the last half of the fiscal year, as the rest of the financial picture begins to gel.

- Year-over-year revenue and expense comparisons. Are there revenue categories that are well below a similar period last year? Are there expense categories for this year that exceed last year's totals at this time?

- Net surplus or net shortfall. Does the agency have a net operating surplus (revenues greater than expenses) or shortfall (expenses

---

Definition

Cash Versus Accrual Accounting

Cash accounting recognizes revenues on the date when they are deposited into the organization's account and expenses on the date a check is cut to pay a bill. Cash accounting is best used for less complicated and smaller organizations.

Accrual accounting recognizes revenues when earned (as opposed to when deposited into the bank) and expenses when they are incurred (as opposed to when the check is cut). This method tracks accounts receivable and accounts payable.

Most organizations use accrual accounting. Beware! You should know that your organization could show a large net surplus but have no cash in the bank. Why? With the accrual method, a $100,000 grant that was awarded but not yet collected would be recognized as revenue before it actually makes its way to your bank account.

greater than revenues)? If it is early in the fiscal year, it is quite possible that you will see a net loss. If that's the case, how does that shortfall compare with last year's numbers at this time? Might this be a seasonal shortfall that will be made up soon? If the organization is ten months into the fiscal year and showing a large net loss. . . that's a red flag!

What Are Financial Checks and Balances?

To help ensure financial integrity, which in turn impacts the integrity of financial statements, your board will want to implement some form of checks and balances. A good system assigns financial functions to multiple people: One person should not be handling the money, counting it, depositing it, cutting the checks, and reconciling the bank statement. When one person does all the financial work, that's when mistakes are made and not caught, and you leave your organization open to inaccurate financial statements and even more serious issues such as embezzlement or theft.

When there is plenty of staff, it is easier to spread out the financial functions among multiple people. If your agency is smaller or relatively new, it is possible that checks and balances are less formal and possibly nonexistent. However, they are no less important. It is imperative to find a division of labor. A few ideas:

- Have the board treasurer generate and sign all checks.

- Require two signatures on check amounts over, say one thousand dollars, or whatever amount the board decides.

- Require that the organization use a web-based accounting system and provide the board chair and treasurer with usernames and passwords.

- Ensure that the ED gets board approval before signing for any debt, including a credit card, in the organization's name.

- Provide the board chair and treasurer with usernames and passwords to all online banking accounts.

💡 Require that the ED notify the treasurer before transferring funds between accounts electronically.

💡 Have a hard copy of the bank statement mailed to the treasurer, who will review it and sign off before staff reconciles it.

Larger organizations are more likely to spell out formal checks and balances in financial policies, which will be detailed in Chapter 14. Even if your organization is small, document your procedures in writing. This does not have to be a fifty-page policy document, but the text should provide enough detail for an outsider to understand who is responsible for what and when. This document will ensure that board and staff are on the same page, and it can be used by the auditor to determine whether your organization adheres to its own checks and balances. Speaking of auditors. . .

What Is an Audit and Should Your Organization Have One?

When it's all said and done at the end of a fiscal year, you'll want some kind of independent assessment of your organization's finances. That usually takes the form of an audit, typically conducted by a CPA or accounting firm. If done well, an audit can identify ways to improve internal financial controls as well as give the staff, board, and the public peace of mind that the agency is well managed financially.

An audit task force or committee typically handles the details from the board

Audit Your Auditor

One ED—to save money—asked his next-door neighbor and good friend to conduct the agency's annual audit. The board was not informed of the connection between the two. A few years later, when the ED resigned, the board discovered that the books were in total disarray. The board completely overlooked its responsibility to hire the auditor and ensure that there where no conflicts of interest between those enlisted and the nonprofit. The auditing team reports to the board, usually the treasurer or other designated board member.

Uninspired

side. The ED is an important partner in this process by helping to identify and research appropriate firms and soliciting bids. However, board members select the auditor and should execute the contract.

When the process is underway, the ED and staff provide information and documents needed by the auditing team. The relevant committee and ED then review the draft audit, seeking full board approval. The auditor then presents the final document to the board and takes questions. While you don't need to be a CPA to feel confident about approving the audit, the points below will give you some added perspective.

Opinions Matter!

A foundation's program officer read a potential grantee's opinion letter, which cited five significant deficiencies. While there was no evidence of wrongdoing, the fact that internal controls had been breached was a major concern. During a site visit, the program officer discovered that some of the findings had still not been resolved and the board was not engaged in holding the ED accountable for fixing the issues.

The result? The foundation declined the proposal request and informed the ED that once a "clean" opinion letter was provided by the auditor, the organization could submit a new funding request for consideration.

WATCH OUT!

On the financial side, you will see that the financial statements discussed throughout this chapter will also appear in the audit—they may just look a bit different than what your staff produces. Use the bulleted points throughout this chapter as guides to review the financial statements in the audit.

What will be new to you will be the *opinion letter*, a statement as to whether there are any problems with the financials or with the procedures in place to ensure checks and balances. An unqualified or "clean" audit is an important part of establishing financial credibility.

If the auditor has concerns, those will be outlined in a separate management letter. Those are referred to as "significant deficiencies" or "material weaknesses," the latter being the more severe of the two. It is the board's responsibility to ensure that any issues stated in the management letter are resolved. Depending on the issue or finding, financial policies or other written procedures may need to be created or revised to satisfy the auditor's concerns.

Audits have limitations. While a clean audit is wonderful, board members must be mindful that the audit process merely samples transactions that have occurred throughout the year. A clean audit signifies that the auditor found the financials to convey a fair and accurate picture of the organization. However, it is quite possible that the process could miss embezzlement or other serious issues. To help strengthen the audit process, it's important to have an approved set of financial policies; the audit team can use these as a guide to determine if staff is in fact following protocols spelled out in those policies.

Does Your Nonprofit *Need* an Audit?

This is an especially important question given that they can be expensive. If your organization is small and does not have significant government contracts, yours might not need an audit. Your board, in partnership with the ED, will largely make this determination based on whether its major funders require it. Sometimes, the IRS Form 990 will suffice. Other times, a nonprofit can spend less money by using a financial review.

A *financial review* is less rigorous than an audit, as it does not include any on-site transaction testing or validation, nor is an "opinion" issued. While a financial review might save money, it is not always an acceptable form of financial examination from a donor's perspective. For example, government agencies typically require audits with grant applications. The board and ED must weigh the pros and cons of conducting an audit; evading one just to save money can result in missed funding opportunities that end up costing even more than the audit itself.

You've done it. You've reached the end of the financial section. While these topics might seem overwhelming, they will quickly begin to feel routine as you use them in context with your organization's financial realities. Continue to learn, ask questions, and request group training when you sense that your peers have some of the same questions as you.

To Summarize...

- Basic financial literacy is a must for all board members.

- Make sure someone on your board does a deep dive into the financial statements. However, that doesn't mean that no one else needs to pay attention.

- Spend some time understanding the cash flow projection, the statement of financial position, and the statement of activities.

- Create a system of financial checks and balances, regardless of the size of your organization.

- Audits or financial reviews are an important part of your financial checks and balances, but are only a sampling of information and do not always uncover serious financial issues.

Chapter 12

From Ambassador to Advocate

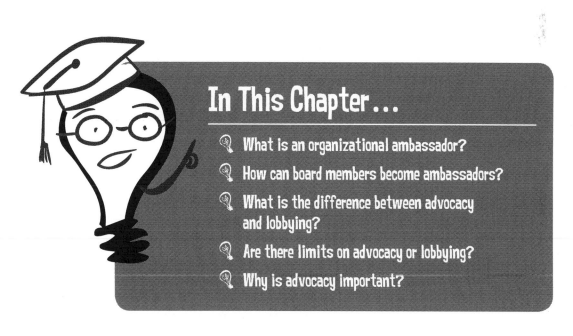

In This Chapter...

- What is an organizational ambassador?
- How can board members become ambassadors?
- What is the difference between advocacy and lobbying?
- Are there limits on advocacy or lobbying?
- Why is advocacy important?

You will be happy to know that board membership is not all about financials. We will pause from the factual side of your job to focus on an equally important aspect, one that will allow you to harness enthusiasm for the mission.

When most of us think of ambassadors, we think about those who represent our country abroad. Those representatives are national symbols in *all* of their undertakings. Your role as an organizational ambassador will hold similar weight. People might start to recognize you as a board member, ask questions about your organization, and even expect entrée into your nonprofit's circles. On that last point, you can expect to encourage others to become involved in ways that best suit them. You will be a matchmaker of sorts. In that way, your ambassador role can be one of your most fulfilling as a board member.

What Does It Mean to Be an Ambassador?

Being an ambassador means actively representing your organization in the community, talking about it with family, friends, colleagues, your spiritual community, local businesses, even your hairdresser. Your goal here is to help broaden your organization's web of support by linking your relevant networks to the organization. Notice we said "relevant." You should not feel pressured to invite all those in your circles to give time, money, or even thought to this mission. If Aunt Bessie is allergic to cats and has recurring nightmares about being attacked by dogs, by all means, refrain from asking her to volunteer at your animal shelter! Instead, selectively approach those who have relevant interests and then, again selectively, decide which organizational opportunities might align with their preferences. It's true that you won't always know someone's interests, so we provide some tips below.

To be a good ambassador, you and your board colleagues must know enough about your nonprofit to talk intelligently, persuasively, and even emotionally about your organization, who it serves, and why you have decided to devote your time to its mission. You must also have a good understanding of the organization's needs, so you can help plug new supporters in where their time or contributions are most valuable. Every organization will have its own list of opportunities for its supporters; these are among the most common:

- Volunteer

- Attend an event

- Provide in-kind goods

- Make a financial gift

💡 Open the door to a corporate, government, religious, or individual contact

💡 Promote the organization's work in the community

These actions help to identify tomorrow's pro bono professionals, donors, and yes, board members.

How Do You Create a Board of Ambassadors?

If you begin to speak of your organization's value in public, imagine the snowball effect when your board peers do the same. Of course, your ED does this work every day. When you all work together, the web of people, businesses, and resources connected to your agency will flourish.

The Power of Ambassadors

An enthusiastic board member spoke of her human rights organization whenever she got the chance. Her corporate employer hosted a social action committee for its employees, and during one of its brown bag lunches, she touted some of the nonprofit's success stories and a few volunteer opportunities. A colleague inquired and began to volunteer. Soon after, this new volunteer joined the board. Several years later, after the first woman completed her board term, her recruit assumed the presidency.

Pure Genius!

Typically, board leadership sets the tone for how engaged members become. Those officers, along with the governance committee, can encourage budding ambassadors by sharing some success stories of their own, and offering some training. If your chair is focused elsewhere, there is no stopping another member from taking a leadership role on this front. It really just takes a regular series of board-level conversations until these activities become part of the culture. The goal here is to develop an "ambassador corps" that engenders regular outreach to the community. Here are a few ways to get started:

💡 Emphasize the board's role in community outreach during the recruitment process.

💡 Include it as a responsibility on your board commitment form.

- Be clear about ongoing expectations associated with this role.

- Ensure that your organization's messaging remains compelling, timely, and clear.

- Engage in training and role play to build knowledge and confidence.

- Provide tools, such as brochures, annual reports, and a solid website, that will help board members become effective ambassadors.

Messaging

The most successful boards ensure that their messaging is consistent, so that all members head out of meetings whistling the same tune. Since it can take time to both develop and internalize your nonprofit's external message, consider suggesting it be a topic of multiple board agendas. What board members will crave are short communications that will help convey the mission in various situations, with comfortable delivery:

- A thirty-second "elevator speech" about what your organization does

- A short retelling of why it is that you are involved in this organization

- An anecdote or two about the nonprofit's impact, in the form of a client story or an amazing performance

Elevator Speech

One of the most important things you can do is practice your elevator speech, which is the couple of sentences you will relay in brief encounters with those who know little or nothing about your organization.

First-Person Accounts Equal First-Person Engagement

Personal stories engender more attachment to an organization than any video, storyboard, or informational packet. Why? Because you are a trustworthy source to those in your circles. Your concise, compelling account of a formerly homeless mother who learned to cook and now works as a sous chef is a story you may well have witnessed with your own eyes. That means the world to someone who, presumably, has developed a relationship with you because you share similar values.

Inspiration

Why not just memorize your mission? Sometimes, that does help. But if your mission is long, or if the language is too formal to fit into casual conversation, you and your peers can tweak it.

This kind of pithy communication comes in handy when, say, you and a colleague are mixing your morning coffee in the company kitchen. Your coworker, Jess, asks what you did over the weekend. You reply that you attended a tennis tournament in your role as board member for Tennis Teens. You then see that Jess has finished stirring his cream and sugar and is slowing heading for the door. With just a short time to respond, you proclaim, "Tennis Teens uses sports to propel physically disabled young people to new levels of strength and confidence." Maybe Jess stops and wants to learn more. Maybe you have planted a seed for future conversations. The important thing here is that you are prepared to convey a short, compelling statement of purpose.

Personal Case Statement

If Jess asks for more information, it will likely take one of two directions. If he knows a young person who is physically disabled, he might ask some factual questions about Tennis Teens' programs. Otherwise, he might ask how you became involved in this cause.

This personal case statement is likely the simplest of the three messaging staples because it retells your own story. Maybe you have a child or other family member with a disability. Maybe a friend drew you to this organization. Whatever the reason, be prepared with a brief, compelling story. It can be a little longer than the elevator speech, but it must be specific. Phrase your story in personal terms. Relive that first encounter with your organization—the one that really pulled you in and made you want to stay. Your goal here is to express the emotional pull that led to your current level of involvement. As simple as it sounds, it's worth thinking about in advance.

Impact Story

Something else you will want to consider in advance: a story that conveys the impact of your organization. If your nonprofit directly serves clients, then you will come upon compelling, emotional stories when you *experience* the mission—through first-hand accounts or activities with clients. If you get out on the front lines of your nonprofit's work regularly, you might have an abundance of anecdotes to convey. Prepare yourself to speak about one particular client whose story encompasses all that your organization has to offer—ideally, a transformation. The more you practice telling that person's story, the more you can hone the finer points of his or her renewal. The key here is to tell just enough detail to draw the listener in and position that person—if so inclined—to want to learn more.

Maybe your organization doesn't serve people directly but is a legal or advocacy group, an industry association, or an umbrella organization. Do those kinds of nonprofits lend themselves to emotion-filled client or impact stories?

Sure they do.

Legal work, advocacy, and support services all affect individuals, even if they are several steps removed from those served. If your nonprofit is a national organization whose beneficiaries the board does not see regularly, ask staff or volunteers with knowledge of the grassroots impact to share what they have seen. Better yet, suggest inviting one or more beneficiaries to speak at

Inspiration

Making It Personal

An advocacy organization was committed to increasing wages for restaurant servers who earned $2.13 per hour, plus tips. Efforts to get a law passed through the city council were not going anywhere. The nonprofit decided to focus on putting this issue before voters as a ballot initiative. The measure passed and the minimum wage for these workers increased to $6.50 per hour, plus tips. The ED asked several workers who benefitted from the increased hourly wage to come to a board meeting and share how the agency's advocacy directly impacted them. These personal stories were used by board members to convey to others, in a very emotional and personal way, the impact of the organization's work.

an upcoming board meeting. That way, if yours is an agency that advocates for patients' rights, you can hear directly about the impact of your agency's health policy work on patients.

Role Play

With the information above, you will be fully prepared to bring people into your nonprofit's family of supporters. The trick is, as simple as these three items sound, you need to learn to convey them briefly and with passion. That takes practice. So, if your board doesn't do so already, you might suggest that members devote twenty minutes at a meeting—or a few—to role play. Imagine that you are Joe, water cooler socialite, or Tricia, fellow PTA member. Create five-minute scenarios whereby you and a board peer can engage in dialogue sparked by questions such as, "What did you do this weekend?" or "I heard you're on the board of ABC Charity. . . ." Pair up, and while one of you plays the board member role, the other serves as colleague, acquaintance, or fellow congregant. Create a setting, and get everyone talking! While some boards shy away from role play, it provides a chance to hone your message, get comfortable finding your voice, and even have a little fun.

Tools of the Trade

Once you have sharpened the message, a few tools can aid your ambassador role:

- Business cards. The front might list your name, "Board Member" or your board leadership position, email address, and phone number, along with the organization's physical and web addresses. On the reverse side, include the nonprofit's mission.

- Name tags. When you and your peers wear name tags at events that identify yourselves as board members, the recognition can spur conversations with other event attendees.

- Website. Take some time to familiarize yourself with your organization's website. That way, you can direct interested parties to specific pages, such as a calendar of events, strategic plans, or client testimonials.

How Do You Unleash the Ambassador in You?

Serving as an ambassador is easy for some and not so easy for others. This is one of those jobs that each member will interpret differently. Each will use personal judgment to determine how the ambassador role will unfold. Bottom line: Every board member can and must do it.

After you engage in the role play and introspection suggested above, it's time to create a plan for yourself. In most cases, you will simply talk about your organization when the opportunity presents itself, as it did with our fictional Jess.

You can also learn about the different ways in which potential supporters can become involved in your organization. Once someone shows interest in what you have to say, be ready to invite that person to come see your site, volunteer at Saturday's Save the Bay event, or attend next month's graduation ceremony. If it isn't apparent to you which introductory

Who Can You Bring Along?

Good board members bring their relevant contacts to the nonprofit. So, start giving some thought to the many people in your network who might be interested in the mission:

- Family
- Friends
- Colleagues
- Your employer
- Small business owners you know
- Neighbors
- Fellow congregants
- Houses of worship
- Fellow hobbyists
- Alumni
- Social networks
- Former coworkers

Perspiration

options are available, that would be a great topic of conversation to suggest for a board meeting.

If you still find yourself lacking confidence about, say, your nonprofit's complex work, take some time to learn from the pros. Your ED and any other senior staff often spend countless hours in the community as the ultimate organizational ambassadors. Ask to join them. Not only will this activity benefit you as you listen to your ED talk about your organization, but external stakeholders *love* to see board members out and about on behalf of their nonprofits. After all, your time speaks volumes about the pull this agency has on its community.

Consider attending visits with government officials, donors, individual supporters, and potential nonprofit partners. Sometimes, funders will even come visit your nonprofit's site, another great way to learn the kinds of

Perspiration

Spread the Word!

Make the ambassador role fun. Consider setting goals for individual members and for the entire board. Ask a board volunteer to monitor measures like these:

- See how many of your board members will host facility tours by the end of the fiscal year.

- Count how many members share organizational information with corporate leaders or employee groups during the next fiscal year. Can you reach ten? Twenty? Thirty?

- Challenge each other to introduce at least five new people to the organization—through events, program activities, and conversation from one board meeting to the next. Can your fifteen board members each commit to spreading the word among at least three new people? That would be forty-five potential supporters, all in a relatively short span of time!

Consider rewarding the winner—or group—with a fun prize or outing.

questions outsiders have about the agency and how your ED answers them. These opportunities also allow you to talk about why you are involved in the organization.

What Is a Board Member's Role in Advocacy and Lobbying?

Once you are a stellar ambassador, you can take it to the next level and do some advocacy or lobbying, using many of the same skill sets. These pursuits sometimes get a bad rap. But increasingly, if a nonprofit wants to create the greatest impact on its community, it must engage in regulatory or policy change or push for adequate resources. That kind of activity is not for every organization, but if yours does not currently engage in either advocacy or lobbying, it's worth a board-level conversation to make sure that your decision is an intentional one.

Both activities are designed to influence decision makers. The main difference is that *advocacy* uses education or public campaigns to influence the views of policy makers and the general public. It increases awareness around a particular issue with the goal of creating some kind of change, usually political. *Lobbying* is designed to pass or derail a specific piece of legislation. It usually involves direct contact with elected officials. Grassroots lobbying uses public campaigns to influence an outcome for a piece of legislation. Both advocacy and lobbying are permissible regardless of an organization's mission.

It's important to note that staff tends to take the lead on advocacy. But, board members can play important roles when they either have connections to legislators or when they speak on behalf of the organization in their roles as volunteers. No matter what kind of connections or enthusiasm you have around advocacy, be sure to work closely with staff before you move forward.

For the most part, advocacy is permitted without limit. Lobbying is a different story. To comply with IRS regulations, lobbying efforts must not constitute a "substantial part" of the organization's overall activities. To help define this, the IRS limits a 501(c)3 organization, for example, to spending 20 percent of its budget on direct lobbying and 25 percent for grassroots lobbying. Nonprofits that lobby are required to submit additional information with their IRS Form 990 to show that lobbying efforts remained beneath these levels. There are also prohibitions on the use of federal funds for lobbying. It might make sense for your organization to pursue this line of work, but it's important that your board and staff have experts who fully understand its limits.

While lobbying is allowed within limits, it is important to note that a 501(c)(3) organization is prohibited from endorsing any political candidates. Be very careful if your organization is engaged in politics of any sort, since missteps can result in a revocation of your tax-exempt status. If your agency wants to be politically active, you might need to establish a separate nonprofit entity that is permitted to lobby for or endorse candidates. Seek legal advice before wading into these waters.

Below are some examples that help distinguish these terms from each other:

Advocacy versus Lobbying

Examples of Advocacy	Examples of Lobbying
Testifying before a government committee on a subject that you are considered expert	Asking a legislator or council member to vote for or against, or to amend, proposed legislation
Educating a local, state, or federal legislator about the effects of a policy on your constituency	Emailing or using social media to issue a "call to action" to your supporters, members, or stakeholders urging them to contact their elected officials in support of or against pending legislation or regulations
Helping policy makers find solutions to problems that your organization is adept at handling or solving	Preparing materials or organizing events (e.g., sit ins, protests) in support of lobbying efforts
Writing a white paper on an issue that includes recommendations on how to solve that issue; distributing that paper to policy makers,legislators, and the general public	

To be an effective ambassador who advocates or lobbies on behalf of your organization, you need to be well steeped in the issue at hand. You will likely require training about the latest trends and the external environment. To aid in this process, the executive director or another key staff person might:

- Develop talking points for you to use with particular audiences

- Draft a letter for your signature that will be submitted to the appropriate government officials

- Provide research-based articles that support the organization's position

While we have only scratched the surface here, hopefully you are beginning to understand that your enthusiasm for the mission can have broad impact in the community. You have the power to attract people's interests, draw them to attend events, and—in the form of grassroots lobbying—even rally them to change the course of the law. As you are about to find out, you can also harness that same passion for the purpose of keeping your organization financially sustainable.

To Summarize...

- As a board member, expect to be a messenger for the organization, educating others about the mission, cultivating relationships, and inviting those in your circles to become involved.

- Good board leadership devotes time to unleash the ambassador in everyone.

- Spend time getting comfortable with your elevator speech, personal case statement, and impact story.

- Board members may assist with advocacy and lobbying, but IRS guidelines restrict the amount of lobbying an organization can undertake.

- 501(c)(3) organizations are prohibited from endorsing candidates for public office.

Chapter 13

The "F" Word: Fundraising

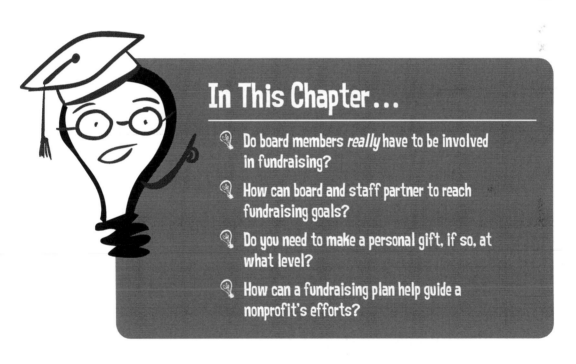

In This Chapter...

- Do board members *really* have to be involved in fundraising?

- How can board and staff partner to reach fundraising goals?

- Do you need to make a personal gift, if so, at what level?

- How can a fundraising plan help guide a nonprofit's efforts?

Fundraising is a dirty word to many board members. They don't want to hear it, they don't want to utter it, they hope it just weasels its way out of the board lexicon. Suddenly, talk of financial statements sounds pretty good! Yet, it is an expectation that nearly every board and ED have of their members. As a matter of fact, it's one of the few roles that most would agree are explicitly shared by both board and staff. Without board members' fundraising assistance, those financial statements stand to look much shakier.

While it may take some time for you to overcome your hesitation to raise funds, once you begin, you will learn how terrific it feels to succeed. After all, the process helps advance the mission you adore. Thankfully, there are many approaches to fundraising. Most are natural progressions of your role as an ambassador, so surely, at least a few will fall within your comfort zone.

What is Fundraising, Really?

Every nonprofit has a particular mix of income streams that funds its programs and services. *Earned income*, for instance, includes revenue on the sales of products or services. *Contributed income* comprises donated funds, income that does not require the nonprofit to directly provide goods or services in exchange for the gift. *Fundraising* is the process of securing that contributed income. This chapter focuses on contributed income, including:

- Individuals' gifts of cash, stock, planned, and in-kind gifts
- Foundation grants
- Government funding
- Corporate grants, in-kind products, pro bono services, and sponsorships
- Contributions from charitable, religious, and civic organizations

A healthy organization benefits from diverse funding streams. That way, if one dries up, the organization will not find its entire coffer depleted. You will find your organization's current mix of gifts and grants in the budget. There are several ways to secure that income, among them:

- Web-based donation pages
- Grant proposals
- Direct mail
- Personal solicitations

- 💡 Email

- 💡 Social media

- 💡 Special events

- 💡 Workplace giving campaigns, including the United Way and the Combined Federal Campaign

- 💡 In-kind gifts, which are contributions of goods or services, as opposed to cash

Fundraising is a central board role, no matter what level of experience you bring to the table. When you help bolster fundraising, you help make those income lines on the financial statements healthier. That's *certainly* a core responsibility. You also help ensure your organization's long-term sustainability, because today's ten-dollar donor might leave a million-dollar bequest a decade from now. You really never know what a new donor is capable of doing, so take pride in each new supporter who relishes your organization.

How Can Your Board Cultivate a Culture of Philanthropy?

If you're anxious about asking people to contribute funds, you're not alone. Many people begin their board service most nervous about this very thing. If you're lucky, your board—and your organization—regularly inject fundraising into their work. That's called a *culture of philanthropy*. It doesn't mean that you will be opening your wallet at every meeting (although if you do, you might win your nonprofit's Board Member of the Year Award). It means that fundraising is embedded in nearly everything that your board does. Leadership helps you get comfortable with the idea of raising funds and gives you the tools and the training to get started. It becomes second nature for members to consider how each community outreach effort might support the bottom line. Staff—at all levels—understands that all it does impacts fundraising.

Fundraising can be akin to healthy eating: If you diet regularly, you likely dread Diet's Eve, when you say to yourself, "The diet starts tomorrow." But

The ABCs of Fundraising

If you have these fundraising terms in your toolkit, you will quickly begin to grasp this fundamental topic.

- *Annual gifts* come to the organization on a yearly basis. They can arrive via direct mail, email campaigns, phone, or social media campaigns.

- *Major gifts* are large contributions. Each nonprofit defines what's considered "major" based on the range of gifts it receives.

- *Planned gifts* are major gifts that are structured to achieve a donor's personal, financial, and estate-planning goals. They often include gifts of stocks, bonds, or other assets and are made via a will or trust.

- *Grants* are contributions made by institutions, such as foundations, the United Way, or government agencies. They tend to require a written proposal and detailed reporting.

- *In-kind gifts* are donated goods or services such as computer equipment or food donated to a homeless shelter.

- *General operating*, or *unrestricted, support* refers to funds secured to benefit the entire organization, including salaries, utilities, and programs.

- *Restricted support* refers to funds that must be used for a particular project or purpose. Also called project support.

- *Campaigns* are time-limited initiatives that raise funds through a variety of means to fund general operations, endowments, or capital investments.

- *Cultivation* is the process building relationships with donors and prospective donors. It includes educating and inspiring them to invest in the mission.

- *Stewardship* refers to the process of maintaining good relationships with donors once they have contributed to your organization.

- *Solicitation* is the process of asking for gifts.

Fundraising Registration

In order to solicit funds from individuals or conduct fundraising in general, most states and the District of Columbia require nonprofits to register. Requirements vary by state, so look to your attorney general's office or secretary of state for more information. While it is a staff function to file the paperwork, it is the board's responsibility to ensure that the agency is in good standing with the states where it solicits donors. If your organization solicits nationally, that can be quite an investment of time and money. It's worth considering an upfront investment in specialists who can help with your initial registrations, since you will want to follow the right process to avoid penalties.

IMPORTANT!

if you modify your habits and eat well regularly, the "diet" becomes more palatable—a regular part of your behavior. A culture of philanthropy infuses fundraising into your daily board diet. It makes fundraising palatable. It is one sign of a healthy board.

If your nonprofit has an executive director, chances are, that person regularly loses sleep around issues of fundraising. It's important for you to know that even the most adept fundraisers are seeing their government grants decrease, individual donors lose their ability to contribute, and foundations change their funding priorities. You will do your ED a world of good if you come in with some sympathy for the unpredictable world of philanthropy.

The fundraising buck really does stop with the ED. A good board member, however, will pitch in wherever practical. Even if your nonprofit is lucky enough to have fundraising staff—often first in the form of a development director—the weight of income generation does not disappear. Usually, this level of staffing just indicates that the budget is large enough that the ED cannot both oversee operations *and* all of the money-raising efforts. A good ED is still very involved in fundraising.

Staff should not shoulder this burden alone. The typical ED works with the board chair to strategically determine how to best leverage members' skills, talents, and time to help secure financial resources. This is a team effort, and one that requires a fair amount of strategy.

As a board member, expect to find fundraising opportunities and education at your meetings and even during special training sessions. If there are tools or information that you desire, mention them to your fundraising or development committee members. Contrary to popular belief, those groups are not designed to raise funds *in place* of the board but to nurture their peers' success. We've seen board members who were terrified of fundraising become fantastic ambassadors, and in turn, raise plenty of funds for their organizations.

So, our focus here is not to help you master the art of asking for big gifts. Our goal is to provide some basic tips that suit the comfort level of most beginning board members.

Why Is Fundraising Less Daunting Than It Seems?

It's easy to assume that after a few board meetings, the board chair will expect that you ask your best friend for a $1,000 gift.

Not so.

Let's begin with a paradigm shift: Fundraising is the process of empowering your nonprofit's friends to support a cause they love. Most of those supporters are *looking* for a worthy mission where they can invest their charitable dollars. That's right, they are already planning to make philanthropic gifts this year and want to invest their money in the smartest way they know. They are shopping around for the right opportunity.

You may be wondering, "Wait a second. I receive no fewer than a dozen charitable solicitations a week—via email, social media, and snail mail. Who could possibly be shopping around for yet another charity to support?" It's true—it seems like there is no end to the requests we receive. It takes a committed ambassador—a board member!—to help transform a nonprofit from one of many into *the one* worthy of a donation.

Most likely, your organization has multiple ways it cultivates donors. As a board member, you can assist in these efforts without formally asking for a gift—at least not until you are ready. We know that it can be scary to wade into the fundraising waters. There are ways to build your confidence while signaling to others that this is an investment-worthy nonprofit. Here are some steps you can take, in the approximate order in which most new board members feel comfortable getting involved.

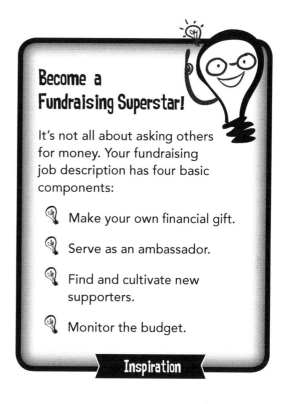

Become a Fundraising Superstar!

It's not all about asking others for money. Your fundraising job description has four basic components:

- Make your own financial gift.
- Serve as an ambassador.
- Find and cultivate new supporters.
- Monitor the budget.

Inspiration

Make Your Own Gift

In your first months on the board, it is imperative that you make a financial gift. Hopefully, someone filled you in on that expectation during the recruitment process. Your gift of time is tremendous, but it does not pay the electric bill. And while many boards are coy about asking members overtly for money, institutional funders, especially foundations, often ask about board giving participation. They expect to hear that 100 percent of members make annual contributions. So, your gifts must occur yearly—at a minimum—and they must be generous.

What do we mean by "generous"? Some boards will *tell* you the minimum gift you need to make. This idea of whether or not to require members to contribute at a minimum level is one of the most debated issues in many boardrooms, so if you come onto a board with that policy in place, don't expect to change it in the very near future. Setting a minimum amount can be controversial for a couple of reasons: It can prevent less affluent members from joining the board, or result in more affluent ones not giving beyond that minimum—even when they have the financial means to do so.

If the gift-making minimum is left to individual members, the notion of generosity is a relative one. Plan to give within your means, but we recommend this gift be among your top three charitable contributions for the year. It should even cause you to stretch your typical charitable giving. Aim to be a model for the community. It's possible that few others will ever know how much you contribute, but you should feel confident about revealing that figure in meetings with potential donors. Of course, if your organization produces an annual report that lists all individual donors by levels of giving, it is possible that this data will be very public indeed. The real reason you want to first make a gift is that you want to be able to shout from the rooftops,

"My board colleagues and I are so passionate about this organization's work that we're funding large portions of it with our hard-earned money. Yes, it's that good! Come join us!"

Observation

Give, Get, or Both?

Some boards have what they call "give or get" policies. They specify a minimum dollar amount, and members must raise that figure through some combination of personal financial contributions and/or by securing it via their networks. Boards that enforce such policies often struggle to accurately track all of the giving and getting. So, if yours is a give or get board, advocate for a simple system whereby board and staff create a document in the cloud or other format that allows both parties to track relevant contacts who have attended events, made gifts, or appear ready for further attention. Better yet, do all you can to encourage a culture of philanthropy where board members inspire each other to constantly raise the bar on their own giving and getting. Not everyone is cut out to be a fundraising superstar. It's fine to work under the premise that some members will take to the "getting" of gifts more than others. While we are not big advocates of give or get policies per se, we certainly do advocate that board members make regular financial contributions and encourage others to do so.

Slow and Steady

The fundraising team —a.k.a. the development team—at a veterans' organization encourages its board members to bring their networks into the fold in a very deliberate way. The staff gives board members a list of annual events and volunteer opportunities each year and gives the members time to consider which people in their circles might be interested in each activity. That way, board members can engage their circles in a strategic way, rather than just submitting a list of friends' contact information to the development team—a perpetually unsuccessful strategy that is used all too often.

Pure Genius!

If your board wants to take its giving to the next level, systematize it. Everyone is more likely to give more generously—and within the fiscal year—if there is a prescribed period of time when they are asked to give. Typically, the development committee and board chair, in partnership with staff, spearhead this process. In many cases, the executive director and chair contact members individually to solicit annual gifts.

Serve as Ambassador

You will be wearing your board hat wherever you go. Once you have followed the steps in Chapter 12 about becoming an ambassador, you will have set the stage for supporters to take the next logical step—charitable giving. The elements in your ambassador's toolbox will inspire others to consider supporting your nonprofit:

- Education—in the form of a story about your personal involvement

- Engagement—as you extend invitations to volunteer or attend community events

- Inspiration—in the form of a story about your organization's impact on a community member

These pieces might not always come in this order, but together, they form the foundation for a customized case for support. Once someone has attended an event or otherwise taken interest, there will come a time when your new supporter is so enthralled with your programming that this person is awaiting an invitation to invest in your organization. That happens when a board does its job well. Really, it does.

Engage Your Supporters

This is where you can link your role as ambassador to raising funds. There is a whole spectrum of activities available here, depending on your comfort level. Some executive directors work with each board member to develop an individualized, annual fundraising plan. The plan clearly outlines how that board member will secure resources in tandem with staff. Even if your organization doesn't yet use this approach, you can use one yourself in your quest to be a model board member. Then recommend it to the group! See Appendix C for an example of an individualized board member fundraising plan.

Yes, donors need to be asked for contributions, and the larger the potential gift, the more likely that the request must be made in person. But donors of all sizes must be *cultivated* (prepared) and *stewarded* (thanked). Between cultivation, asking, and stewarding, there exist nearly endless options for board member involvement. The importance of your role is one of putting a face to your organization's volunteer leadership, commitment, and giving. People really do pay attention to board involvement.

Put the "Fun" in Fundraising

Your board can transform otherwise mundane fundraising activities into a challenge. Some groups respond well to contests (Team One and Team Two compete to bring the most guests to the gala), fun prizes for bringing in the most new supporters, or just board-level acknowledgement of gifts secured from one meeting to the next.

Pure Genius!

Cultivation Activities

As soon as you or another stakeholder has brought a new individual into your nonprofit's circle, every interaction that person has with your organization serves as a cultivation activity. Each point of contact creates a judgment in that person's mind about the agency. If everyone does their jobs well, all of these cues combined will energize your new supporter to become increasingly involved. Here are some of the activities that aid in that process and how you can help:

- Talk about your nonprofit whenever appropriate.

- Invite interested parties to mission-focused events, whether organized by your nonprofit or self-initiated. You can tailor even a small event to your network's interest in art, food, or outdoor adventures.

- Take a few selected guests on a personal tour where they can see your programs in action.

- Make calls after events. Ask attendees what they thought and whether they have any questions. These can be brief calls. Mostly, say "Thank you for coming."

- Work with your employer's human resources office to create an employee volunteerism event, often the first step toward corporate giving.

If some of these activities sound like those of an ambassador, that's true. Cultivation is the point where that role begins to flow into fundraising.

Solicitation Activities

This is where your organization's fundraising systems come into place: After you introduce potential supporters, *someone* must make an "ask" in order for the gift to come. Whether by email, letter, phone call, or verbal request, you can help determine how best to channel a prospective donor's interest and turn it into dollars and cents. Securing a gift takes a coordinated effort between staff and board, for sure, but you don't necessarily have to be the one doing the asking.

If you are new to fundraising, remember that not all gifts come in the form of cash. If asking for cash initially makes you nervous, start by securing the human and in-kind resources that can help the bottom-line just as much as monetary donations. These might include accounting or printing services, laptops, or office supplies. Even asking has its range of activities that allow for nearly any board member to find a comfortable starting point:

- Encourage individuals, companies, or vendors to make in-kind gifts on your nonprofit's wish list.

- Use your networks to bring professionals to the table who are willing to offer pro bono services. Check with staff to determine which services are most in need at a given time.

- Personalize a solicitation letter by handwriting a message, especially for recipients you know.

- See whether your employer matches its employees' charitable gifts.

- Attend foundation, government, or corporate visits with staff, where the ask will have already been made in writing and you will help further the case.

- Solicit a gift from a service or civic group, house of worship, or other organization with which you are involved.

- Ask relevant acquaintances, companies, or other organizational supporters to sponsor the next special event.

- Visit the home of a major donor—or a potential major donor—and make an ask alongside a staff member.

Ask Before You Ask

Before you approach any potentially major sources of funding, check in with your ED, development director, or other staff point person. Staff members cringe when they learn that a board member has requested $10,000 from a company when the ED has already asked for $25,000 from the same firm. While staff will appreciate your intentions, the company might question the effectiveness of your organization's communications and fundraising systems.

WATCH OUT!

The items at the top of this list often come across as less intimidating to novice fundraisers.

Stewardship Activities

Once someone has made a gift, the work does not end. The competition for charitable dollars is fierce, so it is imperative that you continue to demonstrate a personal touch. You and your staff cannot take for granted that even the most enthusiastic donor will remain in your circles unless you work to keep that person close. These are among some of the most gratifying, and effective, ways for board members to assist:

- Call donors to thank them for their gifts. Even if they do not answer, leave a message that identifies you as a board member and express thanks. If you have received one of these calls, you know how special they can be.

- Ask staff which donors might receive a hand-written note from you. We all know that personal letters are increasingly rare, so your biggest supporters are worthy of that special touch. This activity is ideal for

Uninspired

Dropping the Ball... On the ED's Foot

One novice board got very excited about the idea of hosting its own fundraising event. The group set a date, chose a location, and planned to invite guests. The ED was thrilled that her board showed such enthusiasm but made it clear that the selected date fell during her busiest time of the year and that her ability to pitch in would have to be limited. Board leaders promised to surprise their executive by executing the event themselves. Sure enough, members became too "busy" in the lead-up to the event to follow through with the promised food, sound equipment, and enough confirmed guests to fill the room. This ED took it upon herself to scramble around in the weeks leading up to the event to put all of the pieces in place.

introverted board members who might not prefer personal meetings or calls.

🕯 Attend or stage a donor appreciation event, designed to acknowledge your most loyal and generous supporters in person. Thank as many attendees as possible and let them know a few examples of how their gifts have impacted your nonprofit's work.

The Best Event Is an Intimate One

The best "event" often involves a staff person, a board member, and a potential donor sitting down over coffee and discussing a customized gift. The cost of that activity is minimal, and the return can be surprisingly great. In fundraising jargon, this is considered asking for a major gift.

Inspiration

Monitor the Budget

When the board approves the budget, it essentially produces a basic fundraising plan. The revenue side of the budget will likely include many of the fundraising sources listed earlier. Each will link to a targeted amount that needs to be raised that year. As you monitor that budget throughout the year, you help ensure that income goals are met: Is the organization on track to raise the projected foundation goal? Corporate? Individual? If not, why? Can the board help bolster results? One of the revenue line items might be "board giving," which enables the group to hold itself accountable, as well.

The budgeting process can also spur discussion about which income areas merit more board focus. Sometimes, the group might coordinate much of the annual gala or auction. Some years, there might be a particular emphasis on increasing giving from members' employers or houses of worship. In any of these areas, once the group commits, it must follow through. There's nothing more disappointing—or stressful—to staff than picking up the pieces of a major board undertaking.

Where Do Special Events Fit into the Mix?

Special events can be tantalizing because they can appear to magically transform curious onlookers into donors. Some organizations execute those metamorphoses superbly. Those groups select events and venues well-suited to their supporters, while meeting these goals:

- Showing net profit from the event (gross revenues greater than gross expenses)

- Highlighting the mission

- Engaging people outside the organization's typical reach

Truly successful events are surprisingly rare, as they can be very time consuming and expensive. Remember, they are fundraising vehicles, and their goal is to generate a net profit. Many, however, struggle to deliver the revenue to cover their hefty food and venue costs and long staff hours. While special events can—and sometimes do—rally a whole new group around your mission, it's worth spending time hammering out projected revenues, expenses, and net income. Be sure that the net funds raised warrant the amount of time and money expended to stage the event.

Many nonprofits hold galas, auctions, and wine tastings with too little forethought. If your organization holds events based on tradition and not cost-benefit analyses, consider questioning why each continues, especially if the effort yields a net loss or just breaks even.

What Is a Fundraising Plan and Is It Necessary?

A *fundraising plan* builds upon the revenue side of your budget, by including not only sources of revenue, but strategies for raising those funds, timelines, deadlines, and responsible parties. A fundraising plan can take a large financial goal and break it into manageable parts. The level of detail varies by organization, but even very basic ones can help an organization make sure that plans are in place to raise what can seem like overwhelming sums of money. Here is a snippet of a fundraising plan's important elements:

Funding Source	Goal	Tactics	Timeline/ Deadline	Key Personnel
Individual Giving	$50,000	Quarterly appeal letter will be sent to approximately 500 donors	March mailing June mailing September mailing December (holiday) mailing	Development director with assistance from ED and staff
Spring Event	$50,000 gross $25,000 expenses $25,000 net	This year the spring event will celebrate the organization's 25th anniversary; ticket sales and a live/silent auction will be the main revenue sources	Event is scheduled for May 15	Development director will spearhead, with support from anniversary task force
Foundations	$65,000	Request renewal funding from the following foundations: Flush with Money Foundation $50,000 Cash Galore Foundation $15,000	Application deadlines: March 1 May 15	Development director

Plans are usually developed by those most involved with fundraising: development staff, the ED, and members of the fundraising committee. If your organization is new to this kind of planning or doesn't have adequate staff to create a plan, you can hire a consultant to help. This can be especially useful if you need to increase revenues from a particular source or desire to raise funds from previously untapped resources.

Like your strategic plan, elements of this document might undergo revision as circumstances change. What's important is that the document serves as a tool to help define everyone's collective roles. When your board begins to put its fundraising activities into a written plan and uses it as a working document, then you *know* that a culture of philanthropy has taken root!

To Summarize...

- Both the board and staff engage in fundraising. They can create a culture of philanthropy by regularly injecting fundraising into their work.

- A healthy organization benefits from having diverse funding streams.

- Every board member should make a cash contribution that is personally meaningful and significant to that individual.

- Board members' fundraising responsibilities also include serving as ambassadors, engaging supporters, and monitoring the budget.

- A fundraising plan can take a large financial goal and break it into manageable parts.

Chapter 14

Risk Management: Covering Your Assets

In This Chapter...

- Why is risk management important to board oversight?
- What kind of insurance does a nonprofit need?
- How do policies help manage risk?
- How does a board decide which policies are necessary?
- Who should draft, review, and approve the documents?

Risk management touches nearly all of a board's work. It encompasses identifying potential hazards, prioritizing them, and deciding how to best manage or even eliminate them. One obvious way to protect your assets is to purchase insurance. But what about those intangibles like retaining good staff and letting go of the not-so-good? What about ensuring that there is money in the bank? What about making sure that your IRS Form 990 is complete, accurate, and filed on time? Or that documents are retained as required? What about protecting your organization's reputation? All of these things, and many more, make up the spectrum of risk, because if your organization doesn't tend to them properly, there will be consequences.

The best way to manage risk is to develop—and use—solid policies. Writing them is not enough. Boards must adhere to the rules they set out, so that they keep any legal, ethical, or performance-related issues in check. Policies are central to guiding a board's work and letting the public know that the group takes its work seriously.

What can get complicated is the process used to draw up the policies, and the decisions about which ones to develop and when to develop them. The list of potential policy topics can be long, so it's good to know which should be prioritized, who should create them, and how best to use them. It won't surprise you to hear that the answers to all of these questions vary from one organization to another. So our intent here is not to provide hard answers but to foster informed decision making.

How Can Risk Management Protect a Nonprofit's Reputation?

Most people tend to think that risk has purely legal or financial repercussions, but it can also affect a nonprofit's reputation. *Reputational risk* is the loss of stakeholder confidence due to poor decision making, ethical or stewardship lapses. It can result in a loss of donors or clients or negative media attention.

In this social media age, even the perception of wrongdoing can have long-term impacts on the way a community views a nonprofit. In short, a board must do its job well to protect the organization's reputation.

Of course, things can and do go wrong. The way your organization handles a crisis can make the difference between the situation blowing up or it being a minor setback. Ideally, you will have a plan in place, typically a media policy or a communications plan that includes a crisis management section. If not, the board *and* ED must assess the amount of damage the issue has caused or may cause in real time without a response strategy. It may be entirely possible that it will blow over. . . then again it might not.

If it seems that the most prudent way forward is to respond, then the organization needs to quickly develop a course of action that is well suited to this particular situation. An important piece in all of this is to respond promptly, and as much as possible, take control. Consider following the steps below:

Analyze the Situation

Are the story's facts accurate or inaccurate? Does your nonprofit need to own any of the blame or responsibility? What are the facts from your side of the fence? The executive committee, along with the ED and any public relations specialists on the board, can begin to flesh out the answers.

Develop a Message

Does your organization need to respond to the entire story or only specific points? What will be the tone of your outreach? Apologetic? Staunch? Defiant? Develop a message around your response. Be sure that everyone understands the agreed-upon messaging, including staff. Everyone should

---

Pure Genius!

Correcting the Record

An upstanding nonprofit received a city grant. An inaccurate news article stated that this organization, along with several others, collected the full amount of the award but had only served a fraction of the clients it was contracted to serve.

The executive director contacted the journalist who wrote the story as well as the city agency that supplied the numbers to the newspaper. The city got its figures wrong.

To manage the crisis, the nonprofit pushed the city to admit it had made a mistake, and the city issued a letter of apology to the organization. The nonprofit quickly wrote a letter to the editor and sent printed copies to its biggest financial supporters. Because of the nonprofit's swift actions, there were no financial repercussions.

know in advance what will be said, how, and why. If events are breaking too quickly to pull the whole board into the decision-making process, the chair can communicate with everyone regularly about the latest news. If this is an issue that seriously threatens your reputation, consider seeking professional public relations help.

Identify Key Spokesperson(s)

Who will be the main contact or contacts for this situation? Spokespersons might include the ED, the board chair, another board officer, a board member who has PR experience, or even a public relations firm that is handling the situation on your agency's behalf. If anyone other than the appointed spokespeople is asked to discuss the situation, those folks will want to refer the inquiring minds to the spokesperson(s).

Get the Message Out

You might choose to write a letter to the editor or an article as a rebuttal to a story. Maybe you get another media outlet to present your side of the issue. Or you might take to social media, or contact your supporters via email. You might choose a combination of the above.

What Kind of Insurance Should Your Organization Have?

Board members hate to think about this, but in this litigious society, you must actively protect your organization—and your board—from lawsuits. That's right, there is a chance that you can be named in a lawsuit, even in your volunteer status. Thankfully, there are ways to protect yourself and your peers who are acting in good faith.

While the ED might help to seek out policy quotes and make sure that premiums are paid on time, it's up to the board to make certain that insurance is in effect and that the coverage is adequate. A committee or designated board member can verify that existing policies are sufficient.

Commercial Liability Insurance

Also known as general liability insurance, this coverage is a must if your organization has a physical presence. Policies tend to be fairly standard, covering things such as a slip and fall at the agency or a car accident involving a client being transported in the organization's van. Most policies have $1 million coverage for liability and $1 million for medical. Some states may dictate the minimum amount necessary, so check with an insurance broker for details.

Workers' Compensation Insurance

Employers purchase workers' compensation insurance to provide benefits to employees who become ill or injured on the job. Premiums are based on gross payroll and the range of illnesses or injuries that an employee might experience. Many states require employers to have workers' compensation policies and specify minimum coverage amounts. Check with an insurance broker or your state insurance office for specific requirements.

Lessons in Liability

State laws may limit personal liability when a nonprofit suffers due to volunteers' unintentional actions. Yes, this does apply to board members, so consult an attorney or your state regulations to learn more. However, board members can be penalized with fines or even jail time if they act in bad faith or knowingly take advantage of their insider status to use an organization's assets for their own benefit.

WATCH OUT!

Disability Coverage

Disability insurance provides coverage for the ED when a temporary, or even permanent, absence occurs due to health issues. It is the board's responsibility to put adequate coverage in place so that members can make sound staffing decisions without having to worry about the economic impact associated with continued payment of the ED's salary. It may also be prudent to provide coverage to other staff as well.

Directors' and Officers' (D&O) Liability Insurance

As a representative of the public interest, the board as a whole can be subject to lawsuits. Most of these suits stem from either employment-related claims or mismanagement of assets:

🕯 A staff member thinks her employment was unfairly terminated.

🕯 An employee claims sexual harassment was committed by the ED.

🕯 Donors of a nonprofit sue the board for allegedly misrepresenting its financials.

And, while it's not very common, there are instances when an individual board member can be held personally liable. This is especially true in cases of misconduct, such as a member causing injury to a staff person or client, or causing harm through fraudulent actions. Another way an individual member might be held liable is by personally guaranteeing a loan made to the organization that goes into default. However, if the organization defaults on payroll or other government taxes, the IRS may hold individual members liable for any outstanding tax bills. Each state has its own rules around individual board member liability, so seek legal advice from someone versed in your jurisdiction's nonprofit laws.

Whether a suit is brought against the board as a whole or an individual, the bottom line is to ensure that your organization has D&O coverage. Some exclude employment-related suits, so make sure that your board reads the fine print. If you want to sleep well at night, ensure that your board has secured sufficient coverage even if your nonprofit is small. Legal fees can add up even if a court throws out a case.

Other Considerations

Depending on your organization's line of business, additional policies, such as auto, product liability, professional liability, or property insurance might be in order. Every few years, your board should revisit the policies it holds and the coverage for each.

Why Are Policies a Central Tenet of Risk Management?

Now we're getting into those other kind of policies—ones that might not count technically as insurance, but when written and followed properly ensure that your nonprofit acts in principled ways. Policies can guide both out-of-the-ordinary situations and everyday procedures. Ideally,

Policy

A policy is a statement, principle, definition, regulation, or procedure used to guide actions and decisions. It creates parameters within which the board and staff make decisions and take action.

Definition

organizations write them up proactively, so that when an unusual situation arises, leaders can thumb through their handy-dandy policy manuals to guide behavior.

Many boards do not use their policies to full advantage. Documents get drafted and are shelved. Or, they are not drafted in the first place. Or, they are not drafted until an issue arises. But a well-crafted set of succinct policies can save a board time, money, and headaches. Here are some examples of how updated policies can save the day:

- *It's time for annual staff evaluations.* A sound personnel policy will outline the process for all staff. It will answer questions such as: Does the executive director conduct all evaluations or does senior staff evaluate direct reports? How are salary increases calculated?

- *A board member wants to be paid for providing a service to the organization.* A conflict of interest policy outlines what constitutes a potential conflict of interest and a process for assessing and determining if, in fact, a conflict exists.

- *A donor wants to make a generous gift of real estate.* You don't want to seem ungrateful, but what if your organization is not prepared to maintain or sell a large plot of land hundreds of miles away? An updated gift acceptance policy might exclude real estate from your list of approved gift types. It would preserve your relationship with the donor if you can ground your refusal in a policy, rather than just say "no."

- *It's time to evaluate the executive director.* A policy around executive compensation lays out any guidelines your board has used in previous years. It precludes the board from making ED salary decisions that might come across as arbitrary to your funders or as stingy to your chief executive.

A client accuses an employee of sexual harassment. Many insurance companies require personnel policies in order for the relevant riders to take effect. Without them, the board might be found negligent if a claim is filed, harming the organization's finances and its reputation.

What Parameters Should We Follow in Creating Our Policies?

It's important to establish some baseline principles around what kind of policies your board creates, and when. Most boards write policies when they have the time and inclination to do so. Unfortunately, time is often short and inclination is often brought on by negative events. Ideally, you want to create policies that will both guide unfamiliar situations *and* predictable, recurring ones. Here are a few suggestions that might help you create policies before it's too late:

Be Thorough

The number and complexity of your policies depends on the size and complexity of your organization. A new or small nonprofit likely does not need dozens of policies. A large, national organization doesn't want to get caught off guard with fewer than necessary. There is no magic number for

Pure Genius!

Proactive Policymaking

The board of a program for formerly incarcerated youth knew early on that its young clients risked future brushes with the law. The group foresaw the day when the media glare might shine on this organization, so it drafted and approved a media policy. This short document cemented procedures for how the board and staff would handle media questions should a crisis arise. It outlined who would be allowed to speak with the media and when, how the rest of the board would be notified about the incident, and how those not authorized to speak with the media should deal with reporters. It was several years until the media picked up a story, but when it did, events flowed relatively smoothly because board members knew how to respond.

each stage of a nonprofit's development, so create the ones you think you will need over the next few years.

Be Proactive

You want to stay one step ahead of your organization's needs. That way, if the unexpected happens, you and your peers have already put those "what if" preferences to paper. Granted, you can't always foresee every organizational quandary, but the content of your board meetings should be a good gauge as to when an issue is on the horizon and when it might be time to take minor concerns and turn them into written policies. Let your mission, your internal environment, and the external climate guide your decisions.

Be Current

Just as growing organizations cannot always anticipate their needs, more mature ones cannot rest on their laurels when the basics are in place. Policies are evolving documents that need reexamination and revision. Every three to five years, relevant committees should ensure that existing documents are still current.

Which Policies Should We Absolutely Have in Place?

Let's first state that policies can be too vague or too much in the weeds. Each organization must find the right balance. For one nonprofit, fundraising policies might begin and end with a statement about what is expected around board members' personal giving. That might work for a small group with little infrastructure that receives gifts from one or two predictable streams, say foundation grants and direct mail. For another organization, the impending construction of a building might spark the need for donor acknowledgement, naming, and gift acceptance policies, in addition to board members' personal giving expectations. Again, the art here is to project a bit ahead of the curve. No small feat!

The most essential policies will fall under each of your organization's core functions. These include the umbrellas of administration, fundraising, volunteerism, and community outreach. Each of those topics might necessitate one or several policy documents, depending on the level of detail your organization requires. While it is impossible to cite must-have policies in every case, below are some of the most basic, along with the general topics they should cover. Get legal advice to ensure that your policies are adequate for your organization's needs.

- Conflict of interest. Gets at the idea that your board members should examine any competing interests they may have with regard to their role on the board. For a sample, see Appendix D.

- Document retention, management, and destruction. Specifies the types of documents your organization maintains and for what length of time. Also outlines how documents will be disposed of and precludes those actions when the organization is involved in litigation. For a sample, see Appendix E.

- Executive review and compensation. Details the process the board will use to evaluate the ED, as well as principles that will guide salary increases and bonuses, if applicable.

- Financial procedures and financial checks and balances. Lays out things like who opens, signs, and deposits checks; who balances the books; loan restrictions and procedures; travel reimbursement; credit card usage; and how much the ED can spend in excess of any one budget line without board approval. This document can be very useful to auditors, who verify whether the policy is being followed by staff as prescribed.

- Personnel. Stipulates that execution is delegated to the ED, with board review and approval of elements such as workweek, holidays, paid leave, workplace environment, equal opportunity, and sexual harassment. It might also include the ED's job description, required qualifications, lines of authority, evaluation process and forms, volunteer policies, and grievance procedures.

- Succession planning. Dictates staffing and logistics for planned or unplanned ED departures, including requirements for staff to keep key account/policy numbers and passwords that make information accessible to interim leaders. Good policies also include procedures

Conflict of Interest

What would you do if a board member:

- Wanted to provide paid consulting services to your organization?

- Had family members bid on a contract to do business with your nonprofit?

- Offered to make a loan to the organization and charge above-market interest rates?

A conflict of interest (COI) arises when a board member's activities have the propensity to take on self-serving motivations. A COI policy allows your board to be clear about how it will handle these situations if they stand to negatively affect your organization.

This is a special policy: It's standard on many boards to ask members to sign a copy of the policy annually, to ensure that no conflicts have arisen since the previous year. As part of the signing ritual, ask members to list any organizations, businesses, or other interests that might present a possible conflict with your organization. When a possible conflict arises, these are sound steps to take:

1. The member with the potential conflict discloses the situation as required in the policy.

2. The board votes to determine whether the situation constitutes a conflict. The board member in question is recused from the discussion and voting and may be required to leave the room as the discussion and vote take place.

3. Meeting minutes should highlight that a potential conflict of interest arose and the actions taken to address it.

Not all conflicts of interest are negative. Consider a slightly different spin on the two examples above, when a board member:

- Offers to provide consulting services at a rate well below market rate.

- Convinces relatives to bid on a contract, charging just enough to cover the cost of materials and supplies.

- Makes a loan at zero interest or at a rate far below market.

Situations like these are not always clear cut. The board must decide where it will draw the line.

See Appendix D for a sample of a conflict of interest policy.

that the board will take if the chair's position is suddenly vacated. See Chapter 22 for more details on succession planning.

 Whistleblower protection. Protects employees who report unethical or illegal practices. The policy should include a reporting protocol, so that employees know exactly who to speak to, and how the report will be handled. See Appendix F for a sample policy.

Consult an attorney to review your policies. If you have one on your board who is familiar with these issues, terrific. Otherwise, try to find someone who will do it pro bono. If you can't, these core policies are worth the investment of a few hours' time from an experienced lawyer since the consequence of writing them on the cheap might be the expense of a devastating lawsuit.

Which Policies Should More Advanced Boards Have in Place?

Okay, the first thing we need to clarify here is what we mean by "advanced." These are more mature groups in terms of age and complexity. Depending on your organization's level of sophistication or core activities, you might want

---

WATCH OUT!

The 990 Can Guide Policy Creation

One good rule of thumb: Keep tabs on the policies that are inquired about on the IRS Form 990. Granted, while the IRS does not mandate the policies it lists on this form, if your group checks "no" on the form's questions about whether specific policies are in place, you create a bright red flag for all the public to see. As of this writing, the form asks about the existence of these written policies:

 Conflict of interest

Document destruction and retention

 Whistleblower

The Corporate Conundrum

An afterschool program's gift acceptance policy stated that it would not accept any gifts from alcohol or tobacco companies. When a cigarette maker offered to fully sponsor a new organizational program, the board was not tempted by the offer. That ethically minded policy—developed long ago—served the organization well . . .and avoided possibly hours of debate on the subject.

Inspiration

to invest time to create policies around these common issues, or others that pertain to your line of work:

- Disaster planning. Prepares your organization for natural disasters, data breeches, technology losses, or other major threats that stand to get in the way of your work.

- Data security. Outlines how your organization will safeguard all sensitive data (client information, personnel, financial, etc.).

- Facilities maintenance. Guides the operations and maintenance around buildings, grounds, and equipment.

- Gift acceptance. Lays out the types of gifts your organization will accept and the way in which they will be handled and acknowledged.

- Investments. Establishes the circumstances under which a reserve might be created and the goals, investment options, and parties responsible for monitoring the portfolio.

- Media. Outlines who may speak with the media and under what circumstances.

- Social media. Gets at who may represent the organization through social media and how those parties are expected to present themselves on behalf of the nonprofit.

If yours is a grassroots nonprofit with little staff but a heavy emphasis on social media, you might create that social media policy before an investment policy. Or you might have to create policies not found on this list to accommodate your innovative business model or changes in technology.

Who Should Create and Develop Policies?

Staff can play a part in helping to draft and even recommend needed policies, but it is the board's job to ensure that all polices are current and implemented. Whether the subjects are explicitly governance-related or administrative, the buck stops with the board on both fronts.

Committees can be a terrific resource in this process. The full board is responsible for reviewing and approving the policies but can leave the details to committee members who delve into them more efficiently. Since those on your committees presumably have some expertise in the subject matter, that experience will come in handy. A few steps these groups might follow when developing policies:

- Collect sample policies from other organizations or from state nonprofit associations.

- Update the text for your own use and draft new language when your organization's circumstances differ from the samples.

- Seek input from staff, lawyers, accountants, or fellow board members, as needed.

- Send the draft to the full board for review and approval.

When the draft goes to the board, encourage the group to discuss whether the policy:

- Meets current needs

- Adheres to your core values

- Is forward-looking enough to anticipate some possible next-stage issues your organization might encounter

Policies Are Not Proprietary

If you need to develop new policies, consider asking to see those from like-minded organizations of similar size and maturity. Importantly, try to secure samples from organizations you respect. There are many bad policies out there. Other good sources include your state's association for nonprofit organizations.

Perspiration

Granted, that last piece is tough to do, but the best boards regularly stretch their imaginations through strategic planning, visioning, and yes, policy creation.

Policy Review and Renewal Schedule

Policy or Document	Date Last Approved by Board	When to Review or Renew
Commerical Liability Insurance		Annually
D&O Liability Insurance		Annually
Audit		Annually
Conflict of Interest		Every three years; should be signed annually by key employees and all board members
Disaster Planning		Every three years
Ethics		Every three years
ED Review		Annually
Governance		Every two years
Whistleblower Protection		Every three years; should be distributed to all staff and board annually
Document Destruction and Retention		Every three years
Emergency Planning		Every three years
Facilities Maintenance		Every three years
Gift Acceptance		Every three years
Investment		Annually
Media		Every two years
Social Media		Every two years

How Should We Use Our Policies?

It's amazing how much time boards can spend writing and reviewing policies, only to forget they exist when a relevant situation arises. The hours spent rehashing a previous debate about, say, how the group wants to handle an investment decision, can easily be spared if someone brings copies of a comprehensive policy manual to each meeting. These days, a board member—ideally the secretary—can tote a binder's worth of policies to a meeting on a tablet device, a flash drive, or via cloud storage.

The table on the prior page lists many of the policies and documents suggested in this chapter. Your organization might have others. Your board can decide when to review each, but we have suggested some standard intervals. Review your policies on a rolling basis so that you look at just a few each year.

While it can seem overwhelming to put policies into place, they really will establish yours as a board that has thought through its procedures and values. That kind of introspection lends confidence to funders, staff, prospective board members, and hopefully to you, too.

To Summarize...

- At a minimum, your organization should secure commercial liability and directors' and officers' (D&O) liability insurance. Depending on your nonprofit's business lines, consider other types of coverage as well.

- Boards and staff work collaboratively to draft policies, while boards review and approve them all.

- Reach out to other respected nonprofits and support organizations to request copies of their policies. Use them as a starting point for your own.

- Create a schedule listing all of the organization's policies and when each is due to be reviewed.

- Once your board has taken the time to write and approve policies, don't forget to use them!

Chapter 15

Measuring Organizational Success: The Board's Role

In This Chapter...

- Why is program evaluation important to boards?
- How can your board define organizational success?
- How might the group identify and use a set of outcomes?
- What if results don't measure up?

All of your tinkering with policies, financials, and even fundraising has absolutely no relevance if your nonprofit's services are not meeting their intended goals. While many boards are either not involved or very remotely involved in program evaluation, they do have a responsibility to ensure that offerings are sound. The best ones have a very good idea of program performance, without meddling too much in any staff management of those programs. A fine balancing act indeed!

It's important to remember that societal goals are fraught with elements that are hard to measure. How can you quantify the impact of an art gallery on a community? Or an advocacy campaign on the general population? Most of these evaluation efforts aren't perfect, but they are important to undertake nonetheless. The nonprofit sector—and the world—are moving rapidly toward data-driven results, so your organization should too!

Why Is Program Evaluation a Board Function?

At first blush, program performance sounds like a staff role. Yet, there are a few reasons for boards to wade into program waters: They are the organizational lifeguards. They are not there to jump in the water and teach the backstroke. They are there to oversee, to keep things moving along *swimmingly*, as it were. The board is fulfilling its basic oversight role when it can assure the public that programs are, indeed, fulfilling the mission, making continuous improvements, and having an impact. That approach helps guarantee that the funds your organization collects and spends benefit the mission in substantial ways.

The board's oversight of ED performance is another good reason to pay attention to programs. What more important role does the ED have than to strengthen the agency's offerings? A board with little connection to program performance can't really say that it has a firm grasp on its ED's effectiveness. And it's the strength of programs that bolsters fundraising, finances, advocacy, and nearly all other functions of a nonprofit. When boards delve into programmatic success factors, you and your peers are better able to tackle many basic responsibilities:

- Allocate scarce resources more effectively (financial oversight role)

- Convey more accurate and compelling stories to community members (ambassador role)

- Feel more confident about making your own financial gifts and encouraging others to do so (fundraising role)

- Ensure that programs adhere to the mission (mission focus)

Yes, programs can lead boards down many paths. Before you and your peers attempt to go too far down any of them, it's worth asking a basic question: How does your organization define success?

Let's begin by looking at that elusive idea of what it means to achieve nonprofit success.

How Might Your Organization Define Success?

In the corporate sector, boards know that their primary focus is the bottom line. In the nonprofit sector, financial health is important, but so is mission. If an early education program served fifty children last month, and that's 15 percent more than the same time last year, is that a success when there are dozens of additional at-risk preschoolers on the wait list and even more who don't know about the program?

Success in the short-run often refers to the progress your organization makes in pursuit of its mission. In most cases, it encompasses end results (e.g., job placement) and interim steps along the way (e.g., employment workshops completed, interviews obtained, etc.). To gauge how well your board defines success, the group might give thought to the questions below. And, if your organization operates multiple programs, spend some time answering these questions for each of them:

- Is the agency making a difference?

- If you were to describe an organizational success story, what would it sound like?

- Is your organization achieving success in the way your board defines it?

- Is your nonprofit able to articulate its success or impact to its various stakeholders, each of whom may need to hear the information slightly differently?

Here are some examples of how agencies might define success, which you will see, can vary greatly:

💡 A theater might define success by the number of tickets sold or the number of returning season ticket holders.

💡 A homeless advocacy organization might define success as getting the local government to expand the amount of affordable housing units available to low-income residents, or the number of local residents reached through an advocacy campaign.

💡 A literacy organization might define success by the number of participants who advance reading and math levels or the number who obtain high school credentials.

There is not necessarily a wrong way to define success, but you do want a set of parameters that is focused, impactful, quantitative, compelling, and ambitious—yet achievable. So, for a question with few wrong answers, there's plenty to think about!

How Might a Board Identify Outcomes?

It's possible that your organization keeps tabs on a whole range of measures, like those listed above, but that doesn't necessarily mean that it has well-defined outcomes. It's the board's job to work with staff to define those outcomes by narrowing the field down to a few of what it considers the most important measures.

On the opposite end of the spectrum from groups that collect too much information are those that collect little to none. If your organization is new to data-driven analysis, a task force might develop a set of outcomes that gets discussed and approved by the full board. You won't want the resulting list to be dozens of pages long. Instead, focus on a core set of outcomes that align with current priorities. These are the kind of

Outcomes and Impact

Outcomes are the changes, benefits, learning, or other effects that result from an organization's services. Outcomes help define the organization's path to impact.

Impact refers to change that occurs as a result of services over a longer period of time.

Definition

A Drive Toward Data

An education organization prioritized the value of data enough that its board approved funding for a new position on the small staff: that of data analyst.

Pure Genius!

high-level achievements that you would love to communicate both internally and externally. Some of the most efficient tools to arrive at these ends:

Strategic Plan

If your organization has a current strategic plan, this is the simplest place to begin. After all, you have done the hard work already. Pull relevant outcomes from your highest priority areas and refine them, if necessary.

Evidenced-based Research

Depending on your mission, it's possible that research exists that identifies a core set of outcomes that can be used to evaluate and measure program impact. This kind of information can lend tremendous credibility to your efforts and help you compare your outcomes to others in the field. Contact any of your industry's professional associations or look at the work of esteemed researchers in your field to learn more. Use scholars' work as a basis to set outcomes for your own.

Umbrella Organizations

If your nonprofit is accredited by a governing body, that institution likely defines its own set of outcomes for your organization. Or, maybe your organization belongs to or follows a membership group that sets standards in your particular field. While you don't want to feel captive to these outcomes, the reality is that you might already need to meet them, and they may well overlap with your board's priorities. They are worth serious consideration as to whether you should integrate them with your nonprofit's independently set outcomes.

Like-minded Organizations

Perhaps an organization that is doing similar work is willing to share its outcomes. You might also look at annual reports or websites to learn how comparable nonprofits measure and report success.

What Is the Division of Labor in Program Evaluation?

If the board is the organizational lifeguard when it comes to programs, then it cannot expect to jump in the water with every minor splash. Much of the detail relating to program evaluation falls to staff. The ED suggests measures and realistic targets. Staff collects data, conducts relevant analysis, and makes needed changes to strengthen programs.

What does that leave to the board? The group draws a holistic picture of how the organization is carrying out its mission. It focuses on the aerial view—defining what success means to the organization—then homing in on a subset of the data staff collects to gauge success.

Examples of Outcomes and Measurements

Organization Type	Outcome Example (Approved by board)	Measurement Example (Developed and executed by staff)
Museum	Increased awareness among local teachers, who view the museum as an effective resource for instructional support	90 percent of teachers rate the museum as an effective or highly effective instructional resource
University	Increased student retention	60 percent of freshman students will graduate
Hospital	Improved safety education for children in three rural counties	20 percent decrease in the number of emergency room visits for children from the targeted communities
Advocacy	Growth in the number of partner organizations in support of first amendment constitutional rights	A) Twenty-five new groups involved in coalition B) 20 percent increase in attendance at coalition meetings

Ideally, these exercises create a cycle of defining, evaluating, and recasting goals to meet changing times and priorities.

Outcomes change with time, with experience, and with good data. So, help your board remain diligent about not only monitoring outcomes but also revising them when necessary.

The Cycle of Program Enhancement

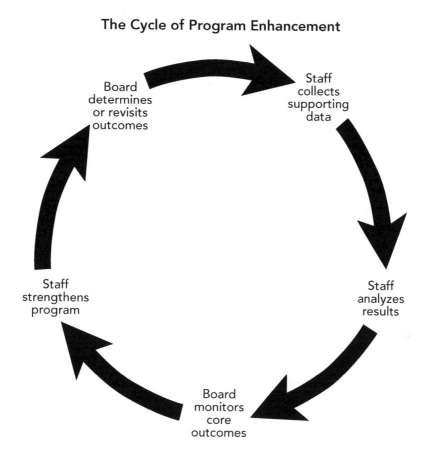

What If Your Organization Is Not Data Driven?

You have probably gauged by now that organizations with some propensity toward numbers have a leg up in the evaluation arena. Some nonprofits are born collecting data. Some collect it and don't get around to analyzing it. Then there are those that run programs based on instinct. Don't be surprised if your staff—and even much of your board—is not in the position to immediately pivot to an outcomes-focused culture. Many are not.

You or a board peer might serve as a champion on this issue by ensuring that the group is committed to ongoing learning. Your ED must also share this value. Together, you can work toward developing a data-driven approach to your work. Like other cultural changes, this can be a very gradual process, but it's one that deserves an advocate. Suggest training sessions or articles that emphasize the importance of evaluation in today's competitive environment.

You can also spearhead efforts to review existing infrastructure. If current systems are not adequate, the board might raise or allocate resources for an appropriate database or other data-supportive system. Your organization might even require additional staff to support your efforts.

How Can a Board Evaluate Programs and Monitor Impact?

The board must determine how and when it will monitor outcomes. And while the details of data analysis might fall to a small group, the full board might study trends somewhere between quarterly and annually. Those responsible for monitoring will want to:

IMPORTANT!

The Systems Behind Data Collection Systems

If your organization doesn't have the ability to collect and report on data, then your monitoring efforts might go to waste. So, you and your peers will want to back reasonable infrastructure that supports performance. A simple "yea" vote to purchase software is only the beginning. Plenty of organizations invest in databases only to find that staff didn't get adequate training on the software, there was insufficient staffing to fully utilize the data, or the system itself wasn't flexible enough to support the changing needs of the organization. Board members with relevant expertise can help staff identify and implement affordable software that is able to collect, track, and report on required data. While such systems can be expensive and require additional board time, they make everyone's job easier and more effective in the end.

🔦 Track key data points

🔦 Ask whether the organization is meeting its intended outcome goals

🔦 Determine whether the organization is doing what it needs to do to meet those goals

🔦 Provide reports and updates to the board

Staff is responsible for collecting, tracking, and sharing information and data. With board input, your chair can work with the ED to discuss the types of reports that the board finds useful. This is an area that can easily prompt members to make requests directly of program staff. In keeping with your good intentions to be a diligent board member, remember to follow protocol and feed any staff-related requests through your chair, who will speak with the ED.

The resulting reports might be in the form of dashboards, spreadsheets, or simple bulleted one-pagers. No matter the format, the documents typically include current outcome information, as well as any efforts undertaken to improve upon prior outcomes.

How Might Your Board Review Data?

It's likely that your organization will keep both quantitative and qualitative records of its work. When nonprofits track hard data alongside appropriate subjective information, boards can begin to gauge effectiveness. The quantitative side often deals with clients' demographics and the before and after effect of your programs on those users. Qualitative data might take the form of surveys, testimonials, or anecdotal feedback from those you serve.

A childhood obesity prevention agency might collect data in the following areas as it monitors its community education program:

Quantitative	Qualitative
Number of people who inquire about the program (via internal record keeping)	Reasons why people take interest in the program (via surveys)
Number of people who attend educational programs (via internal record keeping)	Most valuable information attendees get out of the educational program (via surveys)
Attendees' relevant change in behavior (rated on a scale of 1-5 in follow-up surveys)	Attendees' long-term awareness of childhood obesity (via follow-up surveys)
Percentage change in local childhood obesity rates (via public records and any relevant internal testing)	Attendees' perceptions of the value of this program (via follow-up surveys)

How might you review the quantitative and qualitative information you receive from staff? Two strategies are presented below: year-over-year comparisons and cost-per-unit of service.

Year-over-year Comparisons

Once your organization has collected data for over a year, the board can be most effective if it focuses its time on not only overall goal achievement, but also year-over-year improvements. In the case of the fictitious organization profiled above, data might be modeled on this format:

Quantitative	Qualitative
Year-over-year inquiries	Changing motivations to participate over time
Year-over-year program attendance rates	Improved knowledge about childhood obesity
Improvements in year-over-year behavioral changes	Improved behavior related to healthy eating and exercising behaviors
Year-over-year change in local childhood obesity rates	Changing community value of the program over time

Such a comparison enables a baseline to see whether your organization's work is improving over time. Of course, even this data is not a guarantee of success. Ideally, you will consider this information alongside the evidence-based research or industry standards discussed earlier to confirm whether your results are aligned with broader measures.

Cost-per-unit of Service

Another approach to assessing effectiveness is to track per-client cost or something similar if your organization does not directly serve clients. Many foundations and government funders, for example, might disregard a nonprofit funding applicant if per-client costs seem excessive or exceed a prescribed threshold.

The following example shows how to calculate a cost per client for two childhood obesity prevention agencies.

	Organization One	Organization Two
Program Budget	$150,000	$75,000
Number of people who attend a childhood obesity workshop during a twelve-month period	150	300
Number of people who report healthier behaviors after attending a workshop	75	250
Cost per attendee	$1,000	$250
Cost per attendee reporting healthier behavior	$2,000	$300

There may be reasons why Organization One's per-client costs are higher than those of Organization Two. Maybe Organization One exclusively serves homeless individuals and behavior change in this group is more elusive and difficult. If, however, the organizations serve the same exact population, then the question is, "Why is Organization Two able deliver more economical services that also have greater impact?" Read on for more. . . .

What If Results Do Not Equal Success?

The board's job is to provide the right environment for programs to thrive, not to fix them. That said, if results are not meeting the pre-set goals, it is worth confirming that the goals are reasonable and attainable. Plenty of organizations set goals haphazardly. That process can happen inadvertently when a program is new and untested. If your board and staff can be honest about whether your benchmarks were set somewhat indiscriminately, you might spend time creating more informed targets. Goals should be ambitious without being outrageous.

If your goals are reasonable but the results are far afield, set aside time at a board meeting to ask thoughtful questions of staff. The chair can even ask the ED whether any program staff might want to join the meeting. You won't want this to come across as an attack, so ask thoughtful questions about the current challenges facing the program.

Board members will want to work with staff on aspects that they might help bolster. Namely, consider whether this program might benefit from:

- Increased human or financial resources

- Newer technology or technology, period

- A different social, economic, or cultural environment

- More competent staff

It is possible that this is just not the right time or place for a particular program. In that case, members might want to consider whether this program, even if a long-standing one, might be dated. Maybe it could benefit from moving to another neighborhood? Maybe the population it served has moved, and the program must now be tweaked to serve another demographic. Maybe, given the poor results, the organization cannot afford to pour any additional resources into it. It's even possible that this particular project no longer meets the mission. The board is responsible for ensuring the best chance for programs to excel. It also has the responsibility to terminate one that might not be working well.

Speaking of terminating, the board does *not* have the right to fire program staff for non-performance. That job belongs to the ED. If the board has done its job well, program performance is part of your ED's annual job evaluation, so it will be up for discussion at least annually in that context. Certainly if a program is dramatically draining resources or underperforming, the board might discuss the issue during a board meeting, or the chair might raise the issue privately with the ED. It becomes the ED's prerogative to take disciplinary action against any subordinates who are in charge of the program. So, be sure to give your ED time to work with staff to strengthen program results. It is the ED who must ensure that the board's goals are met; otherwise, your leader's job might be on the line.

If your ED is the only staffer, and programs have consistently underperformed within carefully set parameters, then the board plays a more direct role to help staff meet organizational goals. Again, the board will want to operate out of an abundance of inquiry and caution before taking disciplinary action around programs. There are fewer objective standards here than there might be in regard to financial or ethical issues, so the group will want to ensure that your standards are reasonable and explicit before you risk the public relations and staffing obstacles that come with terminating your ED.

Well-defined outcomes can be energizing factors that lead to greater success across all aspects of the organization. If your board has a clear definition of program success and retains its "lifeguard" status, it will set the stage for fewer organizational S.O.S. crises.

To Summarize...

- Staff and board partner to determine which outcomes best measure success and impact.

- Board responsibilities include monitoring program outcomes.

- Boards help ensure that the organization has sufficient infrastructure, such as a database, in order to collect and report on impact.

- The board can assess organizational and program performance via the ED's annual evaluation.

Part 4

Behind the Curtain

Now that you know your audits from your assets and your budgets from your bylaws, you've probably realized that an active cast of characters directs this production called a nonprofit board. While the chair is the most visible, there are officers, committee chairs, and other behind-the-scenes folks who are working (hopefully!) to make things run smoothly.

Why is it so important to understand the infrastructure that makes a board function? Even if you are not the chair, you have a say in subjects from recruiting new members to running meetings. You can suggest that these topics creep into regular board meetings if they do not already appear on your agendas. After all, community change—as well as board change—is often most effective from the ground up.

Chapter 16

Board Recruitment: The Dating Game

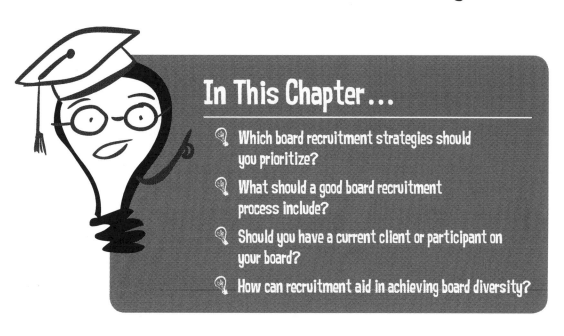

In This Chapter...

- Which board recruitment strategies should you prioritize?
- What should a good board recruitment process include?
- Should you have a current client or participant on your board?
- How can recruitment aid in achieving board diversity?

There's no better place to begin our glimpse behind-the-scenes than with recruitment. Let's face it: Haven't you wondered more than once what kind of discussion took place when the board was considering *your* candidacy? There's nothing more directly tied to quality than the thought that goes into recruiting new members, and unfortunately, that point can escape a fair number of boards.

For many organizations, this activity is done last minute, often with little thought or strategy. An organization serious about developing an engaged board must define expectations, create an opportunity for both candidate and board to decide whether this might be a good fit, and create an on-boarding process that readies new members for service. That's a lot of work in support of a person who's not even on your board yet! But, it's a good use of time if you want to ensure the organization secures and prepares the people it needs.

When Should a Board Focus on Recruitment?

Some boards conduct seasonal recruitment efforts. Others wait until they have newly vacated seats. If you want your board running in high gear, no matter the season, then year-round recruitment is the way to go. With continuous recruitment, your members never lose momentum. They never forget that when they meet amazing people in the community, those people are *all* potential board members. And, since vacancies can occur throughout the year due to resignations or removal of board members, you never know when you might need a candidate. Add to that the reality that most boards do not operate with a full slate of members anyway, and the need to constantly search for fresh talent is obvious.

It's an Honor to Serve

Serving on your board is an honor. While you want to be grateful for someone's willingness to devote time and energy to your organization, a new board member gets to be part of an amazing nonprofit. Don't lose sight of that and automatically vote someone on the board just because that person shows interest.

Inspiration

Who Are Your Ideal Candidates?

You want your new members to have at least a few basic traits:

- Willingness to put the organization above any personal agendas

- Commitment to the organization's mission

- Ability to make the necessary time and financial commitments

Is that it? Doesn't a good board member need to be someone with professional skills—a lawyer, auditor, or the like? Or someone with a big checkbook, or better yet, rich friends?

No.

While all of those traits can be beneficial—even terrific—for a board, they do not, in and of themselves, characterize ideal board members. After all, how desirable is a wealthy attorney if he uses your board only to approach potential clients? Or a well-connected corporate CEO who never attends a meeting or opens her network to help the organization? You'd rather work with someone less wealthy who diligently helps your new school meet county zoning guidelines. Or someone who takes the time to dig into the details of a motion before it goes to a group vote. Sometimes individuals who may not be the obvious "ideal" board members represent long-term value. Seek out a combination of doers and dreamers, socialites and activists.

Who Is Responsible for Corralling the Candidates?

It is the full board's job to scout out potential recruits. But the logistics of bringing those candidates through a formal nominating process usually falls to a smaller group. There are a few common options:

- Governance committee. While this group focuses on overall board improvement efforts, the nominating process is often among them.

- Nominating committee. Sometimes a board will create a nominating committee with the sole responsibility of board recruitment.

- Full board. Especially when the board is small, the full group might recruit, vet, and take turns interviewing candidates.

- Task force. While it's not our preference to operate a seasonal nominating process, some boards form an ad hoc group to oversee that temporary task.

The ED, as an ex officio board member, also plays an important role. In addition to proposing candidates, the ED will want to meet with every potential nominee. If, for some reason, the ED doesn't feel someone is a good fit for the board, that might not be a deal breaker, but the board should place a good deal of weight on the ED's opinion. It's just as important for the candidate to meet the ED. After all, the new board member will likely learn the most from—and be inspired the most by—the ED. If a candidate doesn't feel a connection to the ED, that might be a reason to avoid a particular board.

What Does the Recruitment Process Look Like?

While there aren't any hard and fast rules about how your board goes about its recruitment, it usually follows steps similar to these.

Reviewing the Board's Needs

Either the full group or a subset listed previously analyzes the type of candidates who will best strengthen the board's current make up. To do so, the board—with the ED's help—can identify the needs or issues likely to face the organization over the next several years. Give careful consideration to your organization's needs. Rather than just say, "We need fundraisers on the board," it's better to say, "We need someone to chair and coordinate the annual fundraising gala." That way, you search for someone with event experience and don't inadvertently end up with a "fundraiser" who spent a career solely focused on planned giving. Specificity can help you get exactly what you need.

Ideally, your board monitors its members' strengths and deficiencies, each of which constantly evolves. That way, your members can seek out a range of candidates that lead to a diverse group, one that's well positioned to tackle a range of timely issues from a diversity of viewpoints:

Say What You Need

Be very specific about the skills or expertise you need. If you need a person who has contracting expertise, don't just grab any lawyer and assume that person fits the bill. If you need someone with capital campaign experience, then seek that skill rather than someone with general fundraising experience, which may or may not include campaigns.

IMPORTANT!

- Skill sets. Your board will benefit from finance, legal, fundraising, management, personnel/human resources, and program evaluation experts. Current or upcoming challenges might influence the kinds of skills your board seeks. For example, if your organization will lose its lease next year, you might benefit from someone with knowledge of the local commercial real estate market.

- Networks. Collectively, you will want your board's networks to reach into varying corporate, government, foundation, religious, and social circles.

- Geographic representation. Members should reflect the regions your organization serves.

- Racial and ethnic diversity. It is ideal for members to reflect the client base and the community you serve.

- Age diversity. You will want members who bring varying generational perspectives.

- Gender diversity. Your board might want to achieve a gender balance.

- Other diversity. Depending on your organization, you may include other populations that include diverse religious, sexual orientation, or economic groups.

Many organizations develop a matrix that crosstabs current board members with current and desired skills, demographics, and experiences. The matrix illustrates where the board has too much of one thing, and where gaps exist. It might look something like the one below, which is abbreviated, but lists current board members across the top and the traits discussed as important by a hypothetical board down the side.

The matrix might also include rows for new traits that the organization might not have previously needed. Some current board members might coincidentally possess those very things; if not, those emerging needs might become new recruitment criteria.

Abbreviated Board Recruitment Matrix

	Anne	Bob	Chris	Dan	Evan
Skills/Expertise					
Finance			X		X
Legal	X			X	
Real Estate					
Networks					
Corporate	X				X
Religious		X			

Identifying Candidates

No matter who is technically in charge of the recruitment or nominating process, it is the full board's responsibility—including the ED—to pound the pavement and seek out suitable candidates. While it's easiest to find people in your immediate circles, that strategy often results in people very much like you, and likely, those already on your board. Try to think outside of the box. Look for quality people a step or two removed from your everyday circles to avoid a homogeneous group. You can find them by asking friends and associates who *they* know that might fit the bill. Also, keep your eyes open at social and professional gatherings.

Kicking Board Members' Tires

Before one arts group commits to bringing an interested person onto the board, it requires that the person spend time on one of its committees, as allowed in its bylaws. This system gives members a chance to see whether the potential candidate is a good fit. If things don't work out, the organization hasn't wasted one of its precious board seats on someone who wasn't willing to uphold the board's high standards.

Pure Genius!

Some larger cities have agencies that will help match board members with nonprofits. Those groups also match nonprofits with potential board members who exhibit the skill sets that the nonprofits desire. These matching services often provide training for interested board members, too.

Putting the Pieces Together

By "dating" the candidate, you and your peers can determine if an individual is worthy of a marriage proposal from your board. Try out several strategies that test a candidate's reliability, motivation, and personality:

A Peek into the Boardroom

One advocacy group invites its board candidates to a meeting, to observe and meet the members prior to the official vote on that person's candidacy. This gives everyone an opportunity to meet the candidate in person before voting.

Inspiration

- Information request. Set a deadline for the candidate to submit a résumé or short statement of interest to a designated board member. Watch whether that deadline is met and the quality of information sent.

- Phone call. Schedule an initial conversation to help gauge the individual's interest and commitment. This is a great first chance to discuss expectations and determine personality fit.

- Meeting. Ideally, at least two board members and the ED will schedule a face-to-face meeting with each candidate.

During these communications, consider discussing the following items:

- Your organization's mission

- Why the candidate is interested in the job

- Basic duties and expectations of board members

- The candidate's past board experience

- The candidate's expectations about future leadership roles

- Expertise the candidate has to contribute

- Committee interests

- Expectations around the time commitment

- Willingness to make a financial contribution

If your organization requires background checks of its volunteers, you will want to mention that fact as well.

Using a Board Commitment Form

One particularly good tool to use during all of the above engagements is a board commitment form. (See Appendix A for a sample.) That document will spell out a board's expectations of its members over the course of a year. The governance committee usually drafts the form, and the full board reviews and approves it. Email it to a prospective candidate, and discuss it during your first exploratory conversation.

Each board's form will vary but will focus on major board responsibilities. The most common elements revolve around these member expectations:

- Adherence to the mission

- Attendance at meetings, committee assignments, and events

- Financial monitoring

- Fundraising and personal giving

- Commitment to serve as an ambassador

- Time commitment

Make an Ongoing Commitment

Many boards distribute board commitment forms annually and ask current members to sign them as a reminder of their ongoing dedication to the group's principles.

Pure Genius!

Show this document to potential candidates as a way to clarify what your board wants from new members. It's a great way to gauge whether your board's expectations are in line with those of your candidates. If not, it's a deal breaker. For example, the commitment form usually quantifies the number of meetings members must attend and when. Feel free to ask your candidates point blank if your expectations sound doable. If not, then this might not be the ideal match. Same goes for a candidate's willingness to attend, say, one-hour monthly committee meetings and make an annual financial gift.

If a candidate hesitates or outright balks at any of your requirements, be prepared with another opportunity in your back pocket that might better suit this person. If your board allows non-members to serve on committees, that can be a great consolation prize. The reality is, if you sense a lack of motivation during your first meeting, you can imagine what that might devolve into by your twentieth meeting. By setting high standards up front, you create your board's best chance to secure high-performing people long term.

Final Criteria

Those who have met with the candidate might ask themselves whether this person has shown these qualities:

- Met deadlines and shown up for recruitment meetings on time

- Came across as enthusiastic, committed, and even passionate about the mission

- Void of an obvious personal agenda as a reason for joining the board

- Showed a commitment to give time, financial contributions, and other requirements of board service

Sample Board Recruitment Process

Task	Comments	Responsible Party
Solicit potential board nominees	Ask board to identify individuals for board membership who have previously identified skills/experience.	Governance committee chair
Place "ads" or information in ABC Organization's newsletter and on website	Ads will recruit both board members and nonboard members to join committees from existing circles.	Executive director
Develop outreach strategy to advertise for board members	Identify publications or resources to promote board vacancies that are outside the board's current network.	Governance committee chair
Conduct follow up	Contact board members who did not provide any names or from whom more information is needed.	Governance committee members
Contact prospective candidates	Make initial calls to prospective candidates, requesting résumé and to discuss timeline.	Governance committee members
Review initial slate of candidates	Board member who contacted each potential candidate briefs the group on the conversation. Candidates' résumés will also be reviewed. Based on discussion, decisions will be made as to whether to proceed with each.	Governance committee members
Conduct face-to-face board interviews	At least one, ideally two, governance committee members meet candidates.	Governance committee members
Meet ED	ED provides organizational overview, discusses vision and programs, and provides a facility tour.	Executive director
Review slate of candidates	Decide which individuals will be recommended to the board.	Governance committee members
Vote on slate of candidates	Governance committee reviews recommendations with board. Board votes on recommendations.	Governance committee chair

How Does the Process Conclude?

After meeting the candidate and reviewing any information submissions, the overseeing committee decides whether or not to recommend this person for board service. If the process moves forward, the committee sends each board member the candidate's résumé and statement of interest as part of the next board packet. At the meeting, it is also helpful for someone who met the candidate to highlight why this person should receive approval. The board then engages in any relevant discussion and votes—hopefully in the affirmative!

The relevant committee chair typically then calls the candidate with news of the board vote and, likely, the date and time of the next full board meeting and any orientation sessions. See Chapter 17 for more about orientation.

Should Program Beneficiaries Serve on the Board?

Many organizations strive to include a client or constituent on the board. Plenty do so successfully, especially membership organizations, whose entire boards typically include those who benefit from the agency's services. There are situations where having a current client on the board can provide invaluable insights and perspectives for everyone. For health and human service groups, depending on who is served, it may or may not make sense to follow the same path. Consider why your board might want to include a current client. Is it realistic for one of your program benefactors to serve in this capacity? Just as you would any other candidate, give thought to the personal obligations and other challenges that might interfere.

Remember, despite your best intentions to be inclusive, board service is serious business and must be reserved for those who can make the full slate of commitments. Some boards do not include clients on an ongoing basis but invite the occasional individual who seems truly interested and able to give back in this role. Your board might also invite a program graduate, rather than a current client, to serve on the board. In that case, any obstacles that prevented service earlier might be lessened.

Involving Former Clients

The board of a workforce training organization wanted nothing more than to include a client in its midst. But, most were mired in personal issues as they worked with the organization. It then nominated Sally, a program graduate, to the board. In this role, one of Sally's duties was to serve as liaison between a client advisory committee and board members. This strategy excelled in bringing candid feedback from current clients to assess organizational impact.

Perspiration

If you do not have clients on your board, then ensure that their voices are heard in other ways:

- Survey them, and share feedback with the board.

- Conduct periodic client focus groups, some run or attended by board members.

- Create a client advisory committee that focuses on program feedback, not governance, with a board member and staff person serving as liaisons.

- Ask a client to serve in an ex officio role on the board or on a committee.

How Can You Achieve Board Diversity?

Diversity of many kinds is essential to a well-rounded board. The greater the mix, the greater the reach to groups of donors, policymakers, and future board members. And, a range of perspectives leads to healthy debate, which often results in better decisions. Maybe most importantly, a variety of backgrounds is essential in the race to adapt to an ever-changing environment. Diversity literally gives your board a competitive advantage.

One board's definition of the word will vary greatly from that of another. So, the group must be clear on what it wants to achieve. If, by diversity, the goal is to increase racial and ethnic diversity, then be clear about it. If it's Millennials you need on the board, then say so. For that reason, it's important for the group to regularly discuss its ideas on this subject. Some boards even take the time to create a diversity statement that provides a vision around diversity on the staff, board, and other areas of the organization.

If your group is currently homogeneous, or even if it seeks diversity in some new realms, it can be challenging to find the right candidates. As stated earlier, it is imperative to search the landscape in new places, including local:

- Chambers of Commerce

- Small business or professional organizations

- Community leadership posts

These tactics will require you and your peers to spend additional time networking. Even when you meet what might seem like the ideal candidate, you will want to ensure a good fit. When you take the time to go through a transparent and thorough recruitment process, it will also solidify—to both your board and its potential candidate—that you are not interested in tokenism but in an authentic fit.

Increasing board diversity should not be a process separate from your other recruitment efforts. If the goal is to seat more Native Americans on your board, then recruit a Native American who has specific skill sets needed on the board. Ensure that everyone who joins the board brings meaningful contributions. That guiding premise both propels board functioning and keeps good board members engaged and happy.

To Summarize...

- Assign board recruitment to a committee, ideally as part of a year-round process.

- Be strategic with recruitment. Be clear about needed skills as well as any diversity goals.

- The board commitment form can be a useful tool to help spell out priority commitments for a prospective new board member.

- Allow time to get to know a candidate before getting down on one knee to propose.

Chapter 17

Orientation: An Essential Beginning

In This Chapter...

- Why even bother with new-member orientation?
- Who should manage orientation?
- What should be included in an orientation session?
- How can a board supplement formal orientation efforts?

How was *your* orientation when you joined your board? Didn't attend one? Or, was it sandwiched between a busy ED's late-afternoon conference call and the evening board meeting? Maybe it consisted of a thorough two-hour introduction with plenty of time for questions. The orientation says so much to new members about the character and priorities of your board. It really is the responsibility of every board member to ensure that your board's first impressions are ones of professionalism and inclusion.

A well-thought-out orientation session, or two, helps reemphasize important expectations and gets everyone on the same page. It can help affirm that a new member made the right choice in joining this board.

Why Is Board Orientation So Important?

At its essence, orientation provides new board members with the basic information they need to become engaged and productive as quickly as possible. Even if a new member has served on other boards, orientation can help acclimate this person to the culture and expectations of *your* group.

Without it, a new member walks into board service having to pick up on many complex issues mid-stream. To fully orient a novice member can take months. Many will tell you that it takes a full year to get a good grasp on the ins and outs of an organization. A good orientation speeds up this process immensely.

Novices become much more productive—much earlier—if you offer them these welcome gifts:

- A brief introduction to programs, services, and organizational structure

- The opportunity to review responsibilities and expectations, including any giving or fundraising expectations

- A preview of current issues or challenges facing the organization that will likely appear on the next meeting agenda

- Overview of current budget and year-to-date financial information

Who Takes on Orientation?

While the executive director typically leads the orientation process, a board that oversees content and facilitation does its newest members a great service. After all the time spent creating that board matrix, noodling over the best prospective candidates, and finding and interviewing nominees, why miss the chance to introduce newcomers to your organization in a way that befits your board's particular style? No doubt, your ED has a rightful place in the process. But don't miss the opportunity to inject some of your board's history, humor, and traditions into the process.

Inject Fun from Day One

There's no end to making orientation creative and engaging. Consider some behind-the-scenes tours, an organization scavenger hunt, staff introductions, and even some social time during the formal session. Since orientation is a first impression of sorts, pepper it with stories and accomplishments that deepen novices' bonds with your work. In short, reinforce the fact that this new member made the right decision to join your board!

Pure Genius!

Members of the governance committee, or other group responsible for the recruitment process, can envision what your board's orientation session will look like: Will it be formal or informal? What kind of materials will attendees bring home? Will additional visuals supplement those takeaways? The lead committee can manage the materials, logistics, and players who will take part in the actual event. Ideally, your orientation will include a variety of people: board members, key staff, and possibly a client. Additional faces emphasize the group's enthusiasm for its newest member. They also give a newcomer a larger circle of support in those early weeks when questions abound.

What Content Is Most Important?

Orientation should excite attendees. It's board orientation, not "bored" orientation! Be creative. Make it fun and interactive. Attendees often benefit when a variety of people take turns presenting information. Most importantly, don't bombard new members with too much information. No matter how you present your content, limit the session to a maximum of about two hours. Those time parameters force a focus on the most important material:

- Review of history, mission, and programs

- One or two client stories

- Review of board and staff roster

- Overview of a typical meeting agenda

- Contents of board packets

  - ◆ Emphasis on the need to read materials prior to meetings

  - ◆ Overview of financial statements

  - ◆ Review of any dashboards

- Strategic priorities for the upcoming year and what the board has been assigned to do as part of the strategic plan

- Discussion of elements in the board commitment form, which attendees might sign as part of the orientation process

  - ◆ Meeting attendance requirements

  - ◆ Committee responsibilities

  - ◆ Fundraising expectations

- Q&A

What Are the Benefits of a Board Manual?

A board manual contains all of the documents most important to a board's operations. It can serve a dual purpose: a textbook of sorts for the orientation and a resource for all board members—new and old. When this information remains at the board's collective fingertips, members can refer to it during board or committee meetings when questions arise. The board's vice president or secretary can take charge of keeping the contents current. This can be an important job, since it ensures that when members refer to what they think is the latest policy, they are indeed looking at the most recent one. Among the topics and items you might consider for inclusion:

☽ Governance and accountability

◆ Mission and vision statements

◆ Board commitment form

◆ Current strategic plan

◆ Work plan and timeline to accompany strategic plan

◆ Any current dashboards

◆ Committee descriptions

◆ Board officer job descriptions/roles

◆ Current year's approved board budget

◆ Last year's budget with year-end results

◆ Most recent IRS Form 990

◆ Last two audits

◆ Bylaws

☽ Program descriptions

◆ Overview of programs and services offered

◆ Discussion/description of target population

◆ Table that shows metrics for the past couple of years

☽ Policies

◆ Conflict of interest

◆ Personnel

◆ Whistleblower

◆ Document management, retention, and destruction

◆ Other policies

◆ List of insurance policies held, with brief explanations of coverage and effective dates of each

🔍 Board and staff information

◆ Board roster that shows each member's board position, business affiliation, contact information, and term of office

◆ Board bios in short, one-paragraph statements

◆ Staff roster and key bios

🔍 Last couple of annual reports

Orientation Abomination

Even the best orientations can be overwhelming—there is so much to learn! One new board member came away especially frazzled when the ED proceeded to spend over two hours talking at—not with—this unsuspecting volunteer. There was no invitation for interaction, no organizational takeaways, no additional stakeholders present. This orientation had the unintended effect of making the board member more anxious about his first meeting. . . not less.

Uninspired

As you can see, the contents make for a nice orientation agenda. If your board is diligent about keeping this information current, it won't take much additional effort to conduct a thorough orientation. Just plug the relevant speakers in to discuss the topics about which they are expert.

The board manual can take many forms in this electronic age. Some boards still utilize an old-fashioned binder, while others maintain their most important documents in the cloud, on a flash drive they hand to new members, or on a password-protected web page.

Even if your organization stores the information electronically, consider printing out those documents you would like your new members to focus on the most. That's the best way to encourage a deeper review of them. Those that might take on that kind of importance include bylaws, the budget, any dashboards, the board commitment form, and the most recent annual report.

Which Strategies Can Supplement Orientation?

Orientation is just one strategy to get members learning and growing. Our favorite ways to engage new members focus on a personal touch.

"Board buddies," or mentors, can make a novice feel at home. If new and veteran members are paired, they can decide together whether they will speak by phone before meetings or meet for coffee afterwards. The two might even sit together at meetings so that the learning process can continue. Even if the novice has no pressing questions, proactive engagement by the veteran member is key. It communicates an interest in bringing new members into the fold and cultivating a tight-knit community among members.

And, the board chair and ED really can't contact board members enough. While they certainly have plenty of other things to do, it often follows that meetings with individual board members result in new insights on members' expertise and ignite members' renewed commitment to the organization. When a group can keep that personal contact going over years, you're bound to nurture dedicated members.

To Summarize...

- A well-thought-out orientation helps reemphasize important expectations and gets everyone on the same page.

- Orientation equips new members with the basic information needed to be engaged, productive members.

- The format can involve several speakers, each covering a few topics from a board manual, the equivalent of a customized board textbook for your organization.

- Be creative and make your orientation fun.

- The chair, ED, and a "board buddy" can welcome new members with personal outreach and support.

Chapter 18

Make Meetings Magical

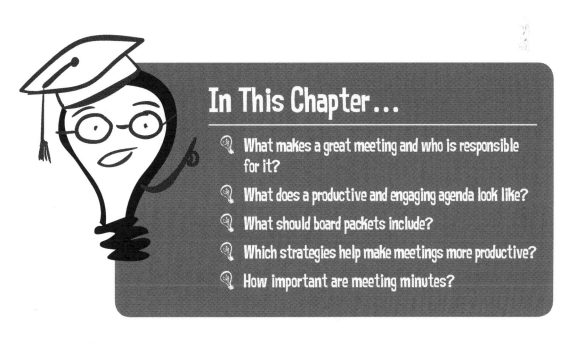

In This Chapter...

- What makes a great meeting and who is responsible for it?
- What does a productive and engaging agenda look like?
- What should board packets include?
- Which strategies help make meetings more productive?
- How important are meeting minutes?

No one likes a dull meeting, or a long one, or one that doesn't start on time. And, meetings that are unfocused or that are dominated by one person can really take a toll on morale. All these factors ring especially true for volunteers who spend many hours sitting through board meetings on behalf of a nonprofit.

So, the ED and board chair must work together to create an enjoyable and productive meeting environment. They must develop an agenda that engages members and encourages them to focus on strategic issues. That's no small task, considering the varied personalities involved, the complexity of the subject matter, and the need to air conflicting points of view. Despite the obvious barriers—we haven't even mentioned those board meetings that take place in cold, or damp, or otherwise less-than-comfortable "grassroots" sites—there are some simple ways to make meetings satisfying.

What Makes a Great Meeting?

Let's begin with the ideal. Take any regular group meetings that have gone smoothly in your life. (We know, there have likely been too few.) Chances are they share most of these traits:

- Convenient, agreed-upon meeting time and location

- Prompt start and end times

- A realistic agenda, focused on substantive issues

- Participation by the full group

- Ongoing dialogue

- Opportunities to learn

- An environment of trust, transparency, respect. . . and humor

- A regular vehicle for feedback about the meeting

- Food

- A sprinkling of fun

Things are no different for board meetings, with one exception: Regular connection to the mission, or "mission moments," are also critical. See the sidebar on the next page for more information.

Why does this list of traits seem so simple and yet so hard to attain? There is so much to be said about running good meetings. We will limit much of our focus here to good *board* meetings and what members—yes, even those who are not in the chair position—can do to help improve the quality of these get-togethers.

You'll remember that the work of the board can only be accomplished as a group, and that group work takes place during meetings. So, if your meetings are unproductive or uninspiring, chances are that your board's work is suffering for it.

Who Is Responsible for Creating Magical Meetings?

All board members play a role in being prompt, participatory, and polite. And all shoulder the responsibility of speaking up when meetings aren't hitting the mark. But, it's the chair and the ED who are responsible for the execution. Consider yourself lucky if your leaders strive to make each meeting slightly better than the last. What a fantastic goal! They might regularly ask things like, "Did our meeting just run late again? If so,

Inspiration

Mission Moments

Nonprofits infuse their meetings with mission in some very creative ways, which reminds members why they agreed to do this work in the first place:

 A theater holds its first board meeting of each year on its stage—a clear reminder of mission if there ever was one!

 A program that teaches culinary skills to teens surprised the board by having a group of clients shop and cook dinner for board members. A treat for all!

 A dance troupe invites members of the company to occasional meetings…to teach board members to dance!

Even if someone affected by your organization's work tells their story—or the ED tells it for them—you are likely to gain understanding for the mission that would otherwise be hard to glean from even the best board packet.

why, and what can be done? Is participation during the board meeting minimal? How can the meeting become more hands-on, interactive, and engaging?"

You may be wondering, "If it's called a *board meeting*, why is the ED involved?" The ED has a better grasp on most issues facing the organization than even the chair, and can help prioritize agenda items. During meetings, the ED often injects data and anecdotes that would otherwise not be known to those who have other responsibilities by day. The chair facilitates the meeting, with the ED injecting relevant insights. If you're assuming that the weight of a good meeting really rests with the chair, you are right.

Many others play a role in meeting mechanics, but when the ED and chair lay some basic groundwork, board members tend to fill in needed gaps naturally. If meetings are filled with important work, members will prepare adequately and put forward their best selves. Otherwise, members quickly lose motivation: They often begin to show up late, unprepared, or not at all, and things generally spiral downward.

Meeting Makers

Meeting Role	Responsible Parties
Create the agenda, along with necessary supporting materials for the board packet	Chair and ED, with possible input from others
Design mission moment and/or other learning opportunities	Chair and ED, with input from governance committee
Prepare board packet, based on the agenda, and distribute it	Chair and ED
Facilitate meeting	Chair
Take meeting minutes	Secretary (or designated staff member if secretary is unable to take notes)
Collect feedback on meetings and suggest improvements	Governance committee chair

In addition to that dynamic duo, see the table on the previous page for the rest of the people who play a role in making your meetings marvelous.

On the back end, it's usually the governance committee, the committee on trustees, or something similarly named, that creates systems designed to improve meetings. While the chair and ED certainly keep their eyes on attendees' reactions, they can be too close to the ground to remain objective. They can easily miss flaws that have become entrenched in the board's culture.

So, encourage a tradition of regular feedback loops, which can take several forms:

- Board assessments, in the form of email surveys, online questionnaires, or in hard copy (see Chapter 24 for details)

- Regular opportunities to contribute to a board suggestion box either via paper or through an electronic platform, such as SurveyMonkey

- Open dialogue at governance committee meetings, which any board member may attend

As part of the feedback loop, regularly encourage your members to comment on the things they think are going well, and those that could stand improvement. (Consider using criteria from the "What Makes a Great Meeting?" section above to create a simple survey.) Committee members who collect the data can then deliver the good news and any constructive criticism to the chair and ED about how to strengthen facilitation, efficiency, and content.

What Does a Productive and Fun Agenda Look Like?

Hopefully, your agenda focuses on items that require board input or decisions. The biggest meeting-related flaw is likely a habit of "reporting out," or regurgitating information already found in the board packet. Your chair and ED must do a delicate dance around creating a *decision-based agenda*, or one that keeps the meeting focused on discussion and voting around issues that require board verdicts. So, the chair must ensure that members have enough information in advance of the meeting to make good decisions *at* the meeting.

Standard agendas include a call to order, approval of the previous meeting's minutes, and the welcoming of new members or guests. Consider including time estimates next to each subsequent item. The times may deviate a bit, but by committing to timeframes, it becomes easier to determine whether the chair needs to get the meeting back on track.

The sample below suggests an outline for a good board agenda.

ABC Organization
Board Meeting Agenda

June 21, 2016
7:00 p.m. to 9:30 p.m.

1. Welcome (7:00–7:05)   *Chair*

2. Mission Moment (7:05–7:15)   *Program Graduate*

3. Board Learning (7:15–7:30)   *Treasurer*
    a. How to read a cash flow statement

4. Consent Agenda (7:30–7:35)   *Chair*
    a. Approval of minutes from the May 19 meeting
    b. Executive director's report
    c. Governance committee report

5. Review of Financial Statements (7:35–7:50)   *Treasurer*

6. Fiscal Year Budget Draft (7:50 – 8:10)   *Treasurer*
    a. Final review and discussion
    b. Board vote

7. Governance Committee Action   *Governance Chair*
    Items (8:10–8:25)
      a. Bylaws
        i. Final review

> ii. *Board vote*
> b. *Recommendation of two new members*
>>   i. *Review*
>>   ii. *Board vote*

8. *Explore Facility Issues and*   *Facilities Chair*
   Strategies (8:25–8:55)
   a. *Current situation*
   b. *Potential options*
   c. *Board feedback*

9. *Closing Remarks, Adjournment (8:55–9:00)*   *Chair*

10. *Executive Session (9:00–9:30)*   *Chair*
    a. *Review executive director's performance evaluation*

These are among the most substantive elements of any good board agenda:

⚲ Board development. This might include a ten- to fifteen-minute mission moment or another opportunity for the board to learn about its job. Ideas include financial literacy training, fundraising training, or a presentation about a political or economic issue that may affect your organization. Of course, a client's first-person account of personal growth is also a terrific educational tool.

⚲ The big picture. There is almost always a major issue looming, be it the impending loss of a large funder, the shift in government interest away from (or to!) your nonprofit's focus area, or even talk of a pending merger with another agency. It is good to give the group time to flesh out its most pressing issues—ideally, before those issues become too urgent.

⚲ Decision points. Outside of that one big picture item, much of the rest of the content can focus on any topics that require board decisions or strategic input. Those often include review and approval of the budget or strategic plan, ED evaluation or compensation issues, or items about relocating or renovating the physical space.

Executive Session

An executive session is a closed meeting that generally includes only members and possibly invited guests. It usually takes place for a limited period during the board meeting, so that board members can confidentially discuss things like ED compensation or disputes between board members. When these sessions occur, they should be cited in the minutes as having occurred but not include any detail. Notes from these sessions should be kept separately by the chair and maintained securely.

Definition

Fun! A few light moments can help break up what might otherwise be a long meeting. Some boards create team-based contests to see who can bring the most guests to the annual event, while others are lucky enough to have recruited a candidate who keeps the group laughing regularly.

The agenda can help keep the board focused where it needs to be: governance and big issues. Even if you're not the one creating the agenda, feel free (sometime *after* your first board meeting) to provide gentle feedback about it to your chair or governance committee.

What Does a Good Board Packet Look Like?

Board packets flesh out the agenda. They provide necessary data, background, updates, and thought-provoking articles that prepare members for each agenda item. Every board must decide the amount and depth of information it needs. While the chair and ED put together the conceptual framework, any member should feel free to suggest tweaks to the current format. Most are continuous works in progress.

Some of the basic elements:

- Meeting agenda

- Minutes from the previous meeting

- Financial statements (statement of financial position, year-to-date budget information, etc.)

- Committee reports, summarizing any activity since the last full board meeting

- Program updates

- Executive director's report

Each organization's board packet will vary. Some members like dashboards, for example. Others don't. Some prefer to receive their packets on their tablets or via another online medium. Others stick to hard copies. There are no hard rules here, so long as members can easily read the contents, and those contents illuminate the current state of organizational affairs. Each new group of members will feel differently about how to achieve those goals, so encourage dialogue about the contents of your packet. Those conversations are affirming signs that members are actively thinking about the best way to provide organizational oversight.

Inspiration

Setting the Right Tone

Culture

While true that board members often look to their officers and committee chairs as role models, any member can suggest revisiting the group's values. So if your leadership hasn't done so recently, and your meetings are in need of some heightened decorum, consider suggesting that the group spend some time brainstorming the guiding principles that will characterize your time together. They will hopefully come out something like this:

- Transparent. Information is available and freely shared.

- Respectful. Everyone's time, views, and input are valued, even when disagreement exists.

- Educational. Continuous learning is key.

- Fun. Social bonds and humor keep members coming back for more.

Ideally, board packets should arrive in members' hands at least three days ahead of the meeting, giving them enough time to review the information and prepare. Be open to the preferences of others whose work or personal schedules might require additional time. The window for preparation shouldn't be too long before a meeting, otherwise, the board risks that the packet's data will become dated before it ever gets discussed.

Which Voting Options Exist?

It would seem that voting about board issues should be straightforward. But in these days of phone-in meeting participation, Skype, and email voting, it's no longer a simple "yea" or "nay." Or is it?

Robert's Rules... or Not

Most boards still claim to use Robert's Rules of Order to run their meetings. These rules require strict procedures be followed in the lead-up and process of taking a vote. If your board is small or somewhat informal, less stringent rules might suit you better. There is nothing that ties boards or their committees to using Robert's Rules. As a matter of fact, more informal rules—those that engender greater discussion—tend to make board members feel more comfortable expressing their opinions, likely because they are focused on the content of the discussion and not on how they must present their ideas leading up to a vote. If your board does decide to adhere to this longtime standby, then you might suggest that someone, likely your secretary, have a working knowledge of those procedures and keep a copy of Robert's Rules of Order on hand at each meeting.

If you decide to use a less stringent method, often a *consensus model,* consider creating your own simple set of rules. Generally, consensus models allow members to offer ideas and modify them during the flow of a discussion, rather than taking an up-or-down vote on a motion. Instead of voting "nay," a member might say, "I don't mind this idea, but I'd like to suggest we change one point...." When the idea is tweaked, nods and verbal agreement bring the group to closure. Typically, a quiet room indicates agreement. It doesn't hurt to restate the final idea. The chair might facilitate, but the process allows for decentralized leadership, as any member can move the issue toward closure. For the purposes of meeting minutes, a vote must ultimately be recorded, but the process you use to get there may be as formal or informal as the group prefers.

Voting by Email

Email can be a terrific way for board members to communicate between meetings. It can help keep members informed, in the loop, or used as a decision-making tool. Rules for email voting vary by state. Most states allow it so long as the results are unanimous and documented in writing. That means that, when email voting is used, board members should send a copy of a signed consent form rather than merely expressing their consent via electronic message. Some states don't have such stringent requirements. Be sure that your bylaws and written voting procedures comply with your state laws.

Email voting is best used when your board has vetted an issue completely and is just one data point away from making a decision on a time-sensitive issue. In this case, an electronic vote may be the most efficient way to put the topic to rest.

It does have some drawbacks: It can lessen dialogue and debate, and it can be challenging to get the required number of members to vote in order to comply with your state laws. And often the tone of emails can be hard to decipher, leading to possible misinterpretation. For these reasons, we recommend that email voting be used sparingly.

Participating by Phone

Geography and busy schedules can make phone-in participation seem a better option than no participation. Most of us have experienced meetings with one or more people listening in via speaker phone, so you likely know the inherent advantages (greater participation) and disadvantages (difficult to hear and get adequate feedback from those on the line). Astute chairs can make a point of asking those on the phone for their opinions, but this is an option that boards should discuss. First, states have greater variance on the legitimacy of board phone participation than they do on email votes. Second, don't let this option snowball on your board: If you live in Wisconsin, beware the avalanche of phone requests your board might receive in the dead of winter! Consider placing limits on the number of times members can participate this way each year.

What Time-Saving Devices Can Make Your Board More Productive?

Even if you're a new board member and not yet part of the leadership, you will want to do all you can to ensure that your time is well used. This means that meetings must run efficiently. Feel free to suggest some of these time-tested strategies (pun intended!) if your board does not already use them.

Committee Reports as Homework, not Boardwork

Many board meetings are filled with committee chairs reporting on the most recent activity within their committees. Your board meetings can be literally transformed in terms of productivity if those oral reports are moved to written form alone. Committee chairs can write up one- to two-page summaries of their meetings that simply list the date, members in attendance, those absent, and a sketch of the topics discussed and actions or decisions needed from the board. They can then submit their reports to the chair or ED a specified number of days before the meeting for inclusion in the board packet. Members can then read, rather than hear, about committee work.

Saving Time by Tracking Time

Consider listing the amount of time allocated to each agenda item next to that line item. By committing in writing to that time allotment, the agenda becomes well thought-out, and it can help pace the meeting.

Perspiration

If a committee requires no action from the board, then its report will be included as part of a consent agenda (more info below). The committee report will provide all the information needed. Of course, members can still raise questions about the written report during the meeting. If the committee is making recommendations to the board, or if some kind of action is required of the board, the committee chair can request time on the agenda for group discussion and action.

Voila. That simple step can save a half-hour, an hour. . . sometimes more.

Consent Agendas

Consent agendas are exactly what their name implies: They are lists of items that require board action that are grouped together because they will likely engender easy agreement. A piece of the full agenda, consent agendas typically contain routine, procedural, and noncontroversial items that can be voted on together. Their contents generally do not require discussion or debate. Of course, before the vote takes place, the chair can ask whether there are questions about any items—it's always possible that a topic thought to be noncontroversial is controversial after all. If discussion or debate persists for a particular item, the item can be moved from the consent agenda to its own line item.

These items are ideal for most consent agendas:

- Committee reports that require no board action

- Immediate past meeting minutes

- Executive director's report, if no board action is needed (although typically the ED will still provide important highlights)

- Approval or confirmation of an issue that was discussed at length at a previous meeting and just requires a formal vote for approval

These are among the items that should not appear in a consent agenda:

- Audit review and approval

- Financial statements

- Review of executive committee decisions or actions

- Contract or loan approvals

Consent agendas streamline the meeting and free up time for substantive issues. How much time? On some boards, half of the meeting can be routinely dedicated to the standard procedures listed above.

Dashboards

This next tip can make your oversight duties as efficient as they get, saving time and elevating the quality of the board's work. Just like your car dashboard, the organizational *dashboard* displays key performance information. It can help you quickly assess whether the organization is firing on all cylinders or whether it needs to be brought into the shop for repairs. A dashboard can consolidate vast amounts of information in one place. It doesn't excuse you from studying financial or programmatic information, but it can help your board focus its limited time.

A dashboard displays key information so that you can quickly identify potential problem areas. The key is to identify those indicators that, when taken together, can provide an accurate snapshot of what is happening within the organization. These topics work particularly well in dashboard form, especially if they include comparison data from the previous year:

Financial. Indicators might include the amount of cash in the bank, number of days of cash in the bank, receivables, year-to-date revenues, expenses, and operating surpluses or losses. Since this is the most common use of dashboards, we include a sample below.

Sample Financial Dashboard

Financial Indicators	Target	This Year-to-Date	This Time Last Year	Take Action?
Number of days of unrestricted cash on hand	90	45	100	!
Months of operating reserve	3	3.5	3	
Accounts receivable > 90 days divided by total accounts receivable	Less than 10%	25%	5%	!
Accounts payable > 90 days divided by total accounts payable	Less than 10%	30%	10%	!

🔍 Programmatic. Benchmarks might include the number of clients enrolled and three to five key milestones that represent impact. This dashboard might tell you that last year at this time, five hundred clients received services, and this year that number is three hundred. The obvious question is, "Why?"

🔍 Seasonal topics. Maybe your organization is having a big event, so for a period of time, your dashboard might include a few items that relate to the event, such as number of tickets sold and sponsorships secured.

To use a dashboard effectively:

🔍 Determine key indicators to be tracked. Ensure that you limit the data to a manageable number of categories.

🔍 Discuss the performance targets for each indicator. For example, some boards strive to keep ninety days of cash on hand, while others aim for six months' worth.

Perspiration

Public vs. Internal Meeting Minutes

The board should approve a "public" version of the minutes that is shared with the auditor, IRS, or other agencies that may request your minutes. The public version of the minutes should be an overview or highlight of the meeting, issues voted upon, and the outcome of those votes.

Internally, a more detailed set of minutes may be retained that includes further details about the board's discussion and all of the reports or documents provided in the board packet or at the meeting. In this electronic era, creating a PDF with the minutes and all of the attachments is a relatively easy task. Having all of the information together creates an electronic paper trail of the meeting, which can be important information if needed later on.

Identify which staff and board members will be responsible for maintaining the dashboard.

One cautionary note: Someone has to keep the information current Therefore, the more complex the dashboards, the more difficult they can be to manage. And, depending on the kind of data included, they might require more than one person to maintain.

How Important Are Meeting Minutes?

You might be inclined to think of *minutes*—those notes taken by the board secretary—as a memory-inducing record of board events. That may be true, but if the IRS or a court ever comes a-knocking, those minutes will serve as official documentation of your board's discussions and actions. . . or inactions. Along with bylaws and articles of incorporation, minutes are one of the documents that nonprofits are required to keep indefinitely, an indicator of their importance.

So if you're not the secretary (not yet, anyway), what do you need to know about meeting minutes?

Minutes serve as an objective legal record of board deliberations, discussions, and decisions during your meetings. They are an important resource if questions arise about past actions or decisions, such as whether the board approved a personnel policy, and if so, when. They are also useful tools for absent board members and for those of us with less-than-stellar memories.

The secretary typically drafts the minutes and should distribute them as soon as possible, so that others can make corrections while the meeting is still fresh in their minds. At the next meeting, the full board reviews and approves them as part of the formal record. What you want to see is an accurate account of who attended each meeting, whether a quorum was met, the general discussion around each topic, and any board actions. In some cases, if a staff member helps tackle this task, the secretary should ensure that the tone of the draft is objective and that the notes are accurate.

You can see the importance of making time to carefully review the draft minutes and report any revisions. If you don't receive them shortly after the meeting, feel free to prod the secretary or the chair. You'll want to see the agenda used as a guide for the minutes, with this general content:

- Time when the meeting was called to order

- A list of those who were present, who participated by phone (if your bylaws allow for that), and who was absent

- Actions or decisions made by the board, including issues voted upon, who made the motion, seconded it, and the outcome of the vote (whether a unanimous "yes" or "no," or the number of "yeas," "nays," and abstentions)

- Any presentations and who made them

- Any documents, reports, or other information that were provided to the board

- Time when the meeting adjourned

Minutes should *not* include a detailed transcription of who said what to whom during your meeting. They should provide enough detail to understand what has taken place without implicating anyone for taking a specific stand. Any member of the board should feel comfortable with outsiders reading these documents. It goes without saying that the content should also be objective, free from the author's opinions.

How Might Committee Meetings Function?

Think about committee meetings just as you would full board meetings. Each should have an agenda, developed by the committee chairperson and the designated staff liaison. So, the fundraising committee chair works with the development director. The finance committee works with the CFO. The ED should also be in the loop on all major committee matters. The committee chair is responsible for preparing minutes or notes for the board packet.

Each committee prepares a brief summary of activities since the previous board meeting for the next board packet. A common committee report format can make it easier to highlight important recommendations and next steps. These sections can guide the ED and chair as they draft the full meeting agenda.

ABC Organization

[Name of Committee] Report

Date

Date of meeting and listing of individuals who participated

Committee Activities: Bulleted information that highlights recent activities or conversations

Discussion Items: Listing of items needing board discussion or input

Items Needing Board Review/Vote: Listing of items that require a board vote

Developing agendas and running meetings might seem simple, but between content, culture, and keeping the agenda within time constraints, it can be a difficult job. Yet, it's one worth investing some time. Meetings have the power to retain stellar members. They can also make your time on the board more engaging and productive.

To Summarize...

- A focus on respect, transparency, decision making, and fun tend to keep board members engaged in meetings.

- A regular feedback loop enables meetings to constantly improve in efficiency and focus.

- Board packets support the agenda by providing necessary data, background, and updates that prepare members for each agenda item.

- Time-saving ideas like written committee reports, consent agendas, and dashboards can help squeeze maximum content into a meeting.

- Meeting minutes serve as an objective legal record of board deliberations, discussions, and decisions.

The Care and Feeding of Your Leaders

No matter how stellar your board members, they rarely thrive as a group without an equally stellar group of leaders. This section will focus on those with the most influence: the chair, the ED, and your founder. All of them play different roles in nurturing the development of your board, so we will explore their roles in molding the team. Even if you are not (yet!) an official leader, we have sprinkled throughout this chapter ways in which you can help prod your current leadership toward a position of strength or develop a culture of leadership.

What happens when key leaders fly the coop? Whether they resign peacefully, involuntarily, or in a dramatic scene worthy of an Oscar, it will be your job, in part, to foster stability. So, we will touch on strategies that revolve around hiring, retaining, firing, and planning for that next great leader. When it's all over, our hope is that you will come away appreciating just how important these board dignitaries are—and why it's critical to select the right ones.

Chapter 19

ED–Chair Partnership: The Dynamic Duo

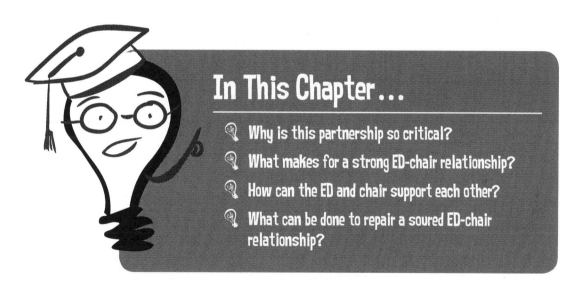

In This Chapter...

- Why is this partnership so critical?
- What makes for a strong ED-chair relationship?
- How can the ED and chair support each other?
- What can be done to repair a soured ED-chair relationship?

As two who served as leaders for the same organization (Bob as executive director, Susan as chair), we understand very well the delicate dance these choreographers must stage. And, we are convinced that the ED-chair partnership is often the key ingredient that drives overall board engagement. It also sets the tone between staff and board. We are strong believers that a chair's commitment increasingly drives a board's work. At the same time, the ED's engagement with that chair ensures that the board's work is informed.

This is a partnership that requires high confidence, transparency, respect, and communication. Hopefully, the two leaders like one another! If not, a professional relationship must prevail. Anything less will affect the organization. After all, this pair is responsible for orchestrating a body of people devoid of many formal rules, required goals, or often, well-defined roles. That means it's up to this duo to set the tone for nearly of all of the board's achievements.

Why Is the ED-Chair Relationship So Crucial?

A strong ED-chair partnership bolsters board performance and long-term organizational stability. Why? Each leader relies on the other for support and ideas, and neither wastes time looking to evade the other when critical events arise. Instead, issues quickly get airtime, and the players find solutions. This reliance enables the organization to weather storms with greater speed and tact than tends to be the case when the board operates in a separate realm from the ED.

This pairing is doubly vital because the board chair serves as the *de facto* boss of the ED. While legally, the full board supervises the executive director, it is not realistic for the executive director to report to a dozen "bosses," which leads to the chair's practical role as primary liaison between the ED and board.

The ED-chair roles can appear well defined:

- The chair leads the board and ensures that it is well managed and motivated.

- The ED leads the staff and ensures that it is well managed and motivated.

- The chair and ED work together to lead the nonprofit enterprise.

Human nature complicates these simple equations. Personalities can quickly deteriorate any one of the elements above, creating a ripple effect that can adversely impact the entire organization. The human factor can even disrupt events if the chair and ED are otherwise doing the right thing. It's like baking a cake: You can have all the right ingredients, but if you bake the cake at the wrong temperature, your prized dessert is toast. The "wrong temperature" in this case might indeed have to do with overheated personalities. Or distrust. Or egos. Or lack of communication. Or divergent priorities.

What Makes for a Strong ED-Chair Relationship?

In most nonprofits, there is a gap between what board members know and the realities of the day-to-day operations. Unless the board is running the organization without staff, it is virtually impossible for these part-time volunteers to know in detail what is happening day-to-day. Members rely on selected information provided by the executive director. While the board does not need to know every minute detail, it does require an intelligent staff "filter" that knows the information best suited for board meetings.

The ED-chair relationship is a bridge that helps close this information gap. The chair often serves as a testing ground for the ED. If the two believe that an issue requires a larger discussion, they will raise it with a committee or the full board. When the board learns what it needs to learn, when it needs to learn it, the resulting synergy transfers to the staff, other stakeholders, and even the mission.

Observation

Information Funnel

An important aspect of the ED-chair relationship is deciding what to share with the entire board. Usually, there's way more information and data available than needed for effective oversight. The leadership duo must decide which relevant information should be funneled through to the board's collective brain for review. Too much could result in information overload and possibly confusion. Too little could result in poor decision making or lackluster governance. The goal is to provide just the right amount to support informed decision making. Funneling information is a delicate balancing act indeed!

The ED and chair must work together in many ways to provide a comprehensive yet manageable set of issues and data that inform the board's work. They must also work to build goodwill between them. The organization relies on this dynamic duo to have their fingers on the pulse of the organization, allowing them to strategically bring new issues and challenges to the board for input and support. Their partnership has both practical and relational aspects to it. The practical parts include:

Information needed. The board defines a set of baseline data that it requires from the executive director on a regular basis, usually during the lead-up to its meetings. This data helps members fulfill their oversight roles. The board chair must believe that the ED is being fully transparent with the chair and, in turn, with the entire board.

Information shared. The ED provides that data and key strategic information, as well as questions that require board input and decisions. These will vary over time. The board chair helps prioritize which issues will come before the entire board.

Strategy. The chair and ED need to work together to frame the strategic issues and goals that will steer the board (and staff) in the same direction and provide measurable criteria to assess progress. These are ideally board-approved goals established during some kind of planning process; however, it is not uncommon for new issues to emerge. See Chapter 9 for guidance on strategic planning options.

A Clear Visual

One particularly savvy ED sits next to her board chair at each meeting so they can easily communicate with each other, even passing occasional notes to each other during meetings. The visual of these two leaders side-by-side also provides a clear picture to the board that the two are working as a team.

Pure Genius!

Board operations. Ultimately, the chair is responsible for overseeing board operations. One major exception comes in creating the meeting agenda. That document represents the collective efforts of the ED as well. The two work together to create an interesting, thought-provoking, discussion-generating meeting. See Chapter 18 for more details.

The relational pieces are equally important, and if not present, can be the undoing of this key partnership:

🔦 Trust. The chair must trust that the ED is forthright and that there will be no surprises. Ethics and honesty is a two-way street: The ED must trust that the chair provides a safety net, so that if something goes wrong (unless it's something unethical), the chair will rally the board to resolve the issue.

🔦 Accountability. The chair must not only strive to partner effectively with the ED but must also hold the executive accountable—and do so in a respectful, thoughtful manner. The ED, then, has a right to expect that the chair will hold the full board and its individual members accountable.

🔦 Mission. With mission at the core of this relationship, the parties gain valuable perspective when navigating issues together.

Communication is both practical and relational in nature. The practical piece includes the information supplied by the executive director, as required to the board. The relational piece will vary by style and personality. For example, one board chair might suggest weekly phone conversations with the ED. The next might prefer monthly or as-needed meetings. However the communication happens, it must meet the needs of both the ED and the chair.

How Can the Chair's Role Impact the ED?

Many board leaders are comfortable taking a back seat to their EDs a good deal of the time. While executive directors' perspectives are important—and are often more informed than those of their chairs—it is a chair's duty to listen to the chief staffer's opinions and use them to propel the board's work. Our goal here is not to diminish the ED, who clearly plays a central role in every nonprofit, but to focus on how the chair can best leverage that leadership position. After all, as the leader of the board and the main board liaison to staff, the chair plays an influential role in the relationship between the organization's two key leaders. By performing the following duties well, the chair stands to gain the ED's trust and confidence, primarily through these tasks:

- Facilitating well-run meetings

- Setting organizational priorities in tandem with the executive

- Recruiting competent, motivated board members

- Holding individual board members accountable

- Ensuring that committees are engaged and functioning

- Mediating conflict among members, either alone or by involving other relevant parties

- Serving as a spokesperson to the greater community

- Guiding the board through crises

- Leading the hiring, evaluation, and firing of the ED

Performing the above duties requires time, commitment, energy, and perseverance. If done well, the result is a strong partnership with the ED that benefits the entire organization.

But, we saved the most important—and one of the most overlooked—duties of the board chair for last: supporting the ED. This role will vary from one organization to the next, but it typically involves ensuring that the ED is being recognized and nurtured. Realizing that the ED job can seem like a nonstop treadmill at full speed, the chair can be the ED's biggest fan and cheerleader! Chapter 20 includes more detailed suggestions and strategies on how the chair (and board) can support the ED. Often, the board follows the chair's leadership on this front, so sometimes even a few laudatory words or a token gift given in public can reenergize an ED's fatigued mindset.

How Can the ED Help Lead the Board?

In our experience, highly engaged boards have this ingredient in common: focused ED leadership. EDs as board leaders keep the board—and especially the chair—focused on attainment of the mission and vision. While the chair may well top the organizational chart, we have come to learn that the ED of a well-functioning nonprofit takes top billing in what we'll call a "leadership chart." There's little denying that EDs must nudge, direct, and cajole the workings of the board in order for management and governance to work seamlessly together.

That doesn't mean that the ED should be the most vocal person at board meetings or that this leader's presence is necessary at every board-level conversation. It does mean that an ED must intentionally work to lead this high-level volunteer group. Otherwise, the board can become directionless, uninspired, and disengaged.

Board members can be quick to define their EDs as either overwhelming the board or being largely absent, providing no focused leadership or guidance. Clearly, neither is healthy for the organization. There is a sweet spot in between these extremes that most often enables a solid, respectful working relationship between staff and board. What are the appropriate tasks for an ED who is seeking to strengthen the board?

Illuminate the Mission and Vision

You already know that the ED conveys the vision. What you might not have thought about is just how much that role can influence a board. The ED's passion for, and communication of, a clear vision reminds members why their focus should be strategic and long-term. And, when the ED regularly illuminates the mission, it often translates into greater board dedication.

Sometimes, these tasks can be accomplished in the boardroom, through mission moments and discussions about the external environment. Other times, they can go further: The ED of a watchdog group set up a pen pal program between board members and those who had been affected by the nonprofit's work. That experience gave them a greater understanding of the impact of that group's work. Another ED strategically schedules meetings with board members when program beneficiaries will be in the building, giving board members a chance to experience the energy of the organization's programs. Other leaders create presentations, share articles, or tell stories that get the board out of the everyday and enable them to see the bigger picture.

Steer the Board's Focus

Most EDs help prepare for board meetings. They compile board packets, help develop agendas, schedule committee meetings, and provide financial information. These tasks certainly keep a board moving in the right direction. They also create the foundation for an ED and chair's work of setting goals and expectations. For instance, each board agenda illustrates the issues delegated to the board under its full authority, versus those that the ED and chair might handle independently or send to committees. If the two players are systematic about delegating work, the bleeding boundaries that plague many nonprofits can quickly diminish.

Help Direct the Leadership Pipeline

Because the relationship with the board chair is so vital to the executive director, the ED has every right to play a part in selecting the next board leader. This process often begins many steps earlier, when the ED plays a role in developing a leadership pipeline for the board. The executive might suggest preferences for board seats, committee and officer leadership, and the chair. Of course, it is the board that votes on the final candidates, but the nominating or governance committee can work closely with the ED to ensure that candidates are acceptable to the person who will work with them most.

Delayed Progress

An otherwise successful ED did not have input into the selection of the next board chair. His organization was just beginning to strengthen financially, so the selection of someone he couldn't work with and who didn't have the skills to be an effective chair caused the organization to lose two years of potential progress. The ED voiced his frustration, and going forward, the ED had input into who would serve in this key role.

Uninspired

Great EDs know when to actively lead their boards and when to let their boards lead. They recognize the skills board members bring and when to tap into those volunteers. How do they gain these insights? In part, they pursue relationships with individual board members. It may seem an impossible goal, but it's worthwhile for EDs to attempt to meet with each board member annually.

A board can expect and even encourage the executive director to provide it with key leadership, motivation, and support. In fact, for many engaged boards, a visionary ED is an essential ingredient.

It is increasingly common for EDs to serve as nonvoting, ex officio members of boards. This structure can bridge the divide between board and ED by legitimately giving the staff leader a seat at the board table.

What If the Relationship Takes a Turn for the Worse?

The likelihood of the ED-chair relationship souring is real. One reason is that, in many organizations, the chair position changes every year or two. Each new one presents a host of adjustments for an already-busy ED. The chair must also adjust when the ED retires, resigns, or even gets fired. Sometimes, one leader or the other remains in the position too long, leading to a feeling of complacency or entitlement. Add to these scenarios any crises that stand to strain the relationship, and you've got a very fluid set of circumstances.

If the ED-chair relationship takes a turn for the worse, hopefully the two parties can have an honest conversation about what has gone amok and the steps that might get them back on track. If the two cannot broker those negotiations themselves, select board members might step in, since an unproductive leadership team directly impacts the board itself. If the situation cannot be resolved internally, it might be necessary to bring in an outside mediator or board consultant to get everyone back on track. Many leadership coaches specialize in getting organizational heads to think through new approaches to their work.

It's typically worth the effort to strengthen even a tottering ED-chair relationship. While a board can plod along for months or even years with a disgruntled leadership duo, it often takes a simple intervention or some professional development to bring the two together and recognize their collective strengths. Those assets are multiplied many times over when they feed board and staff morale.

To Summarize...

- An effective ED-chair relationship requires high confidence, transparency, respect, and communication.

- The chair is the board leader, and the ED is the staff leader.

- The ED-chair relationship directly affects how well the board functions.

- The executive director deserves input about the next board chair.

- If this relationship struggles or sours, it's important to take steps to get it back on track.

Chapter 20

Supporting and Evaluating the ED

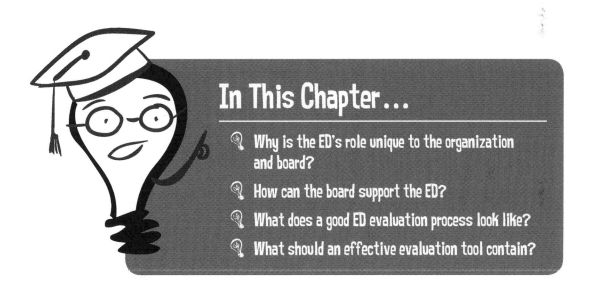

In This Chapter...

- Why is the ED's role unique to the organization and board?
- How can the board support the ED?
- What does a good ED evaluation process look like?
- What should an effective evaluation tool contain?

One of your main roles—while rarely discussed—is to support the ED. Yes, finance and risk management are important, but this might be the most important job you will undertake as a board member. It requires a deep understanding of the ED's roles and your place in making that person successful. . . without micromanaging.

In the previous chapter, we focused on the relationship between the ED and the chair. Here, we examine the board's role as partner. Granted, this chapter also includes information about the ED's performance evaluation, but as you will see, we consider that process very much in line with advocating for the ED, since a solid process demonstrates a keen attention to this leader's work—not to mention the potential pay raise. In short, it's a year-round job to support this most critical staff person.

What Is the Relationship Between the Board and the ED?

The executive director has a unique role in your agency. The ED is sandwiched between the board and staff: reporting and accountable to a multi-person board, and often managing multiple staff. The ED walks a tightrope that can be challenging on even the best of days. So when a nonprofit employs an ED, the most important role a board can play is that of a partner and supporter. You're not likely to find much about this responsibility in board job descriptions, but it can make the difference between a nonprofit that flourishes and one that languishes. The board works with the ED to foster communication, transparency, trust, and excitement over a shared vision. The board cannot achieve those things alone.

It's hard to overstate how easily an adversarial relationship with the ED can creep into the culture, so watch out for it and speak out when you see its

---

Inspiration

Zen Thoughts about Executive Directors

Board members must look critically at their ED's performance, but there are also reasons to support the staff leader:

- Few professionals work so hard, especially given their sometimes below-market salaries.

- Board meetings are just one facet of their very wide-ranging roles.

- Most EDs *want* board members as their partners. Many could work twenty-four hours a day and still struggle to achieve their goals. Just think, if your career vision was to end childhood hunger, you'd have your work cut out for you, too!

signs. That doesn't mean that a board should rubber stamp an ED's ideas or overlook unethical practices. A fine line exists between oversight and smothering, between empowering the ED and letting that person run wild.

When your ED is working hard and working well, it's your job to support the one and only employee who reports to the board. Assuming that you have a well-intentioned, ethical executive at the helm, the board should avoid a "gotcha" mindset. "We've got your back," is more like it.

What Can You Do to Start the Relationship Right?

Because board members often have limited involvement in a nonprofit's everyday workings, the ED is an important link between the board and the organization's struggles and successes. Thus, the ED-board relationship must be built on trust. Board members must trust that the executive will provide necessary information that allows them to govern effectively. And, the ED needs to trust that the board is committed to creating a partnership that is supportive of the position's demanding and unique roles and responsibilities. If trust feels weak on either side of that equation, board members can help to foster regular conversations about it.

How else might you begin to cement a solid relationship between your ED and the board? For starters, be willing to step up and assume responsibility. Don't sit on your hands and wait for someone else to pitch in. Good EDs love proactive board members.

Also, be willing to serve as an ambassador and a fundraiser. A committed group of board rainmakers takes some of the burden off the ED's shoulders. As a bonus, those tasks enable your ED to brag to funders—and even fellow executives—about this organization's stellar board.

Most importantly, no matter how small or large your promises, follow through on everything that you agree to do. If you neglect a task you agreed to complete, you might create even *more* work for your staff leader if you leave the work undone and force the ED to contact you multiple times with reminders!

What Kind of Ongoing Support Can You Provide?

We can't think of a better way to begin your time on the board than to explore how you might support your ED on a day-to-day basis. Here are a few ideas:

- Get to know the ED. Ask questions about the job, its challenges, how that person prefers to work with the board and its individual members, and how you can be most helpful given your skill sets. Offer to attend meetings with donors, community leaders, and public officials, all of which showcase yours as an involved board.

- Know your role. In other words, don't offer advice or otherwise tell staffers what to do. That's the ED's job. The board is responsible for program impact, so if staff is running programs differently than you'd prefer, leave that management to the ED. (The exception, of course, comes if you see something unethical.)

- Provide balanced feedback. Does your board just criticize the ED? Or, is everything wonderful on a regular basis? Most EDs are driven

Pure Genius!

The Number One Way to Keep Your ED

A health organization's board loved its ED but could not find the funds for several years to provide a raise or a retirement contribution. Finally, the ED expressed frustration. The board held an executive session—a meeting without the ED—and decided that it would be less costly to compensate this leader for a job well done than to risk losing her and transitioning to a new hire. A boost in salary, they reasoned, cost less than a search firm, an interim ED, and possible lost funding from donors who adored this executive. Since the ED's salary was already below market rates, members decided that it was in their best interest to ensure that funds were available to adequately compensate their cherished ED. Not only did they increase board engagement in fundraising, but that executive led the nonprofit to a string of new achievements.

people who want to make a difference, so they value thoughtful, constructive input on both sides of the spectrum.

Pay a competitive salary. Many issues of executive turnover stem from a lack of a competitive salary. Granted, this is not the corporate sector, but research what other EDs in your sector, in your region of the country, with your budget, are paid. If the organization's current budget cannot bear the full market rate salary, work gradually toward your goal.

Provide a year-end bonus. If your budget is not stable enough for a salary increase, a bonus might be a good interim step. It's even a smart idea once you have increased your ED's salary sufficiently, as an added incentive. If the organizational budget cannot support a bonus, consider asking each board member to contribute, although that should not count as a board member's donation to the organization.

Nominate your ED for an award or special recognition. If there is an award that recognizes nonprofit leaders in your area, submit an application on behalf of your stellar ED. If none exists, create a certificate and "award" it to your ED at an event or a special staff meeting.

Encourage your ED to take time away. It's important that your executive escapes from the day-to-day stresses of running the organization. If your nonprofit is small, some board members might need to step in and help hold down the fort so the ED can be away for a couple of weeks without worry and anxiety. Make sure this happens! Some EDs will not take vacations because they think that the organization cannot run without them. Send them on vacation and prove them wrong.

Ask your ED for ideas. Hopefully, your ED has a close relationship with the chair or another board member. Have one of them ask the ED how the board can strengthen its support. Also ask what kinds of professional development the ED would like to pursue. Leadership training? A conference? A series of workshops? Ensure that some of those items find their way into the budget.

Evaluate the ED. One of the greatest supports any employee can ask for is a thoughtful, fair performance assessment.

How Can I Play a Valuable Role in Evaluating the ED?

The board's role in supporting the ED is intertwined with its job to supervise that person's work.

For many boards, ED performance evaluations are performed too infrequently or informally. Too often, the board will only initiate the process when it is unhappy with the ED's performance. In other cases, the board acts only when nudged repeatedly by the ED.

If you learn that your board has not performed an evaluation in over a year, ask why. Spur the group to action! It's hard to claim that a board is fulfilling its oversight duties if the chief staffer goes without formal oversight. Providing a constructive evaluation process can be insightful and informative. The process presents an opportunity to provide feedback and sing your executive's praises. If you have a terrific ED, that latter step likely

Pure Genius!

Make a Date to Evaluate

One board keeps a calendar of its activities for the year, including the steps leading up to the executive director's performance evaluation. That last item reminds members that the process must begin months before the chair plans to review the ED's work one-on-one. When the chair first added the evaluation to the calendar, she set a goal of finalizing the ED's new salary by the time that leader was putting together the next fiscal year budget. From there, the chair worked backward sequentially, plotting out the board meeting when the full group would approve the evaluation, the executive committee sessions when members would create preliminary recommendations, and opportunities for the ED to provide feedback on the previous and coming year's performance goals.

does not happen frequently enough. Help make this activity a priority for your board.

How Should the Board Approach the ED Evaluation?

If you work in the corporate sector, you might find some unusual dynamics in evaluating a nonprofit executive. Typically, when an individual reports to a supervisor, that supervisor has enough in-depth knowledge to assess that employee. But when it comes to an ED evaluation, there is likely no one person on the board with a comprehensive knowledge of the ED's performance. Some members may have only seen the ED in action during board meetings—hardly a basis for a comprehensive performance review.

If the ED and board chair have a good working partnership, the chair likely will have the most comprehensive view of the ED's work, including board management. Individual board members might consider spending the greatest time tackling aspects of the ED's job that they know best. The treasurer and members of the financial committee might evaluate the ED's financial performance. Those who help with outreach can speak to public relations. The full board can comment on organizational performance and impact.

The ED evaluation can be a complex process. Assuming that annual goals are clear, there are two equally important parts that will guide your board: an evaluation instrument and a systematic process. Both should be agreed-upon by all parties involved before the evaluation begins.

Evaluation Tools

The most effective evaluation tools combine a rating system with general comments and observations. They can be divided into sections such as: organizational impact and progress, finances, program impact, leadership, and community outreach. Essentially, you'll want to assess items in the ED's job description and annual goals. If your organization has a current strategic plan, those goals can often come right out of that plan. Otherwise, your board can establish annual leadership goals with the ED.

You will find examples of evaluation tools on the Internet, but you might do better to ask to see the forms used by organizations that are similarly sized or that provide like services. Customize any samples to suit your own needs. You will find a sample ED evaluation form in Appendix G.

Evaluation Process

When the evaluation process is transparent and includes the ED's input, it will likely go more smoothly. Below is a suggested framework for such a process:

- Create an evaluation task force. Ideally, a small group of board members will oversee the process. Establish a deadline when evaluation results will be discussed with the entire board.

- Review the evaluation tool. Working with the ED, the committee should review the evaluation document and make any modifications to ensure it continues to be relevant.

- Review the previous evaluation. What were the goals established last year that were to be achieved by this year? What were areas of concern that need to be reviewed as part of the current year's evaluation?

- Solicit feedback. Identify who will be asked to participate and how various evaluators will provide feedback (via electronic survey software, email, etc.).

- Ask for ED input. Let the ED reflect on the year's performance and offer input about it, as well as suggested goals for next year. Some boards interview the ED to garner feedback; others ask the ED to fill out the evaluation form.

- Collect board (and staff) input. Whether or not you plan to conduct a 360-degree evaluation (see sidebar on the next page), provide a deadline for parties to turn in their survey tools. Be clear about whether responses will be anonymous. Typically, the task force can see individuals' names associated with responses, while the ED sees anonymous comments.

Review and discuss. The task force reviews the feedback and writes up a draft evaluation.

Present the draft to the ED. Take time to celebrate achievements and say "thank you," in addition to focusing on needed improvements. A meeting between the ED and the task force is also a good time for the group to draft the ED's goals for the next twelve months, including professional development benchmarks. Give the ED a chance to provide feedback that might influence a rating or comment before the draft goes to the full board. Then give the ED the opportunity to respond in writing to anything that remains a point of contention.

Revise the draft. Based on that meeting, the task force might need to revise the document for its next audience: the full board.

Present to board. During an executive session of the board, the task force presents the evaluation, along with any comments or concerns voiced by the ED. The task force might also recommend a salary increase or bonus. If the board doesn't approve the evaluation, it might require further revision before it is approved.

Sign and file. Once the evaluation has

The 360-Degree Evaluation

Since board member input rarely provides a full picture of the ED's performance, consider asking staff, volunteers, or other stakeholders for feedback. One approach to this is to develop a 360-degree evaluation process. This comprehensive process is lengthy to conduct. Boards must also realize that those completing the survey might have limited views of the ED's performance or may have a grudge against the ED. Given the pros and cons, your board might consider using this approach every couple of years rather than annually. Sample 360 forms are readily available on the Internet.

Perspiration

been approved by the entire board, ask the ED to sign and date the document. Keep a copy of the evaluation in the ED's personnel file.

Assess the process. Debrief to determine any recommended changes for next year.

During the evaluation process, be mindful of whether unmet goals are the fault of the ED or the external environment. For example, if fundraising goals missed the mark last year, was that because a grant proposal was not submitted on time, or because budget cuts forced a key government grant to suddenly disappear? If you enable your entire board to provide input on the evaluation, you are most likely to garner the full range of perspectives necessary to ensure that it is fair.

If your ED falls short in any area, consider offering professional development, along the lines of coaching or training, to help your leader get up to snuff. Many EDs find that kind of encouragement a testament to a supportive board.

There are so many ways to support your ED. Be creative, but don't forget to focus on the primary mode of support: an annual performance evaluation. Your ED—and your organization—will be better for it.

To Summarize...

To The board's goal should be to work as a group with the ED to foster communication, transparency, trust, and excitement over a shared vision.

Find ways to get to know and support your ED.

Supporting the ED is a balancing act for the board: the ED needs acknowledgement and praise but must also be held accountable.

Regular ED performance reviews are one of the greatest supports the board can provide, both for the ED's success and for the success of the organization.

Ensure that the evaluation process is transparent and includes input from the ED.

Chapter 21

Hiring and Firing the ED

In This Chapter...

- Who will take the reins before a new ED is hired?
- What steps should you take to hire a new ED?
- What is the best way to let an ED go?

Executive transitions happen. It's possible you won't be a board member long before you have to hire or (gulp!) fire an executive director. Either task can be filled with anxiety and unexpected opportunity. Even leadership changes less fraught than a firing—a retirement or a resignation—can be filled with angst. When you assist with transitions at the top, you are literally setting the course for the future of your organization. If you and your board peers prepare well, the chances of a smooth transition increase dramatically.

Though hiring and firing an ED are two very important duties, unfortunately, many boards embark upon these processes unprepared or without an action plan. Add to this the likely pressure to get someone in that seat as soon as possible, especially if fellow members are filling the ED's shoes while the job is vacant. So, here we provide some basics to get you through these most important transitions.

Who Will Fill the Gap?

No matter the size of your board or the age of your organization, it's not uncommon to feel some unease when the ED leaves. Why? Because you and your colleagues will be responsible for both the hiring process and for managing the transition. One reason boards may hold onto underperforming EDs too long is that members dread the process of hiring a replacement or fear having to steer the ship until a new ED is hired. That's too bad, because with a little planning and determination, boards actually make their jobs much easier once they have a solid executive in place. It can often be worth the tradeoff to spend a few months in transition, followed by increased results and stability.

Before we get to hiring and firing, let's touch on what to do while that executive seat is vacant. Several options exist when your ED departs. Every board must assess its ability to devote human and financial resources to this phase, the length of which can be hard to determine but can be as long as six months or more.

Board and Staff as Acting ED

Sometimes a board member will temporarily serve in the ED role, especially in smaller organizations where there is no additional senior staff. When an organization can choose from staff with comprehensive organizational knowledge, the deputy director or other senior staff person might lead the organization as an acting ED.

This option of temporarily filling the gap from within the organization— whether from the board or staff side—can be among the smoothest. It allows an individual with knowledge about the organization to come in quickly and quite smoothly. This strategy has two major shortcomings:

Heard It Through the Grapevine

News of executive transitions quickly makes its way into the community. Some of your stakeholders will assume that things are in disarray unless the board communicates otherwise. Consider sending a short note to your most important stakeholders wishing your last ED well and providing a little relevant background about your interim ED. Also include a brief outline of your hiring timeline and process. Then, when you hire a permanent staffer, that person can make a splash with introductory announcements to all relevant community members.

Perspiration

The hiring process may be sped up because board members may feel the need to relieve that acting ED as soon as possible, especially when a fellow member is sitting in the executive seat.

Using an internal person to fill this role, even temporarily, prevents a fresh set of eyes from looking at the organization, which may be valuable information for the board, as it considers needed skill sets.

Interim ED

The growth of the nonprofit sector and the regular turnover of its executives have driven a new specialty of consultants: those who temporarily lead nonprofits during executive transitions. Typically, these are former EDs themselves. If your agency can afford it, good interim EDs can provide these benefits:

- Knowledge about the nonprofit sector, ED transitions, and your local community

- Objective reports to the board about the organization's strengths and weaknesses

- Close working relationships with staff, helping to ease what can be a time of great anxiety

- Continuity with funders

Where do you find these nonprofit saviors? Ask your local United Way, volunteer center, or community foundation to recommend some. Other resources include peer groups that have hired interims, local consultants (although make sure you hire only someone who specializes in these interim stints), and state nonprofit associations.

How Do You Go About Hiring an ED?

While staff, clients, volunteers, and other stakeholders might provide input during the process, the buck stops with the board. Hiring a new leader is a multi-stage process.

Some boards hire executive search firms. This route can be costly and is certainly not a must, but it can make things easier if those on your board are particularly strapped for time and cannot devote the hours needed to find the right candidate. Search firms may also help tap into talent in places not familiar to the board. Hiring a firm can also be practical if you plan to conduct a nationwide search.

Assuming that you are not working with a search firm, the steps below will help your board to think about each step along the way.

ED Search Task Force

Unless your board is very small, it probably doesn't make sense to involve all members in the screening, interviewing, and selection of job finalists. Typically, a task force takes on these preliminary activities, with a goal of recommending a candidate to the full board for approval.

Who should sit on the task force?

 Chair or vice-chair

Dollars and Sense

The salary range and benefits your organization offers can greatly influence who applies for the job. Your task force will want to research salaries and benefits of EDs at comparable agencies. The results vary greatly by region, type of nonprofit, and budget size. *The Chronicle of Philanthropy*, Guidestar.org, and peer organizations' IRS Form 990s provide executive salary information. A cautionary note: What the market demands and what your organization can pay might be two different figures.

Perspiration

> 🔦 Treasurer or another board member who understands the organization's finances

> 🔦 Long-term board member

> 🔦 Relatively new board member

Spice things up a bit when it comes to task force members so there will be lively debate about who will make the best ED.

First Steps

It can seem like there are so many steps to this process, but none is as overwhelming as making that final candidate selection. So be methodical and create solid criteria. If you keep your standards high, chances are that you will come out with an ED who will suit your organization's needs.

> 🔦 Create a timeline. On average, hiring timelines can take three to six months, possibly longer. The entire board will want to chime in on and approve the timeline.

> 🔦 Determine necessary skills. Ask staff, clients, board members, and trusted external stakeholders what they want out of your next ED. If possible, have an honest conversation with the outgoing ED about the skills needed to take this nonprofit to the next level. Qualifications will be determined by the age, size, and complexity of your organization. What your agency required from your ED in the early years might be dramatically different now. So, it's essential to engage in a rigorous and thorough analysis of qualifications.

> 🔦 Revise the job description. Based on the above surveys and conversations, revise the job description to reflect desired skills and experience. Ideally, the board should approve this document.

> 🔦 Settle on a salary range. Do your homework with regard to salary, and consider listing a range in the job announcement. It is a waste of everyone's time to get a stellar application from a candidate who is currently making $120,000 when the most you can pay is $60,000.

Get the word out. Options include social media, the organization's website and newsletter, an e-blast to donors, funders, and volunteers, and nonprofit employment sites such as Idealist.org. Check with other nonprofits that have recently hired and see which forums worked best for them. Get the job description out to as many parties as possible in order to get the best candidates.

Interview Topics

Before actually interviewing candidates, the full board might engage in a conversation about some sample interview topics. The nature of the questions you ask will reflect the values of your board, your organization, and the traits you seek in an ED. You can certainly include most questions that you would hear in a corporate interview. Below we list some that are unique to the nonprofit sector:

Describe your connection to our mission.

This is a multi-faceted position. How do you go about establishing priorities and organizing your time?

What specific experience do you have with nonprofit finance?

Explain your fundraising background. Describe the largest gift you have solicited.

Describe your role with your last board. How did that board evolve during your tenure? What was its greatest accomplishment?

You can use your list of board- and staff-generated criteria to craft questions that pertain to those specific traits, such as capital campaign experience, growing an organization, or working with local politicians. If the candidate is transitioning from the corporate sector to the nonprofit sector, you might want to ask a few questions about the candidate's expectations and motivations for moving to this sector.

Screening Process

Task force members will want to establish criteria to determine who will get beyond the first round of screening. Then, either the full group or various subsets will undertake these activities:

- Identify preliminary candidates

- Conduct phone interviews with preliminary candidates

- Select semi-finalists

- Conduct in-person interviews with semi-finalists

- Identify finalists

- Conduct second round of interviews; these should be in-person (consider including board members who are not on the task force and possibly staff and/or clients in this round of interviewing)

- Select top candidate(s)

- Contact references

- Select candidate who will be recommended to board

The Staff's Role

At multiple organizations we know, senior staff was not involved in the interview process and met their new boss on that person's first day on the job. They were not happy! Board members will want to make clear to staff that the board makes the final hiring decision, but there are plenty of ways to include them along the way:

- Help develop interview questions

- Meet the final two candidates and inform board members of preferences

> Meet the sole finalist, and unless staff has serious reservations, put that candidate forward to the board's vote

> Sit on the search task force, a less common option, but a possibility for one or two very mature staff members

If an internal candidate is applying for the ED position, it does not necessarily mean that the staff should not be involved in the process, but task force members need to carefully think about how to appropriately engage those colleagues.

Making the Offer

You have identified the perfect candidate. Now it's time to make an offer. In one scenario, the board might authorize the task force to identify the top candidate and negotiate a salary up to a certain limit. As long as the task force stays within that limit, it can negotiate a package subject to final board approval. If, however, the limit needs to be exceeded, board approval is required. As soon as possible, the new ED should meet the entire board face-to-face.

Stepping In and Backing Out

The board often becomes more involved in day-to-day operations during the search period. Once the new ED is hired, the board must revert *to* its regular oversight and governance roles. It's easy for the board to micromanage after a new ED is hired. It can be a tricky balance.

The new executive needs space and time to get acclimated and establish leadership. The board should not step away completely and challenge the ED to sink or swim, but work with the ED to determine how best to leverage members' skills, experience, and talent to establish a strong partnership with the new leader.

Boards Beware!

When an executive director is fired, make sure your board safeguards the organization's assets. While rare, the executive stands to become uncooperative or even engage in intentional sabotage. One such ED had held the job for many years. Upon departure, he took critical files and destroyed others. When the new executive director began work, some key information was missing, making the transition difficult.

WATCH OUT!

In either case, the task force chair provides the board with résumés, cover letters, and a brief summary as to why the task force recommends the final candidate(s). Once the hire is finalized, draft an offer letter, which confirms start date, salary, and benefits. Finally, the board chair or task force chair can communicate—preferably in person—with staff about who was selected and why, and when the new hire will begin work.

How Do You Go About Firing the ED?

As the ED's ultimate boss, boards must occasionally fire an executive director. Some of those decisions are clear cut. Others are not. Don't assume that your board will never have to fire the ED: Studies have shown that up to a third of EDs are fired. Even if you don't ultimately terminate your leader, the steps below can help determine when things are not going well.

When boards talk about letting their EDs go, there are typically two reasons: leadership that raises legal or ethical implications, and situations in which the ED falls short on performance. The board should meet in executive session early on when dissatisfaction or doubts about the ED arise, no matter what kind of issue is at hand. If you suspect serious ethical or legal violations, consult an attorney right away. Even if the ED's performance is the reason, your board might seek legal advice to help mitigate a potential lawsuit. The board will also want to prevent the situation from tarnishing your nonprofit's reputation.

In general, firing the ED is like firing most other employees. You monitor, evaluate, document, discuss, and then dismiss anyone who repeatedly falls short of a clear set of expectations. Performance criteria should appear in a job description, annual goals, and in your ED's contract, if applicable.

It's best to be as methodical as possible. Firing the ED is the board's job, and often, no one in the group will have had experience with this particular set of tasks in a nonprofit setting. So, follow the advice of your attorney and these general steps:

- Lay the groundwork. The board will want to meet in executive session to discuss the situation. Depending on the circumstances, the group might decide to consult an attorney, monitor the ED for evidence of indiscretions, hire a specialized consultant to gather information, or discuss performance issues with the ED directly.

- Document, document, document. Your attorney can help you determine exactly what kind of data you will need to maintain. While no amount of information can prevent future lawsuits, the written word can help clarify facts and next steps.

- Follow up. If the issues are performance-related, your chair might create regular check-ins so the ED gets a fair chance to improve. Sometimes, it's this kind of diligence that can turn a potential firing into a new beginning. Boards sometimes realize during this process that communication barriers were as much a culprit of frustration as the ED's behaviors.

- Take action. If you and your peers have documented behavior worthy of dismissal, you might first give your ED the chance to resign. A resignation often allows both the ED and the nonprofit to move on with less drama and preserves the reputation of both.

What are some firing scenarios?

- Immediate dismissal. There may be very clear, undisputed facts that show the ED has acted unethically: Money may be missing, or personal expenses appear on the organization's credit card. If the facts are clear and indisputable, immediate dismissal may be warranted.

💡 Administrative leave. If someone has levied an accusation against the ED, there will be a period when the facts are being investigated. The ED may be placed on administrative leave during that time, drawing a salary while a board task force or outside group investigates the claim. If the illicit act is confirmed, then the ED may be dismissed or placed on probation, depending on the gravity of the situation.

💡 Fired after warnings. If there is general dissatisfaction with the ED's performance, the chair or executive committee might provide written notice that lays out the issue and any required next steps. A copy of each warning gets filed in the ED's personnel folder. If the situation continues unresolved or unaddressed, the board might decide to dismiss the ED.

There are a few things your board can do to make this series of events less tumultuous. If you and your peers follow the steps below, you will put your ED on notice that this board takes its work seriously.

Don't Take It Personally

As much as possible, avoid letting personality rifts between the ED and board influence whether you show your employee the door. While ED-board dynamics can greatly influence your level of enjoyment as a board member, personality differences should not be the sole factor in letting an ED go. Remember, mission is your first priority.

Uninspired

Annual ED Evaluations

A formal, objective, annual performance evaluation, as described in Chapter 20, is critical. If done consistently and according to a prescribed process, your board will have the evidence needed to fire an ED due to poor performance or noncompliance. Pay particular attention to documenting any concerns and laying out specific goals for the coming year.

Ongoing Performance Evaluations

If your board raises issues with the ED during the evaluation or outside of it, don't wait for the next formal evaluation period to present additional feedback. Whether the ED makes positive or negative progress, you will want to revisit the issue at prescribed times and document each meeting.

Personnel Policies

The best insurance you can have—other than hiring well from the start—is a strong set of personnel policies. As with hiring and evaluating, firing the ED should also have some kind of agreed-upon process. Follow many of the basic steps in this section, and consult a lawyer for added refinement. It benefits all involved if the process is in place before it's needed.

While no board looks forward to firing its ED, the courageous group will do so when change is needed to advance the mission. Better to cut ties and move forward than to lose years or risk the nonprofit's reputation on a subpar leader. If you and your peers undertake these steps—and carefully communicate what you expect of your ED—you help avoid this often tumultuous stage in your nonprofit's history.

To Summarize...

- ED transitions are an opportunity for the board to set a future course for the organization.

- When your lead staff position is vacant, the board must consider whether staff, board members, or an interim ED will temporarily lead the organization.

- The board ultimately hires and fires the executive director.

- Both the hiring and firing process require a good deal of planning, and potentially, some outside assistance.

Chapter 22

What If Your Leaders Flee to Cancun?

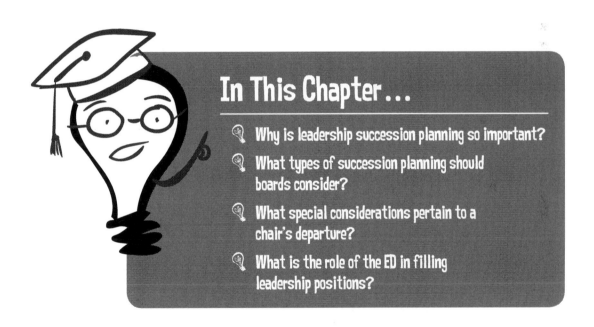

In This Chapter...

- Why is leadership succession planning so important?
- What types of succession planning should boards consider?
- What special considerations pertain to a chair's departure?
- What is the role of the ED in filling leadership positions?

We just can't bear to think that your board chair or ED might get hit by a bus, but our title here gets at a parallel outcome for your nonprofit. If either of your chief leaders suddenly abandons ship, you don't want your organization to sink...or even float aimlessly through rough seas. With morale hanging by a thread, you stand to lose valuable time figuring out your next steps. Better to discuss and plan in advance for leadership transitions.

So we'll focus on the board's separate, but similar, roles in each of those two succession scenarios: that of the ED and the chair. As you can imagine, smooth leadership transitions are some of the board's most critical risk management roles—not only because they ensure continuity, but because you know who tends to fill in for absent board chairs and EDs? That's right, board members! We assume that you need no further persuasion about the importance of this topic.

Why Is Succession Planning So Important?

The best boards treasure their leaders, whether past, current, or future. It's not easy to find ones who excel at management, programs, finance, public relations, and the many other skills we expect of our board chair and ED. Then there's the fact that many lead our sector for below-market or no pay, the latter in the case of most chairs.

Many boards ignore the sticky topic of leadership transitions until they must deal with it imminently. However, those that do tackle succession planning benefit in a few ways:

- Minimize risk. Thoughtful planning provides greater likelihood of hiring or voting in the right candidate.

- Maximize limited time. If the board must both create the succession plan *and* implement it during a time of transition, board members will spend twice as much time filling interim roles as they would if a plan was already in place.

- Attract quality candidates. Good candidates for both board and staff positions can often spot a prepared board from miles away.

- Ensure continuity. Staff functioning and external relations improve markedly when everyone knows what to do in case of a leadership vacuum.

While it might seem like an advanced concept to put transition or succession plans in place, it's often the newest and the smallest organizations that are shaken the most by leadership voids. That's because those groups rarely have adequate staff to take on an ED's roles. And the chair is likely to have the greatest institutional knowledge on what is often a small board.

How Can a Board Prepare for a Leadership Transition?

These days, leadership posts vacate, especially at the staff level, for a variety of reasons, some of which are categorized below.

Leadership Transition Types

	Planned	Unplanned
Temporary	Vacation Sabbatical Surgery Parental leave	Prolonged illness Serious injury Care of family member
Permanent	Retirement Dismissal with warnings	New employment Immediate dismissal Serious illness or death

The planned and unplanned categories above take into account *the board's perspective.* For example, if the board plans to fire the ED, it can begin to prepare for that leader's departure even before the deed is done. Unplanned transitions are unexpected, giving the board little or no time to prepare.

Temporary absences come with the expectation that the ED will return once the events precipitating the absence are resolved. If your ED will miss a week of work, or even two, chances are most operations will be functional during the absence. Even so, your board will want priority measures in place to cover a very short ED hiatus: Who else has the keys to the building? Who has passwords to key documents? When a temporary absence drags on for three weeks or more, in most cases, formal plans must take effect.

Board chairs tend to vacate on a more permanent, planned basis, sometimes due to term limits. Of course, chairs can also decide, based on personal or professional commitments, or a lack of defined term limits, that the time has come for them to step aside. Hopefully when that time comes, they will provide plenty of notice for a suitable replacement to take the reins.

Succession plans will differ slightly depending on whether the plan's authors are talking about vacancies that are planned or unplanned, temporary or permanent. While we will briefly pull apart the differences here, we will largely stick to the basics that define all types of transitions.

No matter which leader vacates—the ED or board chair—a few precautionary measures can make absences, departures, and transitions easier on everyone:

- Discuss transitions before they happen. Many boards prefer to avoid these kinds of conversations, often fearing that they will *inspire* leadership departures. This is rarely the case. As a matter of fact, conversations about leadership transitions during times of stability are often a mark of the strongest boards. The discussions themselves can bolster board members' confidence that their nonprofit can sustain itself during what is a standard organizational life cycle.

- Put a plan in place. You will find many templates on the Internet, and they don't have to be complex. We will suggest some of the more important pieces in the pages that follow, and you can see Appendix H for additional language. A plan ensures that, in a moment of panic, your board has a roadmap and does not forget important steps along the way.

Slate of Candidates or Competitive Elections?

Don't forget to help your board leaders transition effectivity. The process often works most smoothly when the governance committee, in partnership with the ED, identifies the slate of candidates. It's rare that multiple board members will be chomping at the bit to assume each officer role. When that's the case, the committee can talk to each candidate about alternative leadership positions. Competitive elections can have unintended consequences like hard feelings or diminished morale.

Perspiration

🔖 Continue the conversation. Even if your board put a succession plan in place months or years ago, and there is no sign that your ED or chair plans to leave anytime soon, revisit it periodically to make sure that it still adheres to the culture and structure of your organization. Update it if necessary.

🔖 Begin with unplanned scenarios. If talking about a planned transition seems too awkward or threatening, begin by developing emergency succession plans for the executive director and the board chair.

🔖 Create board and staff leadership pipelines. For the board, consider how you can create a pool of talent ready and willing to step into leadership roles when the time comes. If there is sufficient staff, allocate money in the budget for staff leadership development so that senior members can assume key duties during either a planned or unplanned executive transition or absence. Through ED evaluations, you can encourage your ED to get others up to speed on specific critical functions of the executive job.

🔖 Assign roles. As part of any succession plan, be very clear about who will be assuming which leadership roles.

What Are the Key Elements of an Executive Succession Plan?

If your board discusses just one succession planning element, make it that of the ED. A good plan will include most of the elements that follow. Your plan's tone may be formal or informal. Its length may be may be long or short. What's critical is that it spells out clear procedures and priorities.

Permanent Departure

For a permanent vacancy, whether the departure is sudden or planned, the end goal is the same: hire a new executive director. To make the plan as useful as possible, the answers to the following questions will form a good deal of its content:

Who will oversee the plan's execution? If a small board, it will often be the entire group. If a larger board, the group might delegate this activity to the executive or another committee.

Who will serve as acting executive director? See Chapter 21 for ideas, which include senior staff, board members, or a hired interim ED.

How will staff learn the job of the ED if employees are in line to serve temporarily in that role? Lay out expectations for the ED to create a training plan for potential acting executives so that they may learn the ED's priority activities. Those priority tasks may be listed in the plan or in an attached document.

Will the interim ED have full authority to act in that role? If so, you will want to state that. If not, state the job's parameters. For instance, do you want this person to have the authority to hire and fire employees? Take out a loan?

Will the interim ED, if a staff member, receive a salary increase while serving in the ED role? The answer might be no, in which case this item may be omitted. Some organizations offer a nominal, say 5 percent, increase in salary during the time serving as ED.

What messaging will assure external parties that the transition will be a smooth one? Key donors and supporters will want to hear from the interim ED and board chair soon after that person has taken the helm. The messaging might lay out steps that will lead to permanently filling the ED role.

And the Password Is…?

An important addendum to any succession plan is the creation of a document that identifies passwords to key email or financial accounts, bank account numbers, and insurance policies. The file might also include the location of personnel files, grant applications, and accounting information, whether on a computer or in paper files. Keep this document in a secure place only accessible by a few key staff and board members.

IMPORTANT!

> 🔍 Who will serve as spokesperson for the above messaging? The chair often serves in this role, but the interim ED might assist.

> 🔍 The plan might end by stating that the board will appoint a search committee to carry out an executive search. See Chapter 21 for information about next steps in hiring an ED.

Temporary Vacancy

When responding to a temporary ED absence, the biggest determining factor is the length of time your top post will be vacant. Your board might prepare slightly different plans for absences less than three months and for those longer than three months. Whether planned or unplanned, it is quite likely that many of the steps listed above will apply. What will vary is the level of detail and degree to which the outside world will be put on alert.

The Chair's Catch 22

One dedicated chair remained in her post for twenty years. When she finally decided it was time to step down, her board had a terrible time finding a replacement. Members were so complacent when it came to thinking about leadership that the longtime chair ended up staying in her role for a few years longer than expected while new recruits came up the ranks. You can bet that the chair made sure that those up-and-comers understood the need to take on top leadership posts!

Inspiration

How Might a Board Plan for Its Chair's Departure?

This can be a difficult conversation for a board, especially if the chair does not initiate it. In that case, it's likely that others fear that such a discussion will imply a desire to see the chair vacate that seat. Yet this position really is the glue holding its volunteer members together, and if the seat were ever to stay vacant for long, board morale is likely to sink. Members will be apt to consider their board greatly flawed if no one is willing to rise to the pinnacle of leadership.

Few organizations have written succession plans for the chair. So we will focus on a few practical steps that can save a board from floundering in the aftermath of a chair's departure, whether planned or unplanned.

Consider Term Limits

While some boards do just fine without hard term limits for officers, the creation of them does force a board to continuously talk about its own succession planning. Even the best chair, if left in place for many years, can create a feeling of stagnation among members who may believe they cannot rise to that level. To counter that feeling—or the idea that a chair may *want* to step down but can't, for lack of a willing replacement—consider suggesting one or more of these options in tandem with officer term limits:

- A call for all board members to self-nominate or nominate others for the chair position before the chair's term expires

- A period of mentoring—up to a year long—to help the chair-in-waiting learn the job

- A chair who serves as an immediate past chair to help the new one through the first year of service

- A vice-chair who is expected to take on the chair's role in the case of a planned or unplanned departure

All-Around Succession Planning

One board constantly scanned its membership, and particularly its committee chairs, for the next great leader. When it spotted a finance committee member who was especially engaged and active on that committee, the governance committee began to groom that person to be the next treasurer... and future chair.

Pure Genius!

Embed Expectations in Board Job Descriptions

When boards expect that a vice-chair will assume the chair position, that expectation often takes the form of a verbal—or worse, non-verbal—assumption. If your board is relying on the vice-chair to step up, make sure that person is well aware of it. While you may hope that the idea was broached when the vice-chair agreed to take on that job, you might suggest that it works its way into the vice-chair's formal job description. There's still no guarantee that your succession plan will succeed every time, but clearly communicating expectations is essential.

A similar warning applies when giving the board an out if members decide that a particular vice-chair would not make the best *numero uno*: The job description should not guarantee a promotion to chair. The language should set expectations without making a promise.

Empower the Governance Committee

This group can be your greatest ongoing advocate in filling the board leadership pipeline. Members can spearhead leadership initiatives in many forms:

- Keeping tabs on exceptional leadership candidates. When new or veteran members are highly engaged, the committee, along with the board chair, can eye short-term leadership openings for those members.

- Making leadership an ongoing board conversation. From orientation to the annual retreat to standard board meetings, the governance committee can find regular opportunities to encourage future officers and committee chairs.

- Updating and circulating board commitment forms. Make sure the board commitment form includes expectations for individual board members to take on officer and committee chair positions. If signed annually by members, this document reminds them of their commitment to serve in leadership positions.

- Populate bylaws and leaders' job descriptions with succession-related language. These documents can recommend, for instance, that the vice-chair is expected to move into the chair's seat; or that the chair will serve a one-year term as past-chair to help ease the new chair's transition.

Nurture a Culture of Leadership

Most boards are too small to retain a significant number of members unwilling to serve in leadership positions. Think about it: When you include officers and committee chairs, that's up to ten people per organization. The average board has sixteen members. That's more leaders than non-leaders!

Recruitment interviews, board job descriptions, and orientation are great ways to remind new members that your board is serious about its leadership expectations. Then of course, more veteran members will need to walk the walk and willingly step into officer positions. The chair and other current leaders can help nurture such a culture:

🔍 Model leadership behaviors

◆ Ensure that meetings are well run and focus on substantive issues

◆ Hear from all board voices and utilize members' expertise

◆ Cultivate a strong partnership between the ED and chair

🔍 Hold members accountable for duties outlined in the board commitment form

🔍 Identify board members who exhibit leadership potential and encourage their development

🔍 Provide opportunities for board development

🔍 Ensure that conversations about leadership take place regularly

Involve Your ED

The ED is also an important player in the leadership arena. A visionary, charismatic ED can motivate board members to take on new challenges. And the chair and governance committee can actively partner with the ED to identify candidates. From the chair to officers to committee chairs, board members are wise to discuss every candidate with the ED. It's possible that the ED might view board-selected candidates in a different light.

To Summarize...

- Clear leadership transition and succession plans are important risk management strategies.

- Organizations may have planned or unplanned leadership transitions.

- The chair can nurture a leadership culture that results in other members' willingness to step into leadership positions.

- When considering members for leadership roles, the board chair and governance committee should actively partner with the executive director to identify candidates.

- It is important to have planned and unplanned transition plans in place for the executive director.

Chapter 23

Founders and Longtime Leaders

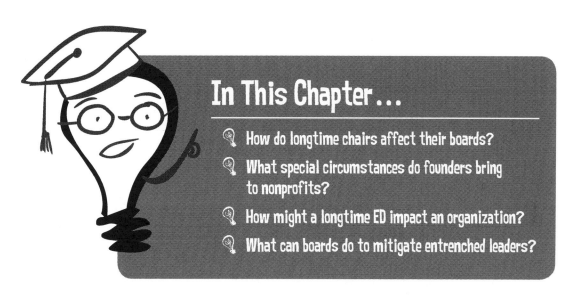

In This Chapter...

- How do longtime chairs affect their boards?
- What special circumstances do founders bring to nonprofits?
- How might a longtime ED impact an organization?
- What can boards do to mitigate entrenched leaders?

There are a few categories of impassioned leaders to which board members owe a debt of gratitude: founders, for their...well...founding of these beloved organizations, and longtime leaders—be they EDs or board chairs—for their prolonged dedication to the mission. It would be lovely if our discussion of these fervent souls ended there, with heartfelt thanks. But often, the sea of issues that gets swept into a long leadership stint creates a title wave of board angst. Some of those issues have merit, and others are grossly misunderstood.

This chapter will explore some of the special circumstances you might encounter if your organization's founder is still at the wheel, or if your ED or chair has been at the helm for many years. Some of these issues deal with intangibles like emotion, control, and passion. Any of these can result in, among other things, a breakdown in governance. In more extreme circumstances, they can be the undoing of an organization.

Our goal here is to prepare you to understand these leaders' impact on your board. If you're willing to roll up your sleeves, you might even make some progress in normalizing some of the anomalies that come with founders or leaders when they have spent a long time in their roles.

How Can Longtime Chairs Influence Their Boards?

This sector doesn't talk about it much, but board chairs—those most dedicated volunteers—can do their boards harm when they overstay their welcome. Maybe you're thinking, "Are you kidding? I'm thrilled that my chair has been at the helm for a decade. That really takes the pressure off of the rest of us."

Precisely.

When non-chair members feel relief that they will not need to step up their leadership in the foreseeable future, the culture suffers. Complacency reigns even for the best boards. Let's face it, if your highest aspiration is that of vice-chair. . . well, let's just say that most vice-anythings take on much less responsibility than the top dog.

Before you know it, generations of new board members come in assuming that they will not need to engage their leadership skills to the fullest. Rumor likely has it that the chair has been there "forever," and that the culture and procedures are slow to change. Taken a step further, members watch their boards stagnate under the weight of a chair who is controlling or ineffective or concerned mostly with ego. Responsible board members will do their jobs, then go home without thinking much about their future leadership aspirations.

If you find yourself in the rare situation where a chair has both a long tenure *and* an incredible ability to maintain energy, leadership, and new ideas, consider yourself lucky. Still, when it comes time for that chair to step down, chances are that those with the strongest leadership aspirations will have left for another board.

If you are a chair yourself and have sat in that post for more than a few years, it's likely that you have had stellar intentions around your service. You probably adore your organization and want to give to it until you have run out of juice. Or maybe you have arrived at the point where you'd love to step down. You look down the roster of fellow members and don't see anyone you think is willing or able to take on this demanding role.

If that's the case, it's possible that, during your long tenure, your board has attracted and even *created* a culture where members are not primed to take on leadership positions. They did not hear about it as candidates during interviews and orientations, or during meetings or retreats as board members. If they did, they soon realized that leadership aspirations ended at the vice-chair slot. The good news is, there are ways to jumpstart a leadership pipeline. The bad news is that it takes some patience.

How Can Boards Stem the Influence of Longtime Chairs?

You can imagine that it's a dicey proposition to suggest an exit for a longtime chair. Such a move might encounter resistance from both the chair and the executive director. These leaders can forge a comfortable partnership that, in their minds, serves the organization well. In other cases, even if the chair is ready to leave, board members might not approach the topic for fear that this loyal volunteer will think the group ungrateful for many years of service.

You can try to stem the influence of a long-term chair with some of the following strategies, many of which are part of the succession planning process:

 Governance committee. An active governance committee can query board members to gauge how they feel about the board and recommend changes. It can also encourage leadership change.

Term limits. If your organization has no term limits—or doesn't enforce them—consider suggesting them as a means to create a pipeline of new ideas and leaders.

Bylaws. Are they outdated? Are they vague on roles, officer responsibilities, or other key aspects of board operations? Insert term limits and other key leadership protocols here.

Recruitment. As part of the recruitment process, stress that all board members must be willing to seriously consider leadership positions, including the chair role. This is your best chance to initiate a leadership pipeline.

Consultant. If it seems that a leadership change proves difficult or impossible, and if it's hard to have honest conversations with the chair, you might hire an impartial outsider who can help move the board forward.

How Can Founders Impact Their Nonprofits?

Founders can be some of the most dedicated people you will meet. They sacrifice time, money, and much of their personal lives to further a social

---

WATCH OUT!

Board Members as Watchdogs

A successful businessperson founded a nonprofit that did construction work using clients as his workforce. The arrangement was a business enterprise in disguise. This founder created a board because he knew that he had to in order to maintain his tax-exempt status, but it met only every couple of years. The founder was afraid to have it meet more regularly for fear that members might learn of his ploy. This enterprise was financially successful, so board members just assumed that things were going well. Warning: Even with the founder at the helm, the group must think and act independently.

cause. After all, they had the inspiration, passion, determination, and motivation to launch our organizations. Theirs is a much harder job than most would imagine. They also become very emotionally attached to their nonprofits; in a very real sense, they are the founders' babies. It's a loving relationship for sure, but you know how a mama bear can react to anyone who gets near her little one!

It's this emotional attachment that separates founders from longtime EDs or chairs. It drove them to devote significant time, energy, and personal resources to this mission. It continues to bind them to their organizations. It can also cloud their thinking. That same inspiration, passion, determination, and motivation can serve as an obstacle to board work.

Founders used to making decisions alone or in the reassuring company of close board-member friends must understandably realign their routines and communication techniques as the board and organization matures. If that transition happens too slowly, boards can quickly become frustrated. Organizations can suffer.

Despite their best intentions, early protocols can set the organization up for future tumult. Below are some of the more common, but not ubiquitous, practices that founders tend to engender and how they can impact the future board work.

Solo Decision-Making

It makes sense that founders seek to fill the inaugural board with people they know and trust. After all, many founders invest their own hard-earned cash into the nonprofit and want only their closest confidents to oversee its management. The problem with filling the board with only the founder's close family and friends is that they have a tendency to rubber stamp their loved one's choices. They also stick around. It can take years—sometimes decades—for the board to understand the importance of including independent thinkers in its midst. And once the board *does* diversify, founders can struggle to abandon their habit of independent decision making.

Reactive Problem Solving

In the early days, focus revolves around clients. Programs prevail over planning. Crises are dealt with as they arise. As organizations grow, and the board begins to look down the road a bit, founders can resist the urge to plan for the organization's future. Often, that inclination is due to our next set of sticking points. . . .

Overemphasis on Programs

Of course, you want your nonprofit to offer excellent programs. But if those IRS forms are not filed on time, or the red ink flows all over your financial statements, your programs will not be around much longer. Sometimes, founders just don't have the talent or attention span for administration. Yet, their passion inspires everyone who encounters their nonprofit. When a founder like this holds tightly onto the reins of a great thoroughbred of an organization, the nonprofit may not get the care it needs. Some founders don't want to discuss finances, or board development, or especially, fundraising. This can lead to a range of work that doesn't get done, *or* such an over-emphasis on programs that no mortal could possibly come in and accomplish the same workload when the founder does decide to exit.

Control of Information

It's understandable at the outset that founders keep mental files. That's a simple, seemingly logical, thing to do. Fast forward a few years and many founders have adopted the practice of keeping information to themselves, sometimes at the detriment of the board and the nonprofit's well being. Records are scarce, and the organization relies on one individual to get everything done.

Fused Identity

All of the dangers above are complicated by the fact that many founder-led nonprofits take on the personalities of their founders. Given their passion and commitment to the mission, it's no wonder that the public begins to equate them with the organizations themselves. That certainly has its advantages: If a founder is a charismatic go-getter, you can bet that people all

How Can You Enable a Smooth Founder Transition?

When the founder decides to transition, change is in the air for the board, too. So, encourage your peers to take a serious look at what life will be like post-founder. Those transitions can take a few different forms:

- Retire. A bona fide retirement means that the founder expects to completely step away from the organization. That can be harder than you'd expect.

- Move to a staff role. The founder may no longer want to serve as executive director because the role becomes more administrative and less connected to direct service. The founder may prefer to focus on delivering programs and let someone else take the helm.

- Remain on board. The founder may decide to no longer be the executive director but may desire to focus on governance.

However the founder transitions, it's important for the board to fully understand how complicated it is for the next ED to step into the founder's shoes and succeed. The board must carefully plan and communicate the next phase, beginning with the founder's new role. After all, this person has likely been the heart, soul, and face of your organization since its inception. Ideally, board and staff will want to secure a year's lead time prior to the founder's departure to focus on these activities:

- Collect historical information and details about relationships with supporters

- Encourage the founder to introduce the new ED to all critical community relationships

- Create a media strategy to announce the smooth transition from founder to new ED

- Enable the new ED to direct strategy

The board plays an important role in assuring stakeholders that the organization will survive and thrive. You and your peers will also help staff, board, volunteers, and clients, manage expectations about the new executive director, who will undoubtedly be very different from your founder.

over town are getting involved with your organization because of this striking personality. In other cases, the "mission" can begin to take on a cult of personality, becoming overshadowed by someone who enjoys the spotlight or stature a little too much. Either extreme makes it hard for nonprofits to one day exist as an entity apart from their founders.

There are plenty of founders who do their research and work with their evolving boards to steer their organizations to ever-stronger heights. Yet each of the above traits can derail board work. If your board struggles because of any of the items here, you are not alone. Keep reading for some ideas on how you can overcome these very common barriers.

What Do Longtime EDs Have in Common with Founders?

Nearly everything, except the establishment of the organization. We're clearly speaking in generalities, but talk to anyone whose ED has led a nonprofit for ten, twenty, even thirty years, and you will learn that they, too, become overly associated with their organizations. They, too, can lack the skills to take the organization to the next level. They, too, purposefully or not, can foster ineffective boards.

Let's be very clear: Our goal here is not to put these dedicated public servants in a bad light. If you were to remain in the same job for fifteen years, you would likely establish patterns, too. You might wonder if your board was a necessary evil, an administrative requirement that caused you to spend many hours a month away from the mission that you love.

While founders, longtime EDs, and boards may have understandable frustrations with each other, the bottom line is that they must learn to work together. It isn't easy to overcome many of the obstacles listed above. Some organizations never do. But you and your fellow board members *can* dedicate yourselves to elevating governance. It's an admirable goal with tangible results.

How Can Boards Manage the Influence of Founders and Longtime EDs?

The board must find a balance between supporting a beloved leader and looking out for the long-term interest of the organization. Below are a few strategies that can help in these endeavors:

🔍 Regular performance evaluations. Boards too often forgo these critical benchmarking exercises, especially with founders or long-term executives. Regular evaluations provide an opportunity for dialogue to occur around issues facing the organization, performance, and even the ED/board relationship.

🔍 Sabbaticals. After a number of years of service, require that your devoted leader take a several-month sabbatical. Time away from the agency can help show everyone—staff, board members, even the leader—that others are capable of stepping up.

🔍 Professional development. When the board emphasizes ED training—through budget line items, in performance evaluations, and in practice—your ED can strengthen skills that can fill gaps in knowledge or leadership.

🔍 Staff-building or development. Hiring more staff can help the ED delegate responsibilities and share institutional knowledge. It can also help to train existing staff to operate at a higher level and take on some of the ED's duties.

🔍 Board recruitment. If the founder or long-term ED does all of the recruiting of board members, your peers might not come with the objective perspectives needed to adequately oversee the ED's performance.

🔍 Outside perspective. An objective professional can help identify how the board and executive director can better partner together. A consultant or coach can make suggestions to the executive director that may be hard for board leaders to raise.

Can a Founder-Led Organization Survive Long Term?

The short answer is "yes," but it isn't easy. It seems counterintuitive, since founders get their nonprofits off the ground in the first place. But they must learn and evolve with their changing organizations. Sometimes, a maturing nonprofit's emphasis on infrastructure and management doesn't jibe with a founder's mindset. These issues can directly lead to some common patterns among founder-led nonprofits. Boards must exercise tough love in order to achieve some ambitious goals. Without these building blocks, founder-led organizations might find themselves struggling. While these same basics apply to any nonprofit, they often come with additional hurdles when founders are still involved.

Funder Accountability

As a public entity, a budding nonprofit becomes increasingly accountable to its donors. All supporters, whether individuals or institutions, will expect to see increasing levels of transparency. So, a board once dominated by its founder must step up its oversight. The organization's IRS Form 990 becomes the most visible report card for any potential donor. Use that form as a guide to establish good financial, governance, and ethical protocols.

Observation

Should You Bet on a Founder-led Organization?

During a ten-year period, a foundation made a total of thirty-nine grants to organizations where the founder served either as executive director or as a board member: At thirty-four of those organizations, the founder served as ED at the time the initial grant was made; five had the founder serving on the board only. Between 2002 and 2012:

 Fifteen of the thirty-nine organizations went out of business.

Eleven of the fifteen were founder-led at the time the organization closed its doors, and three closed with the founder still on the board.

Of the fifteen shuttered nonprofits, *fourteen* had significant founder involvement! Only one organization that closed had no founder involvement.

Twenty-four of the groups from the initial sample are still in business. Of those twenty-four still in business, eighteen still have the founder as ED or serving on the board with only six having no founder involvement. This is a small and unscientific sample, but one that shows how important it is for the board to bring a holistic set of skills and perspectives to the table—and ensure that management and oversight get fair play.

Financial Know-How

Boards function best when members fully understand their agency's financial status. Even "nonfinancial" members will want to regularly review cash flow reports and track revenues and expenses against budget projections. This way, the board can partner with the founder to identify any cash flow bumps before they happen and figure out how to deal with them before they become a crisis.

Impact

The board can insist on understanding the organization's impact. A founder might not realize the importance of collecting data that shows outcomes and impact. This information is not only useful for program improvement but is important input to make a case for grant funding or other donations. The board can work with the founder to develop key output and outcome indicators and develop a process to regularly collect and report on this data and use the data to improve programs and services.

Relationship with the Board

The above topics are fact-based disciplines that come via training and learning from subject-matter experts on your board. There is a psychological dynamic too: Serving on a board when founders are involved can be especially exhilarating and challenging. Founders may:

- Expect the board to rubber stamp their ideas and strategies

- Regard the board as a necessary evil, existing only to meet certain legal requirements

- Regard the group solely as a source of donations

- Have little or no experience working with a board, unaware of how to leverage members' expertise

- Provide unreliable or inadequate information as a result of little financial, fundraising, or management experience

- Be resistant to change

- Believe that the staff should be so committed to the mission that salary takes a back seat

- Hesitate to document key procedures, data, or relationships

Early on, some of the above issues may not be overly disruptive or problematic, but they can begin to challenge the organization's sustainability over time. A founder who has a zest for developing programs may be able to work wonders with a small cadre of volunteers. But once paid staff is hired, grants must be written, outcomes tracked, and financials produced. The founder may be overwhelmed. That's a hard realization for such a passionate, driven soul.

As much as is possible, boards with a founder at the helm will want to adopt the practices described throughout this book. The board will want to encourage—and possibly even insist—that the founder embrace processes and practices that will help strengthen the organization. For example, if the founder's strength is not bookkeeping, then outsource that task or send the founder to a bookkeeping workshop to

The Lending Founder

Some founders have made personal loans to help nurture their nonprofit babies. While making loans in and of themselves isn't necessarily bad, those that continue to accumulate, that mask a dire financial situation, or that are unknown to the board are not good practice. One founder, over the course of three years, made loans to the organization to keep it afloat. The board was kept in the dark about these loans and when they came to light, was surprised they existed. If, in fact, a loan is needed to help grapple with a cash flow crunch, the board should approve it, making the terms and conditions clear to everyone.

WATCH OUT!

learn some basic accounting. As with any other board, there must be a culture of ongoing education. With founding organizations, the learning curve may be steeper.

Of course, not all founder-led organizations suffer from a lack of board know-how. There are plenty of founders who are diligent in their program delivery, staff leadership, and management of the board. It's important to acknowledge that expertise in all these issues is a tall order for someone initially so focused on fulfilling the mission.

What If the Board Wants to Dismiss the Founder?

This is not as uncommon as one may think. While it's possible for the founder to be at the helm for many years, even decades, it is also possible that new skills are needed, and that tensions, disagreements, and resentments develop between the founder and the board. It's understandable, really. When the organization took root, it was the founder's to nurture. It's not easy to cede power and direction to a group of potential strangers or to accept that the organization has outgrown what the founder can do.

This can be the stickiest of dismissals, given many founders' public personas. Whether that person is forced to resign, fired, or "eased out," the board must take solid control of a process that will inevitably present the unexpected.

In making the decision to fire or move past the founder, the board must treat that staffer as it would any other employee, while giving great consideration to the ripple effects this departure most likely will cause. For the most part, the same process discussed in Chapter 21 can be used. Yet, while a change might solve a current crop of issues, it's possible that a founder's departure will precipitate others among staff and board, or a major funding source might back out. This should not preclude you from firing or moving past the founder, but the board will want to consider potential chains of events that such a change might set into motion. This exercise will help prepare all of you for potential consequences and how you plan to address them.

To Summarize...

- Long-serving board chairs can create a culture where others do not step up to lead.

- Founder-led organizations have unique characteristics that boards need to consider and face.

- Boards can become complacent when their organizations have longtime leaders.

- Founder transitions can be trickier and require more planning than other transitions.

Part 6

Taking the Reins

Is there such a thing as board nirvana? No. Even the most mature and well-connected boards push themselves to attain new innovations and efficiencies. So, once you've made it through your first several meetings, your attention might turn to a personal wish list for your board. Whether your fellow members seem disconnected, the culture is less-than-energizing, or your peers could stand to simply participate more, these pages will suggest ways in which you can make a difference.

Even if you're not yet part of the formal leadership—and certainly if you are— there are many paths you can take to help your board make strides. It starts with each individual engaging to the fullest. And it ends with everyone working together in a spirit of diligence, community, and fun. Yes, it can and does happen! It might not be nirvana, but it can be a workable, even enjoyable, way to oversee a community treasure.

Chapter 24

Assessing the Board's Performance

In This Chapter...

- When is the ideal time to evaluate the board?
- What are the steps involved in board assessment?
- How might individual members evaluate themselves?
- What tools are most useful in board assessment?

The best boards got that way because members regularly asked themselves, "How can we take our work to the next level?" You know by now that it's the board's job to regularly evaluate the executive director. But, who looks at the *board's* performance? Who gauges how well individual members are doing their jobs? For better or worse, those are tasks that members must take on themselves.

Too many boards ignore self-evaluation. Some deny their own problems. Others attribute any deficiencies to staff or program malfunctions. When your board begins to evaluate itself and its individual members, and *uses* that feedback to improve, it moves into a prized position of self-awareness. Little is more important to the long-term future of your organization's governance. And, since no board ever attains perfection, the best collective goal you can set is one of continuous improvement.

What Is Board Assessment?

An assessment is an opportunity for the board and individual members to determine what you are doing well and what stands to improve. It provides a forum for addressing ongoing issues. The evaluation process works best when it is broken into two parts: that of the full group and that of its pieces, or members. That distinction is important because, as you've read in these pages, the board's roles differ from those of its members.

Like most other aspects of board work, assessments can be formal or informal, broad or focused, online or in hard copy. What matters is that all members participate and that their responses are honest. Limited feedback results in an incomplete picture. If 60 percent of your members fill out an assessment at a board meeting, you might not realize that those who are absent have a hard time making your 9:00 a.m. Saturday meetings. Yes, something as simple as new meeting times can emerge when you ensure that the full group takes the time to assess its practices. Not only can those simple changes have measurable impacts on your board, but members often feel more connected to a group that asks for—and acts on—their input.

Stickier issues can get resolved, too. Let's say that George is a long-timer who, on paper, meets all board commitments. He makes an annual gift, attends special events, and has good meeting attendance. But during meetings, George is a disaster. He interrupts, argues, and takes the group off-topic. He is the kind of member who is

Macro vs. Micro

While board assessments might raise the issue of an individual member who is hindering the board's progress, the issue itself should be resolved outside of the assessment process. See Chapter 26 for more on dealing with difficult board members.

WATCH OUT!

among the hardest to control—or coax off of the board. Confidential, honest assessments are vehicles to bring potentially taboo subjects like George's behavior to light. If two-thirds of your assessments mention his behavior as an obstacle, your board has solid ground on which to take action.

The assessment process itself does not solve any problems: It's what members do with the results that strengthens the board. All sorts of constructive dialogue can follow, leading to plans of action and assignment of tasks. The results? Improved functioning and engagement.

When Should an Assessment Take Place?

Let's begin with a few thoughts about when it might *not* be ideal to assess the board. At certain points in an organization's maturity or because of external factors, self-evaluation can come off as. . . well. . . self-interested. So, avoid the process during these situations:

- Organizational crises. When the ship is sinking, no one is focused on assessing the value of the captain!

- Member misbehavior. Boards should not undertake assessments to get rid of problem board members, although sometimes, they do have that effect.

- Lack of leadership buy-in. Board leadership and the executive director must agree to use the assessment's results to make positive changes. Otherwise, all that good feedback will sit on a shelf.

- Lack of board buy-in. If the ED is driving the process, change is unlikely. The board must own the process and be committed to improving its performance.

- Expectation of rapid results. Assessments rarely transform boards quickly. Change can take months or longer. Participants can expect assessments to be the first step in a process of ongoing improvement.

That's a long list! So, when *might* it be a good time to initiate board assessment? Every other year is often a good rule of thumb. But if this is your board's first go at it, or if there's a tradition of irregular assessments, you will

> ### Continuous Learning
>
> One highly responsive board uses an online survey tool to gather feedback from members after *each* board meeting. The chair and ED use the information to improve approaches to meetings, committee work, and overall board functioning. Talk about continuing education!
>
> **Pure Genius!**

likely want to conduct the evaluation when things are going relatively well. That way, your board has the bandwidth to be thorough and to make adjustments as recommended via the assessment.

There are, however, a few specific occasions when it might be appropriate to initiate an assessment. These are most often periods when constructive feedback stands to solve the problem at hand:

- Leadership transition. A change in either the board chair or executive director lends itself to new beginnings on many fronts.

- Strategic planning process. As a new strategic plan goes into effect, the board may want to think about how it might work differently or better going forward.

- Waning meeting attendance. If many board members are missing meetings, coming late, or leaving early, a board assessment might uncover reasons why your board is detached.

- Grumbling. When members or the ED appear frustrated about how the board functions, it's time to seek input and take action.

- Continuous crisis mode. If your organization goes through one crisis after another, it's time to take stock. While organizational crises are not always the result of a poor board, they often indicate that the board is not effectively engaged with staff, providing strategic guidance, or providing effective oversight.

It is critical to secure buy-in from the group before the process begins. The chair and ED, in particular, must agree not to take any criticisms personally. It's not a bad idea to remind the board—throughout the process—that this exercise is not about those leaders, but about the entire board.

How can you and your peers convince naysayers to buy into the process? You might bring up an obvious shortcoming, such as a regular inability to make a quorum or the fact that you get only halfway through your agenda before the meeting ends. You might signal the opportunity to strengthen the board as a new chair reaches the helm. You might even highlight a desire by the group to seat more high-profile members and the need to ratchet up your board's game to attract them. If you can begin a dialogue about the advantages of assessments, you are likely to bring others along.

What Might the Assessment Process Look Like?

This is the board's responsibility. The ED might suggest that the board undertake an assessment, but the board should take the lead to implement any recommendations or strategies for improvement. If yours has a governance committee, that group will likely spearhead the effort. If not, a small task force can take the lead. The executive director will, at the very least, want a chance to provide input along the way. As much as possible, strive to create an objective process where honest feedback and input is encouraged and welcomed. A few simple steps will get things off to the right start:

Keep a Group in the Loop

If your assessment process is led by an individual, rather than a group, you set your board up for a much more subjective set of analyses. On one board, just one person volunteered to spearhead the process. When the results didn't jibe with that person's perspective, she conveniently omitted those perspectives in the analysis she provided to the board.

Uninspired

- Create a timeline. Set realistic deadlines for each step of the process and be clear with board members when, and in what form, information is needed from them.

- Develop an evaluation tool. See the next section for information on how to select or revise the appropriate form, survey, or tool.

- Administer the survey. Some boards send their forms electronically. Others do it via paper and pen. You can allow time to fill out the survey at a meeting or as "homework" in advance of one.

- Collect, tabulate, and analyze results. Committee or task force members review information and generate recommendations based on the results.

- Present the findings and recommendations first to the chair, then to the full board. Your chair might have important insights, but you won't want the board chair's comments to influence what gets reported to the group and what doesn't. For boards to improve, it's important that everyone hear the honest opinions of members—whether good or bad. The recommendations are merely suggestions, so these presentations create an opportunity for stakeholders to problem solve, usually at a time dedicated to solutions.

- Conduct a retreat or other time focused on results. After the board gets some time to think about the issues raised, schedule a few hours to flesh out solutions. This can be as informal as time tacked onto a board meeting or a retreat facilitated by an outside party.

- Ensure follow-through. The committee or task force creates a process that guarantees that new systems, educational sessions, or other action steps take place.

How Can You Find or Develop a Good Assessment Tool?

The most useful assessment forms tend to use a combination of rating scales and open-ended questions. The scales, which might ask participants to rank an issue on a scale of one to five, are a simple gauge of satisfaction. Questions that allow for elaboration provide the backstory when someone feels particularly strongly about an issue.

There is no reason to reinvent the wheel. It is relatively easy to find samples on the Internet, from peer organizations, and from state nonprofit associations. You might use one as is or mix and match questions as you see fit. You can also purchase tools. BoardSource is a national organization that provides such resources for a fee. And some governance consultants can customize a tool for your organization, administer it, analyze the results, and offer recommendations.

In general, assessments are often broken down along the lines of the subjects laid out in this book: finance, fundraising, strategic planning, and so on. Get a sense of how prepared members feel in topics such as finance, fundraising, strategic planning, and recruitment. Then ask about the collective job done by the board in those areas. You will also want to home in on some of the core engines that keep a board moving in the right direction:

- Does our board have a compelling, shared vision?

- Do we function under a set of strategic priorities?

- Are we diligent stewards of our organization's

    - Finances?

    - Program results?

    - Clients' interests?

- Do we operate using high ethical standards?

- Do members generally fulfill the duties they agree to uphold on their board commitment forms?

- Are our meetings inclusive, building on a diversity of voices?

- Do we have a respectful, productive relationship with our executive director? Does our chair?

How Might You Analyze Results?

Most boards begin with a simple tally of results, by taking an average of any ranked scores. Averages work well, but consider going a step further and accounting for outliers, too. For example, if, on a scale of one to five, one question's average response is a three, while not a stellar score, a full set of threes is very different than half ones and half fives. The idea here is to present the scores in a way that illuminates them fully.

The committee will want to look for areas of agreement and disconnect among various groups, including:

- Newer versus veteran members

- The ED, the board chair, and the rest of the board

- Any factions that might exist among members

Consider your sources: If you notice that half of the members feel that orientation did not do a good job of preparing new members—and those responses overwhelmingly come from the novices in the group—then revisions to the orientation process will become a higher priority than if that response came from people who went through orientation five years ago.

While committee or task force members can certainly recommend solutions to any problems, it's important to let the full board buy into them. Don't set the board up for failure, but do push the envelope—if your board is disengaged, there are reasons for it, and some of those reasons stand to create uncomfortable situations.

Let the board's own feedback guide any discussions. Conversations that emerge from the assessment process might be difficult but warrant a thorough set of input from the group. Without it, the status quo will continue, which is likely *not* the outcome anyone hopes for during an assessment. So, set aside a decent part of a board meeting to discuss results. Plan to come away with a set of priority actions. Importantly, celebrate those areas that receive positive feedback!

What Is the Best Way to Implement Results?

Once the board identifies a set of priority actions, it's time to develop an implementation plan. Without a determined effort to implement improvement strategies, little will change.

The governance committee, or even a task force, can take charge of developing and implementing the plan. The document can take the form of a simple table, with a list of each "action" item, the responsible party for each, and a deadline. Some actions or "fixes" will be relatively simple. Others will take more deliberation and time, such as developing a comprehensive recruitment strategy.

Be realistic. The best thing you can do is to ensure that the committee or task force that launched the assessment process continues to monitor its implementation. If the board devotes five minutes at each board meeting to a status report on progress made, that will keep everyone focused on goals attained and those yet to be undertaken.

Sample Board Action Plan

Issue	Action	Responsible Party	Deadline
Meetings don't begin and end on time	Assign time limits to each action item	Board chair and executive director; board chair to enforce time limits at meetings	December board meeting
Board members don't have enough financial knowledge	Provide financial training to board	Governance committee will develop a training schedule with board treasurer	Training schedule due by January board meeting; training to be completed by May

How Might Individual Members Assess Themselves?

Assessing the board as a group is just one aspect of board performance. It is just as important to gauge how individual members are fulfilling their duties. If your organization has a board commitment form, then it will be relatively easy to create a tool that measures performance: Ask board members to evaluate their performance against the written board commitments. Are they attending the required number of meetings? Making personally significant gifts? Serving on at least one committee? Members will rate themselves against each listed responsibility and expectation.

Some organizations develop an annual work plan for each member, with the input of that individual. At the end of each year, a governance committee member, the chair, or sometimes the ED, reviews the plan with its owner to assess it for completion and quality. It's best if the board chair, with input from the ED, provides each board member with performance feedback. Such meetings also create the perfect opportunity to set goals for the upcoming year. This approach often builds upon criteria listed in the board commitment form:

> If members are expected to make annual gifts: I will personally commit $___ during the next fiscal year.

> If members are expected to serve on at least one committee: I will spearhead [name of initiative related to that committee].

> If members are expected to take on leadership roles: I will work toward assuming/continue to assume the position of [name leadership position].

And so on. It's possible that meetings like this one might spur the board member to step down. That's okay. These reviews tend to allow board members to reflect on their performance, motivations, and time commitments. If any of those things makes the member feel guilty or overstretched, then a resignation is a win for both that individual and for the board. Or, this kind of analysis just might make members reflect on why they agreed to serve in the first place. . . and commit to take their work up a notch.

To Summarize...

Assessments provide an opportunity for the board and individual members to determine what's being done well and what stands to improve.

The assessment process itself doesn't solve any problems—it's what members do with the results that strengthens the board.

It's best to conduct assessments during times of relative stability.

Along with a performance evaluation of the full board, individual members value the chance to assess their own accomplishments.

Use assessment results to identify priority actions and to develop a board improvement plan. Without a determined effort to implement improvement strategies, little will change.

Chapter 25

Keeping Board Members Engaged and Connected

In This Chapter...

- What does board engagement look like?
- What are some warning signs that it may be waning?
- What are some strategies to hold a board's interest?
- How can you influence board engagement?

We never said that this board thing would be easy. Among the greatest challenges: engagement. After all, we're talking about human beings here. Personalities can be enough to derail a group. Add to that members' competing demands: It can be a challenge to garner attention *during* meetings, let alone outside of them. Then there are those members who join boards solely for prestige, networking, or ego. Some get restless because they expect a level of performance that your board might not provide. Others are easily bored.

We have focused quite a bit on the need for the board's work to be organized well. But without reciprocal member engagement, even the best policies and procedures will mean nothing. With a couple of allies and a dose of patience, even those outside of the leadership ranks have the ability to influence peers.

What Is Engagement and What Can It Look Like?

The above might seem like an obvious question, but boards can be engaged—or not—on a number of levels. The challenge is to optimally leverage each member's limited time to benefit the organization. Below are some categories that paint a picture of board engagement. Some require physical presence, while others entail intellectual or even emotional curiosity.

Fulfilling Basic Requirements

Boards that set out minimum job expectations *and* create accountability systems to track those expectations are the most likely to engage their members. The easiest way to initiate the process comes through a board commitment form that explicitly lays out the criteria. Then, good boards ask a governance committee member or the secretary to keep tabs on whether each person is attending the minimum number of meetings, fulfilling committee assignments, and preparing adequately for meetings. When a member's term comes to an end—or even before—these board watchdogs are armed with the data necessary to encourage improvement... or resignation. The best boards are serious about both options.

Tackling Current Problems

Often, the ED, the chair, or a rank-and-file member spots a problem and includes it on the agenda. Maybe reserves are dwindling. Maybe staff morale is down. Maybe the auditor needs to be replaced. Engaged boards tackle these issues efficiently and adeptly. They respond to these trends with information, discussion, and strategy. Any group that spends its

Does Engagement Equal Retention?

Board engagement is not only the best way to ensure that your nonprofit's oversight is sharp, it's the surest way to retain your best board members. The members most willing to roll up their sleeves will likely walk away if they are not challenged on a regular basis. Take your pick: rolled-up sleeves or walking shoes?

Inspiration

time listening to committee chairs report on their group's activities is looking backward.

Connection to the Mission

We cannot say enough how regularly members must be reminded of the mission. When personalities or other problems cloud the room, a rescued puppy, a grateful patient, or a field trip to a program site renews focus.

Planning for the Future

Boards should also look down the road. Members are expected to understand industry trends, external players, and next-stage innovations—and synthesize them for the good of the organization. These activities take thought and sustenance. When any one of them slips from a board's radar, the domino effect often impacts the board itself, then the staff, then the programs. Nonprofits can, and do, fail.

This is not meant to scare you. Just the opposite: If you decided to sit on a board for the right reasons, then your skills and energy are needed more than ever. You will make a real difference in the trajectory of your organization. Many boards cultivate forward thinking through strategic planning, but it can also take the form of educational sessions at board meetings, articles inserted into board packets, or even off-site workshops. Because you are reading this book, you already understand the importance of raising the bar. You are engaged.

The trick is to move from reading a book to raising issues to taking action. It begins with one person, then a few, then a group. Your full board will never be completely engaged on every subject or activity, but you will feel the energy when people begin to hold themselves accountable to their job descriptions and to the needs of your organization.

What Are Warning Signs of a Blasé Board?

Ask any executive director or board chair how many board members are active and engaged. Few will say 100 percent. It is common for half the group to be active, with the other half somewhat engaged or totally disconnected. There is always room for improvement, but learn to watch the way in which you judge your peers' involvement.

Not all members will participate in the same way. So, while Audrey Accountant might find her niche in the finance committee's work, Carl Corporate might put his efforts into getting the mission out to local companies. And while Ernie the Extrovert might espouse many thought-provoking ideas during meetings, Ina the Introvert might spend time behind the scenes lending her real estate expertise to the ED one-on-one as the organization searches for a new space. All are valid means of engagement, even though some will be less visible to fellow members than others. That said, you will know when your peers are disengaged. Among the warning signs:

- High turnover
- Board chair as primary decision maker
- Poor attendance at meetings
- Little or no response following ED or board leadership's requests
- Little or no committee activity
- Poor follow-through in general
- Little or no oversight of organizational matters

Spreading the Blame

Sometimes waning board activity can point directly to the ED. One board member points out, "I resigned from a board where I felt the executive staff leader really did not want board input and felt my time and ideas were not valued or needed. I am now a member of two boards where the members are encouraged to work together, respected, and engaged." This veteran volunteer knew when to leave an uninspiring board. Others might include feedback in the ED's performance review and work to remedy the situation.

Uninspired

    Lack of responsiveness even during a crisis, with the executive director shouldering the burden

    Infighting and arguing among board members

    Little to no interest in leadership roles

These aren't just signs of a lethargic group. When members are not communicating well or are absent, they are not fulfilling their three duties of care, loyalty, or obedience. They are not doing their jobs. Even if you create all the policies and procedures listed in this book, if there's no quorum at meetings or if everyone defers to the ED, all that work is lost.

How Can You Keep Your Board Engaged?

Board engagement is a learned behavior. It follows a progression. It does not magically emerge with a group's age or status. It can require just one, then two or more members who express an ambition. The best places to do that are from positions of leadership: The chair and the governance committee head are the ideal places to make a difference. Those positions are incubators for strengthening governance.

But change does not have to begin at the leadership level. *Every board member* has the power to influence fellow members, committee chairs, and yes, even the chair.

How?

Some of those who are joining boards en masse—younger adults, entrepreneurs, those in the tech industry—are accustomed to leading from the bottom up. While that might run counter to your board's traditional operations, a gradual shift will help your group adjust to an environment where a flow of ideas must come from more than just a few at the top.

This transition often begins with seeds of knowledge. Someone has read a book like this one, or served on another board, or attended a governance workshop. That person realizes that the board holds greater potential.

That's all it takes: a little information and some focused intent. Spread the word and make things happen. Talk to those at the top as well as the general membership. Be willing to help push the group's boundaries when necessary. Set goals with timelines and follow through.

You might set a goal to strengthen one or more of these areas:

- Basic requirements. These might include meeting attendance, preparation (i.e., advance reading) for meetings, and committee participation.

- Skills-building. This area usually zeros in on one or more activities where members generally need more training, such as financial statements, audits, or fundraising.

- Productivity. Progress here can range from prodding more meaningful discussions, creating inclusive debates, asking more questions, or resolving conflicts more easily.

If expectations were set during candidate interviews and orientation, then the first bullet above might be helped by merely reiterating and enforcing requirements. If your board makes a point of setting expectations high *and* communicating them to its newest members, half the work is done. The other half comes in *showing* those new members that you and your peers are serious about meeting those expectations, which are solidified when the board models the stated behaviors.

The other two items can require training from an outside expert. If your board doesn't have the means to hire someone, there are plenty of other options available. Depending on the issues you are working to advance, consider finding some relevant online videos, TED Talks, articles, books, or other materials to collectively review and discuss. An expert on your board might also pitch in. Give yourselves concrete goals to attain. And yes, if it was your idea to move this group forward, offer to take the lead in selecting materials and facilitating discussions.

If you love your organization and find yourself disappointed that your passion for the mission has not carried over to your passion for this board, there *are* things you can do about it.

Focus on Doing Your Job

If each member proactively contributes time, money, and energy, the collective impact can be powerful. If your board has even a few engaged members, consider creating time during meetings to exchange success stories about how members recently served as organizational ambassadors, advocates, or fundraisers. Exchanges like these can inspire others to act in new or higher-level ways. Some groups circulate board and committee attendance or rates (not amounts) of board giving in board packets. These tactics can provide just enough peer pressure to move other members in the right direction, whether toward action or toward the door.

Speak Up about Board Performance

Candid conversations might start with a trusted board peer, your governance committee, the chair, or the full board—wherever you see a seed of mutual interest. This job can be more pleasant than it seems. It means that you point out the obvious places where enthusiasm is lacking and suggest possible fixes. Some ideas are listed in the sidebar "Engagement Etiquette."

If your personality is quieter and you prefer to tackle this issue behind-the-scenes, you can accomplish the same thing by addressing the chair directly. If yours is not an effective chair, build alliances among other movers and shakers on the board. It's amazing what just two or three people can do to change a culture when they use their collective energies. You can begin by finding tips in this book or in other resources, and suggest, "Here is an idea that might be worth our time." Of course, you should be prepared to help follow through with the solution!

Suggest Professional Development

Especially if expectations are not clear, some board members simply don't know what they don't know. There are speakers, videos, and resources on most any topic. If your board has many issues on which to improve, consider creating an annual calendar with an educational topic for each meeting.

Engagement Etiquette

If you'd like to accelerate your collective engagement, consider these practices:

1. Chair as cheerleader. The board chair can encourage members to step up and follow through with tasks and responsibilities.

2. Check-ins and check-ups. The ED and the chair can meet with each board member annually. These check-ins enable leadership to determine what is going well and what is not going so well. . . and work to fix problem areas.

3. Meeting mechanics. Well-run meetings—those that provide members with opportunities to discuss substantive issues and strategies—help keep members engaged.

4. Tailored experiences. Individual members want to serve in areas of interest to them.

5. Mission. Experiential learning helps connect members to the mission, including client testimonials, program observation, and direct work with clients.

6. Vision. A compelling and exciting vision gives everyone a sense of excitement and direction.

7. Honesty. Members do not like surprises, such as an ED's board meeting pronouncement that there's not enough money in the bank to meet tomorrow's payroll. Members remain engaged if they trust the leadership.

8. Board community. Devote time to socialize outside of board business. Happy hour, a baseball game, or bowling night can deepen connection and camaraderie.

9. Clear expectations. Board members should understand what is expected of them—before they join the board. Board commitment statements and strategic plans solidify expectations.

10. Inclusion. It's the chair's job to include everyone in dialogue and debate. Yet all members should value their peers' perspectives. Leadership can also learn what's on the mind of individual members through board assessments and one-on-one meetings.

11. Recognition. Some EDs are terrific about thanking their board members. But board members can also thank each other. Send a note or a collective bottle of wine to a hard-working chair. Initiate a social to celebrate the group's hard work. Just say "thank you" when a peer has done a good job.

Schedule a Retreat

You can use an off-site gathering to tackle professional development, planning, or to flesh out the results of a board assessment. When members get outside of their typical patterns, the greatest take-away is often trust. It might seem that knowledge would take top billing, but the trust that comes with spending time with people and understanding their values is just as important. When relationships strengthen, people are more motivated to support one another in their collective work.

Join the Governance Committee

A strong governance committee directly influences board expectations. Remember, this is typically the group that spearheads the touch points that can define a member's experience:

- Candidate recruitment and orientation. This is the period when expectations are defined.

- Board job descriptions. As part of orientation, and often, annual retreats, members sign board commitment forms. The committee tends to write and revise them, which serve as de facto job descriptions. The more specific the descriptions, the more precise members' expectations will be.

- Board self-assessments. When members regularly evaluate their own performance, as well as that of the group, ongoing improvement becomes part of the culture. See Chapter 24 for details.

- Board development. This committee often recommends and even organizes learning opportunities for the full group. Many times, the topics emerge from self-assessments and can help give members the tools to better engage.

- Terminations. If all else fails, the governance committee chair can recommend to the board chair the termination of an uncommitted member. That is not a cure-all, but it might help make room for more energetic members.

Board Book Club

One board selects a book each year for its members to read. Selections range from novels relating to the mission to self-help to business books to those focused squarely on governance. All are chosen to spark discussion on a topic that members agree is relevant to the board's current stage. They spend one hour at the annual retreat discussing the merits of the book as it pertains to the board's work. The discussion is followed by lunch, when members often enjoy continuing the conversation.

Inspiration

Aim to Become Board Chair

If you want to have the ultimate sway over expectations, become chair. There's no better way to influence your peers. From meeting facilitation to goal setting to influencing new members, the chair really does have the chance to shape nearly everything. When that role is used properly and to good effect, it can be powerful. A chair can set a tone of inclusion, innovation, and healthy debate—and infuse everything the board does with a goal of continuous improvement and engagement.

No doubt, there is tough love involved in this job. Every good board chair has to crack the whip periodically or off-load inadequate board members. That might sound harsh, but some people just don't take hints. Try as the group might, there will always be members who are both unwilling to learn and unwilling to voluntarily give up their seats. The best board chairs will not be afraid to suggest that the board is moving in new directions and that it needs new members who are committed to making strides in those directions. More on that in the next chapter.

Resign

If the above strategies do not work for you, resign. There is no shame in opening your seat for someone more suited for this position—or someone willing to fight for change. The best thing you can do is request an exit interview and come clean about the reasons for your departure. Sometimes, the most obvious of problems does not garner attention until someone leaves over the matter. It all goes back to that frustrating trait we call human nature.

How Long Does It Take for These Changes to Take Effect?

If you have a couple of allies in the process of strengthening your board, consider yourself lucky. The two or three of you can work together to implement various strategies discussed in this chapter. Blunt conversations with your peers—when expressed diplomatically—can spur others to action. Such discussions can also prompt the less motivated to consider resigning.

Patience really is a virtue when it comes to board development. None of the changes we mention here happens quickly. Changing a board culture can take a few months to a year or two. Sometimes it means recruiting new members with a new mindset and approach. All of this can take time. There are no guarantees. It's possible that you can try everything in this chapter to little effect. But if you have even a couple of members who are chomping at the bit to be more effective, engaged participants, act fast to help change the dynamic.

To Summarize…

- Engaged boards are better fundraisers, ambassadors, and partners.

- Watch for signs that your board is either totally disengaged or becoming less engaged.

- Every member has the potential to positively influence board engagement.

- The best board members are more likely to stick around if they can find engaging ways to participate.

Chapter 26

When Things Go Awry

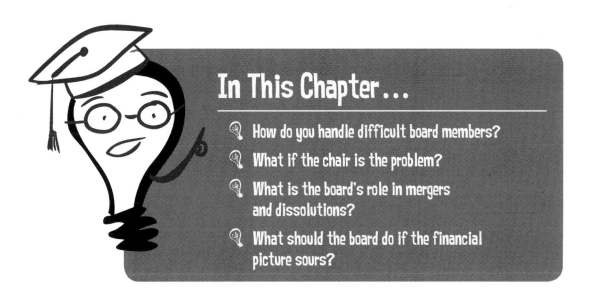

In This Chapter...

- How do you handle difficult board members?
- What if the chair is the problem?
- What is the board's role in mergers and dissolutions?
- What should the board do if the financial picture sours?

Take a group of personalities, put them in charge of a complex organization with sometimes intangible goals, and things are bound to get messy. We have attempted to deal with sticky situations in previous chapters, as the topics have warranted. But there are other common problems boards face that deserve attention. The size, maturity, and structure of your board and your nonprofit will have a lot to do with your range of options. So will those personalities.

If your board has followed much of the advice in this book, your chances for tumultuous moments should decrease. If you have appropriate policies in place (and adhere to them!), educate everyone about financial basics, and hold members to high standards, you are well on your way to a decent volunteer experience. However, in spite of your best efforts, challenging situations can arise that will distract or even derail the board's efforts. We will cover a few of the biggies in this chapter. Hang on, the board doctors are on the way!

How Do You Handle Difficult Members?

It's hard to serve on boards too long without running into at least one unruly, uncooperative, or exasperating member. It's also possible that several members' personalities may clash.

While diversity of perspectives, life experiences, and opinions define a good board, channeling various personalities is a challenge. Scuffles might be public or looming beneath the surface. They might result in someone stomping out of a meeting or quietly disengaging from activities. These behaviors can arise for a variety of reasons:

- Clashing personal agendas

- Dominating board chair

- Disagreements that fester and become conflicts

- Organizational crises, which are breeding grounds for stress

- Members who simply don't like each other

Depending on the situation and the number of members involved, your board might benefit from one of the steps below, or the situation might call for triage.

Establishment of Guiding Principles

Plan to deal with conflicts quickly so they do minimal harm to the board and the organization. When they arise, have an agreed-upon set of ground rules for how members will work together to help mediate the situation. The list can be short and might include some basic etiquette reminders, along with tactics that create a safe space for board interactions to occur. These might be things as simple as "organizational mission over personal agendas" and "respect for others' views." Prolonged distress might prompt the group to discuss how ongoing conflicts will be addressed and, hopefully, resolved. Some of those strategies appear below.

Board Chair Intervention

Assuming that the board chair is not part of the problem, this leader is in a position to mediate a conflict and bring it to resolution, hopefully before it spins out of control. That might mean a facilitated session between the disputing parties, or if the situation warrants it, a conversation among the full group.

The board commitment form can serve as a tool to highlight areas of concern that stray from expectations. That's why it can be helpful for that document to include statements that address decorum, especially respect for each other's viewpoints and respectful listening and communication.

Governance Committee Intervention

If the chair is unable to deal with the situation, the governance committee head, and possibly a committee member, can meet with those involved to mediate a solution.

Executive Director Intervention

In some cases, the executive director can be the best one to resolve a conflict, especially if the board chair is part of the

All's Well that Ends Well

A wealthy board member was used to getting his way. He regularly used his money to steer the organization in his preferred direction. He went so far as to pay for the nonprofit's programs to expand to multiple new sites, all far from this local organization's home base. When his peers finally challenged him, he didn't take kindly to it. He resigned. But he still floated in social circles that touched this nonprofit. He heard about its progress and its needs. After a few years, he began to contribute again and became one of its most generous donors.

Inspiration

problem (more on that topic follows). Depending on who is involved in the situation, a visionary, charismatic executive can be an important voice of reason and refocus attention on the betterment of the organization.

Objective Party

If the organization has ample funds or can get a grant to cover the costs, hiring a mediator or coach can be a great way to bring in a pair of objective eyes and work with the board to get everyone back in sync. This strategy probably makes the most sense if the conflict involves the board chair or if it has the potential to take a serious toll on the board's productivity.

Documentation

It can also help to keep a record of the member's transgressions. Just as an unhappy supervisor documents an employee's misdeeds, the chair can keep written tabs on particular meetings and conversations taken off-course by an individual. Those specifics can help remind both parties of easily forgotten details, and in the rare case that the behavior leads to legal action, it has been documented.

After using one or all of the interventions suggested above, three outcomes are possible:

- The member or members involved might agree to respect rules of decorum.

- The issues might persist.

- One or more members might resign.

Resignation is not a bad outcome. The organization's mission comes before individual pettiness or agendas. If a board member resigns, make sure to end on a note of thanks. Surely this person has contributed in some positive way, and you don't want that person walking out the door with more bad feelings than necessary.

What If the Chair Is the Problem?

If your chair monopolizes your board's discussions, decisions, or direction, you've likely got the toughest of board issues. There can be a fine line between being a visionary leader and a control freak! This person is a volunteer, for goodness sake, and even some of the ones who are hardest to work with contribute countless hours to our organizations. We don't want to come across as thankless, especially in situations where there is no obvious stand-in for the chair. But a controlling or ineffective board chair can complicate life for the board, the ED, and the organization.

A number of circumstances can bring on such a thorny state of affairs. The most common come when the chair exhibits these traits:

- Long tenure as chair, which can create complacency

- Insufficient leadership skills, resulting in poor management of board meetings or an inability to take the group in new directions

- Wrong reasons for pursuing the post, usually status or ego, as opposed to a passion for mission or giving back to the community

- Dominating personality, inhibiting members' abilities to contribute

- Poor relationship with the ED, which can hamper progress on many fronts

This last point is worth sustained thought. Organizations lose their executive

Healthy Conflict

Not all conflict is bad! When a health services group saw its reserves fall, its dedicated board members felt the pressure. They formed factions around strategies related to next steps: Should they continue to pay bills with reserve funds, or cut existing programs? Members argued forcefully—but respectfully. The wise board chair called a special session that focused on finances exclusively. Before that meeting, he sought the opinions of both sides. He requested large amounts of data from staff. On the date of the special session, all felt that their views had been heard. The group used the data collected and guidance from all sides to help mediate a solution.

Pure Genius!

directors regularly because the chair is difficult and other members stand by and watch the discord. So, if you see your leaders heading for serious problems, bring the issue to your governance committee or to other committed leadership.

None of the steps to resolution, in any of the above scenarios, is easy. We recommend that the governance committee review the chair's performance against a written job description and that any board assessments include opportunities to provide feedback on your leadership.

Maybe the chair cannot commit adequate time, as was previously the case. Or maybe your leader is simply burnt out. Having a key governance committee member talk with the chair can be a good approach, so the chair can see that more than one person has concerns. Sometimes though, those committee members can better spend their time encouraging a veteran member—whether on the governance committee or not—to get involved. A well-selected long-timer can often have the most candid conversation with the chair. That person can reflect upon what has worked for the board in the past and provide perspective on how things might work differently now. If that veteran comes across as grateful for the chair's service and appreciative of the amount of time spent working in that position, the chair is more likely to listen.

A fellow officer can also be the right person to tackle the situation, especially if the chair's demeanor has worsened over time. A vice-chair is in a particularly good position to extend a hand, since that post is often set up to support the chair. The conversation might revolve around a statement like this, "I remember when you began your leadership role, you handled [name the situation] so well. I have noticed a change recently and wonder if there is an issue you'd like to discuss. Are there ways in which I can help?"

If your organization is going through a crisis, it's possible that your chair is internalizing some of that stress. Sometimes it suffices for a chair to talk through the big picture with a trusted peer from the board, or outside of it. If the chair feels unprepared in certain areas or just plain overwhelmed, someone might suggest a governance coach. Training through BoardSource or a local or state nonprofit umbrella organization might also be in order.

Just as with the individual board member, the chair might make an effort to reengage differently or resign. A third outcome might be that the problem persists.

If the above strategies don't work, or if your chair is unwilling to listen in the first place, your board might want to start making waves. They can be gentle at first. Board assessments can, and do, include questions about the chair's leadership, especially as it pertains to that person's relationship with the ED. In general, though, if the governance committee includes questions on an assessment that allow for open-ended responses about board leadership, that feedback is a perfect conversation-starter between the governance committee and the board chair. While it is very difficult to "fire" a chair, your board can use the tactics below to encourage your chair to resign.

How Do You "Fire" a Board Member?

This should truly be a last resort. Boards should make every effort to provide constructive criticism and reasonable second chances. If this sounds like a procedure you'd encounter in a workplace, there is certainly a parallel.

The process of removing a board member begins with the governance committee. You never want the appearance of a dismissal being one person's purview. If that group is regularly on top of all members' activities, everyone will expect that their performances are up for review. No talk of off-loading board members should come out of the blue. In most cases, it's only fair to provide one or two warnings before dismissal is discussed. As usual, the board commitment form can save the day. A well-written document will provide the committee with criteria against which to measure behavior, even if it's "treat your fellow members with respect." Give the non-performer a chance to make amends. Committee members can follow up with scheduled feedback on any progress.

It is appropriate for the governance committee chair to offer resignation as an option for troublesome, absent, or unresponsive members. This is a preferable option to blatant "firing." Resignations enable a member to save face. When you let a board member go, that person will likely still be part of your community, even if that just means talking publicly about the organization. So, every move your board makes carries with it the chance to become community fodder. That's why it's important, no matter what the offense, that the committee and others carry out even the stickiest disciplinary actions with dignity and grace. If someone voluntarily resigns, show some sympathy for the member's arrival at that difficult decision. Close by saying, "Thank you for your service."

Of course, optional resignations do not always do the trick. A committee chair must be prepared to lower the proverbial ax when necessary. This can be a brief conversation. You can use a statement as simple as, "Your schedule doesn't seem to permit you to participate like you did in the past. Board service doesn't seem to be a good fit right now. It may be better for us to find another way for you to be involved in our organization."

Sometimes you might need to be more blunt. That delivery, although hard to execute, can be as simple as, "Since you are unable to fulfill your responsibilities, we have no choice but to ask you to step down." And again, "Thank you for contributions to this organization."

What If a Staff Member Does an "End Run" around the ED?

Things can also go awry if a disgruntled staff member goes directly to the board, bypassing the chain of command on the employee side. Consider this scenario:

Carlos, a board member, volunteers every Thursday evening to prepare meals for your organization's dinner program. Because of this volunteerism, he gets to know some of the staff, including Dan, the program manager. One evening, Dan angrily complains to Carlos about a disagreement and subsequent argument that took place between the ED and himself. The scuffle's subject? The fact that Dan asked (at the last minute) to leave early to see his son's choral concert. As told by Dan, the ED reprimanded him, which Dan believes was unfair. Carlos takes this information back to the board and shares it during an executive session, a meeting that excludes the executive director.

Carlos' behavior is acceptable only in cases of executive embezzlement, sexual harassment, or other unethical behavior, and only as the process is spelled out in the organization's whistleblower policy. Those are rare cases.

Grievance Policy Sample

Grievance procedures outline the course of action that stakeholders must follow to address internal disturbances. Below is some sample language:

All employees will treat others the way they themselves would like to be treated. To that end, employees will act professionally when faced with a matter that is troubling.

This grievance procedure may be used to resolve a troubling matter or if an employee has reason to believe that any personnel policy or benefit has been wrongfully denied him/her, or has been applied in an inconsistent manner. No employee will be penalized formally or informally for voicing a complaint or for using this problem-resolution procedure.

The grievance procedure is as follows: The employee should first address the dispute or disagreement directly with the relevant individual. If the situation is still not satisfactorily resolved,

- An informal complaint may be lodged by bringing the issue to the attention of the supervisor within three calendar days of the incident. The supervisor may suggest remedies, or the complainant will be notified of the response, within three working days of the discussion, unless it is determined by the supervisor that the response should remain confidential (e.g., employee reprimand/suspension, etc.).

- If the problem remains unresolved and the employee chooses to move forward with a formal complaint, the employee will write a memo to the executive director who will respond, in writing, to this complaint, outlining the steps to be taken to correct the problem. This response is to be provided no later than ten days after receipt of the complaint letter.

- If the employee is not satisfied with the executive director's plan for resolution, the complaint may be taken to the board chair in the form of a letter. Within ten days of receiving the letter, the chair will appoint a committee with representation from each party to discuss the complaint. The committee will provide a written explanation of the action to be taken within ten days of this meeting.

- In the case that the complaint is lodged against the ED, the complainant should follow the above procedure, except that, after first attempting to resolve the issue with the ED directly, the complainant should then contact the board chair in writing.

Since staff reports to the executive director and not the board, all board members should follow your grievance policy, which will likely require staff to circle back to the ED and attempt to resolve the situation personally. Otherwise, staff stands to create a tangled web of allegations and reporting lines.

What Should the Board Do When the Financial Picture Sours?

What might your board do if your executive director informs you that a government grant was eliminated due to budget cutbacks, resulting in a 20 percent reduction in revenue? Or what if, for whatever reason, the organization cannot make payroll, pay its rent, or otherwise cover significant expenses? What should the board do?

Some financial crises will come as no surprise. When foundation grant money disappears, for instance, that might happen because the funder has planned to spend down its endowment or because it has announced planned changes to its priority funding areas. When you know that financial difficulties are approaching, your board can work regularly with the ED and other relevant staff to diversify income streams, cut expenses, or just strengthen your overall fundraising program. These strategies should work whether your board foresees dark financial clouds or if you are caught by surprise. Here are a few more approaches:

- Work with the ED and staff to scour the budget for bloated vendor contracts, staffing structures, and even program reductions.

- Form a task force to work with the ED and staff to develop several budget scenarios, say trimming your budget by 10, 20, and 30 percent, so that you are prepared to pull the relevant one, depending on how dire the situation becomes. This approach was discussed under responsive planning in Chapter 9.

- If available, vote on a measure to tap into reserves that will cover shortfalls for a specified period of time. As part of this plan, determine how those reserves will be replenished and by when.

- Partner with the ED to reach out to donors and funders to seek additional support to cover the shortfall. This is typically a very short-term solution that would only appeal to your most loyal supporters.

💡 Assist the staff in securing a line of credit, a tactic that might be harder to execute during times of financial crisis.

💡 Seek guidance specific to your particular financial dilemma. Resources such as the Nonprofit Finance Fund offer highly specialized assistance.

Hopefully your agency will be able to weather the financial storm. Once through it, the board can continue to work with staff to revise or develop a fundraising plan that strives to develop new revenue sources or increase revenues from existing ones. If the financial picture sours and stays that way for a prolonged period, it might be time to explore a merger or even close shop.

What Is the Board's Role During a Merger?

This topic deserves more than a few paragraphs, so seek out other resources if your board is considering a merger. Attorneys, peers who have gone through mergers, and a growing cadre of specialists who help shepherd nonprofits through the complex process are all invaluable. We provide a basic overview here to get you started.

Pure Genius!

The Ever-revolving Funding Door

A small nonprofit was warned two years ahead of time that its major corporate funder would cease its giving. The board chair called an emergency session and launched a multi-year initiative to address the coming shortfall. The board and staff conducted retreats and strategic planning to figure out where they could fill the gap. They developed a new fundraising plan, and the board authorized hiring a development director to help the ED execute the new strategies. The time they spent reconfiguring revenue streams served not only to diversify income but also to catalyze a new level of commitment among the players. The nonprofit came out stronger financially and also improved many governance processes along the way.

Boards, funders, or fellow nonprofits might float this option when the going gets tough. But the merger process doesn't let anyone off the hook, not right away at least: The process can take years and requires money and serious dedication. It does not necessarily result in an agency that is greater than the sum of its pieces. Alternatives include collaborating on specific programs, sharing administrative functions, or dissolving to become offspring to a parent organization. Then there's the option to dissolve entirely and cease operations altogether (described in the following section).

If your board has explored the above options with a merger expert—found at consulting firms and some nonprofit umbrella organizations—and decides to move forward, you can expect these general steps:

- Explore possible partners. You can help your ED pinpoint an ideal merger partner. Options tend to focus on nonprofits with complementary missions, such as an arts education program and a community arts center. Members can help initiate preliminary conversations with leadership or contacts at the targeted organizations.

- Delve into the details. Typically, the chair, ED, and another member or two examine the two organizations' finances, program offerings, future funding prospects, and cultures. All of these items must be viewed favorably by both parties for talks to proceed.

- Put it in writing. A formal merger agreement will focus on end-stage logistics: board structure and chair, staffing, mission, corporate structure, program offerings and location(s), financial considerations, and timeline.

- Make it legal. Attorneys will put the written agreements into a formal document and file it with appropriate government agencies. Votes must be taken on both sides to either merge into a new organization or dissolve one organization into the other, the latter being more common. Your attorney can also assist with any notifications required at the federal, state, or local levels.

IRS May Come Knocking

In the case of dissolution, as with most types of nonprofit debt, board members are typically protected by law from personal liability. But, if your organization fails to withhold and/or deposit payroll or other federal taxes, be forewarned that the IRS may come knocking on your home door! This is one obligation where individual board members may have to use funds from their personal piggy banks to settle the debt. Personal liability would depend on the board member's knowledge of and involvement in the failure to pay taxes. The moral of this story: Be sure that payroll and other government taxes are up-to-date.

WATCH OUT!

💡 Integrate and showcase. It's critical to have a plan early on that highlights the benefits of the merger to the community. Often, new funders, clients, and partnerships emerge out of a well-communicated merger. All the while, staff and board get busy melding the operations and cultures of the two groups.

Some funders will provide money for the planning, execution, and even the transition period after a merger has occurred.

What Is the Board's Role When an Organization Dissolves?

This is another painful topic for most boards. After you and your peers have poured your time, energy, and money into an organization, it can be painful for everyone to dissolve it. Of course, staff and clients are affected, too. The most important points are these: 1) The board plays a very important role in a dissolution, and 2) an attorney's help is a must. Below is a short list of items that need to happen and the board's role in each.

Examine financial and legal obligations with an expert. An attorney, who might assist pro bono, can help you assess close-out strategies for your building, leased equipment, grant monies, and taxes.

💡 Comply with your bylaws and articles of incorporation. Follow any stated dissolution provisions, including the number of votes needed to proceed. Carefully document all steps as they occur.

🔖 Notify the state and the IRS. State requirements vary but often include a formal resolution and plan. The IRS will learn of your intentions via the Form 990, which has a check-off box confirming dissolution. The IRS also requires the value of assets and how they were distributed.

🔖 Meet with staff. Board member(s) might attend a staff meeting to help the ED share reasons for the dissolution, a timeline, and how long employees can expect to draw salaries.

🔖 Meet with clients. Board members can also participate in any meetings held with clients to share the news and assist with transitioning them to new service providers.

🔖 Reach out to the community. The chair and ED might co-author a dissolution letter that goes to funders, clients, and other stakeholders. Your website and any social media vehicles should also reflect the news. Be sure to highlight your organization's successes over the years.

🔖 Repay any debts. Working with counsel, the treasurer and ED should identify all outstanding debt and create repayment plans. Notify all vendors and creditors about the pending dissolution.

🔖 Distribute remaining assets. Any remaining assets must often go to another nonprofit agency. In fact, the IRS will ask if anyone with an interest in the dissolving organization will be working or gaining financially from an organization that will receive assets from the dissolved organization.

Don't hesitate to seek legal counsel in the case of dissolution—or any other crisis situation. The resources spent on that advice could end up saving your board even more money—and added stress—down the line. If legal advice doesn't apply, you might require consulting, coaching, accounting, or other professional assistance. Board members of small nonprofits, whose budgets might not allow for consistent professional help, can pool some of their own financial resources or seek pro bono assistance from a trusted source. In any case, don't skimp when your organization is at stake.

To Summarize...

- The board must deal with conflicts quickly so that they do minimal harm to the board and the organization.

- When things go awry, the board's role is crucial to helping resolve the situation satisfactorily. The board needs to be an active partner during these times.

- Written policies and procedures can save time and headaches when crises emerge.

- Don't hesitate to seek the guidance of an attorney when your board is uncertain of next steps in a crisis.

Chapter 27

Board Culture: Boards Are People Too

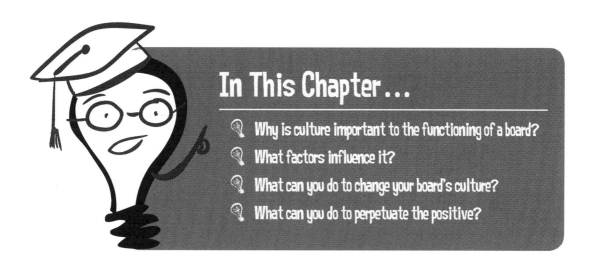

In This Chapter...

- Why is culture important to the functioning of a board?
- What factors influence it?
- What can you do to change your board's culture?
- What can you do to perpetuate the positive?

Human dynamics can lift a board to unimagined heights...or send it hurtling to a fiery crash. Most won't experience either extreme, but it's important to know what helps shape the dynamic. We thought we'd end with some thoughts about culture, because when it comes to your satisfaction with your board service, it is one of the most important—and least discussed—topics.

Board service provides endless issues to debate and a roomful of individual compasses to align. And of course, you're bound to run into that rogue individual or two. Or a tired few. Or a whole group that is simply distracted by their busy lives. Put all of those personality issues together with the fact that boards and staff must regularly examine their relationship to each other. . . and you get a rather complicated animal. So let's close with some thoughts about why culture matters, what influences it, and what you can do to change it.

Why Does the Culture of a Board Matter?

Many of the actions a board takes are influenced greatly by its dynamics. Since a board's work is so multifaceted, its culture is often defined by:

- Values

- Traditions

- Assumptions

- Beliefs

Case in point: a board with an underperforming ED and a history of leadership turnover might be quicker to fire that ED than one with a history of encouraging professional development. The "firing" board might have come to its decision based on a culture of impatience, unrealistically high standards, or—if the firing is warranted—a willingness to act decisively. The "skills-building" board might operate in a culture of professional growth, or a belief that dismissing staff is bad for the organization or not worth the drama. You can see that either of these cultures has both beneficial and potentially harmful components.

Culture matters on two levels: It's a key ingredient in a successful group venture, and it's central to individual participants' enjoyment. Most often, one leads to the other in a prosperous cycle. . . or a bleak decline.

A Real Snoozer

One board of academics sat around a table for years, never bothering to learn its roles or find new members. The result? Board members regularly *dozed* during meetings. Talk about a need for a culture change!

Uninspired

Culture and Success

On some boards, one member's enthusiasm carries the whole group to ever-higher success. An otherwise blasé group of community activists can achieve amazing things under the leadership of a stellar board chair. When one or more people consistently put the mission before their own self-interests, the board as a group takes on the same selfless personality.

And unfortunately, we have seen many groups of energized citizens stifled by an egocentric or disengaged leader, or even a cranky rank-and-file member.

Culture and Happiness

Ideally, a diverse group of people puts personal agendas aside to advance the mission. Members engage in respectful, interesting conversations. They laugh together. They bond. Then there's the other extreme: Board members form factions. Egos prevail. Nothing gets done, and everyone is unhappy.

So, board culture is not psychobabble but a real phenomenon that must be monitored by someone—ideally, more than one person. Rarely do board leaders ask their members: What can we do to make these meetings more productive? More engaging? More beneficial to you? What would you like to learn? How do you learn best? What's currently happening with the board that you'd like to see changed? How can our board become more successful? While some of these questions get addressed through board assessments, their solutions tend to focus more on substance than on culture. That's fine, but without a comfortable environment in place, the group might not even get around to addressing those structural goals.

What Can Influence a Board's Culture?

As complex a subject as culture is, there is really only a handful of factors that influence it. That doesn't mean that it's simple to control!

348 Part 6—Taking the Reins $\bullet$

Organizational Age and Maturity

Organizations in their early stages are typically founder-led and thus tend to take on the personality of that trailblazer. After all, the founder is the organization's greatest cheerleader. Early board members often join because they are Friends of the Founder (FOFs), which perpetuates that person's approach and style.

Founding boards tend to be informal, and the organization's work tends to focus more on programs than governance. As the group matures and creates more policies and procedures, the culture often evolves into one that takes on more structure. The most mature boards lack FOFs, adding diversity and breadth of experience to that increased structure.

Recruitment Strategies

The importance of board recruitment has been talked about throughout this book. We mention it one last time because of its importance in helping transition culture. One way to begin chipping away at a stagnant climate is to diversify the board. By bringing on new perspectives, backgrounds, and beliefs, the culture can begin to change. Members can learn from previous recruiting mistakes and wisely bring on novices with relevant skills and traits.

WATCH OUT!

Passion and Ration Don't Always Mix

Under the influence of a founder, the culture that emerged in one nonprofit was one of austerity. The belief that staff should be "grateful to have the opportunity to serve clients" dominated conversations. One fallout from this belief was a culture of below-market salaries. The board supported this by approving budgets that provided below-market pay to staff. This slowly began to change when a new ED was hired and new members joined the board. While it took a couple of years, the culture began to shift from one of austerity to the belief that the agency had to raise more funds in order to pay staff appropriately.

"But We've Always Done It This Way..."

Major shifts in culture can take a year, two years, or more. One member sat on a board whose mission she loved. Yet, when rank-and-file members suggested new ideas, leaders loved to say, "But we've always done it this way...." Our heroine was patient—but persistent. She worked within the existing culture first. Then she found an ally and worked to garner more and more support for her ideas. She was thrilled when her passion for the cause finally matched her passion for the board. It took a few years but was worth the wait.

Perspiration

Earth-shattering Events

Often it's a jarring incident that forces board culture to change: the founder's retirement or death, a significant change in finances, the firing of an ineffective or dishonest ED. The effect on the board can be immediate, or it might take years for the change to become evident.

Board and ED Leadership

The health of a board's culture will largely be dependent on board and ED leadership and the ability of those leaders to evolve with changing organizational needs. If this pair is willing to push for change, build consensus, make hard decisions, and take action, your board will possess a very different culture than one that lets its problems languish.

Who Can Change a Board's Culture?

It takes a very determined group to change the culture. It also takes a very deliberate decision to intentionally shake things up, diversify, and lift everyone to new heights. It might take months or years to notice a perceptible difference, especially if it means filling or turning over numerous seats. But, a change in culture can be one of the more tangible marks you can make on your board itself.

The ED

The ED should be very involved in helping shape the board's culture. Why? Because an exciting vision, articulated by a charismatic ED, can create energy that translates into board member engagement. Since EDs tend to help select the board chair and committee chairs, this person also has a direct influence on board leadership. Many EDs also help identify and recommend potential new members, which increases that influence many times over.

The Board Chair

Chairs can have the greatest impact on the culture of a board—if they choose to utilize it. Some do not. They look to the ED to set the tone, and that might work just fine. But boards with an inspiring ED *and* chair who work in tandem can create a magical environment where high expectations are met with regular enthusiasm.

What steps can a chair take to help nurture this kind of climate? We have focused on the chair as the most influential piece of the board equation, and that holds true for culture, too. It's worth a quick review of the most important jobs a chair can perform, since all contribute to board culture:

- Create a strong working partnership with the ED.

- Hold board members accountable, so that the group works toward continuous improvement. This is where the various policies and board commitment form come in handy!

- Create an environment where everyone's voice is heard, respected, and valued.

- Make board leadership a regular topic of conversation, during candidate interviews, at orientation, during meetings, and with individual board members.

- Focus the board on mission.

- Make sure that the board understands its roles—and doesn't micromanage staff or activities.

Food for Thought

Food can help nurture a positive, supportive culture. It can be a long haul to sit through a board meeting with nothing to eat or drink. Snacks, drinks, even potlucks have become tradition at many board meetings. Suggest one—or all—of them!

IMPORTANT!

🕯 Coordinate and plan ways for the board to socialize and get to know one another outside of the boardroom.

🕯 Manage founder transitions so the board's culture maintains a semblance of the founder's fingerprint without enabling that departing trailblazer to unduly influence the group.

Governance Committee Members

After reading this book, you might think that governance is the only committee worth its keep! Not true, however, this group does have the most direct impact on both governance and culture. It really can help create a board that is a worthwhile place to volunteer.

Individual Members

Members can be diligent about putting principles over personalities. That sounds simple enough, but executing this core concept must be a continual work in progress. There's a fine line between making the most of your board experience through expanded networks and opportunities, and putting those things above the work at hand.

A few other key items that you can do:

🕯 Be open to other viewpoints and perspectives.

🕯 Volunteer to be on the governance or nominating committee and make sure culture is a regular topic of discussion. Recruit candidates who are likely to move the culture in the right direction, however the committee has defined it.

🕯 If possible, approach the board chair and possibly the ED with concerns about the board, its culture, and its operations. Recommend changes.

🕯 If the board is not being led effectively, step up and lead!

🕯 Build board community and host a get-together at your home or elsewhere to help board members get to know one another better.

- Champion the issue that you feel would most impact the culture. Suggest a task force or other small group, if necessary, to move it along. Research and relay examples of other boards working well in this area. See the sidebar on the next page for an example.

Why End with a Chapter on Culture?

This topic is simply not discussed enough in boardrooms.

And it is critical to boards' success.

By definition, your service on a board is inextricably tied to a group of fellow members. You can collectively choose to slog through meetings and accomplish the bare minimum, running home as soon as they adjourn. Or you can take the lead—no matter how new you are—and inject some pizzazz into your next gathering.

You don't need to be an extrovert to gain momentum. You don't need to make a speech to the group. You don't need to propose a radical new undertaking. You can simply start a quiet, consistent drumbeat with the most mundane tactics:

- Suggest that members begin a meeting by going around the room and telling others something the group doesn't know about them. This is a great way to encourage personalities to emerge from anyone who is straight-laced at meetings.

- Bring a snack or dessert for the group, and when someone thanks you for it, ask whether that person might like to take a turn for the next meeting. You know what they say about breaking bread with others....

- Set a high bar. Advocate that the group learn a new skill, tighten its knowledge of a particular subject, or challenge itself to meet specific fundraising, attendance, or other goals.

- Encourage inclusiveness. If you plan to attend a relevant workshop, invite others to join you.

Cultural Clues

The more items below you can check, the better you should feel about your board's culture.

- ❏ Is communication respectful, inclusive, and engaged?

- ❏ Is healthy debate permitted and even encouraged?

- ❏ Does the board get the information it needs?

- ❏ Are decisions made via consensus whenever possible?

- ❏ Does the group carefully consider the ED's recommendations before approving them?

- ❏ Is accountability enforced by either the chair or governance committee?

- ❏ Are meeting agendas engaging, educational, and focused on decision points?

- ❏ Do board members come to meetings prepared?

- ❏ Do meetings start and end on time?

- ❏ Is the board diverse enough to ensure varying perspectives are heard?

- ❏ Does the board have the bench strength to tackle issues with expertise and confidence?

- ❏ Is there a board leadership pipeline?

- ❏ Is the board partnering with staff to advance the mission?

- ❏ Does the mission guide the board's actions, as opposed to personal agendas?

- ❏ Is there a little humor, laughter, and food at each meeting?

Your approach will differ depending on the existing culture. Some boards operate in a very business-like setting, while others are more informal. But never let that veneer make you feel boxed in. You might be surprised how many boards made up of businesspeople relish the idea of letting down their proverbial hair. We have seen those groups engage in fierce fundraising contests—with only gold stickers as rewards! We have also seen them perform skits, and really ham it up, in role plays that let them improve their jobs as community advocates.

Less polished boards can also take on new lives: Even the most grassroots groups can achieve incredible new things. . . and it doesn't have to mean that they surrender culture. We have seen groups in their jeans and T-shirts learning, doing, and achieving things usually attributed to much more "professional" boards. There's nothing like seeing a grassroots group commit to boning up on finances or raising the bar on their recruitment criteria. The sky's the limit!

That's really the point of this chapter, and of this book. Board service is what you make of it. The more you put into it, the more you will get—in enjoyment, in relationships, in service to your community. Unlike your family, unlike your workplace in most cases, board service enables you to engage in a culture *of your choosing*. What a privilege!

Most of us simply want to make a difference. We want to do so in an ethical, accountable, high-achieving environment. If that includes a little fun, friendship, and shared food along the way, most of us won't complain. So, let your board take you on a collective journey that results in tangible benefits to your community. There's nothing better.

To Summarize...

- Culture matters to the success of your board and each member's happiness.

- Board culture is often defined and influenced by values, traditions, assumptions, and beliefs.

- The group should prioritize principles over personalities.

- The climate can change for the better if those changes are intentional and sustained.

- *You* can propel your board by nurturing sound ethics, community, and camaraderie.

Sample Board Commitment Form

Think of this form in terms of a job description. Consider using it to educate prospective members about your board's expectations. Then, ask members to sign it annually as a sign of their continued commitment. Each board's text will differ, depending on your individual group's expectations.

ABC Organization
Board Commitment Form

As a member of the ABC Organization's board of directors, I agree to support the mission of the organization. I further agree that I will meet the following expectations:

◆ To oversee the programmatic and fiscal well being of the organization, including:

❑ Review and adoption of policies and programs that further the mission of ABC Organization

❑ Review and approval of the annual budget

❑ Work with staff and volunteers to produce the income required to meet budgeted goals

❑ Recognize that the board of directors partners with ABC Organization's staff in carrying out its mission and programs, which exist to serve ABC's clients

◆ To attend at least XX% [or ___out of ___] of regularly scheduled board meetings and be prepared to participate by reading materials provided prior to the meeting

◆ To serve on at least one committee and actively participate in its work, and seriously consider serving on any task forces that may be established

◆ To make an annual financial contribution during the current fiscal year to ABC Organization *that is meaningful and significant to me**

◆ To participate in fundraising events and secure the interest, service, and financial support of others who appreciate ABC Organization's mission and programs

◆ To seriously consider serving in board leadership positions

◆ To propose candidates who will further ABC Organization's work for election to the board of directors

◆ To agree and adhere to ABC Organization's conflict of interest and other policies and its bylaws

◆ To ensure the confidentiality of all board and committee discussions

◆ To get to know ABC Organization's staff members, volunteers, participants, programs, and activities

◆ To support a culture of respectful dialogue and debate

*In recognition of my responsibility to make an annual financial contribution that is meaningful and significant to me, I pledge to contribute $_____this fiscal year and pay my pledge by [date by which pledge will be fulfilled].

Read, understood, and agreed:

_____

Printed Name   Signature

Date:_____

Sample Board Officer Job Descriptions

Consider using these sample job descriptions as springboards for creating your own.

ABC Organization
Board Officer Job Descriptions

Job Description: Chair of the Board of Directors

Title: Chair

Purpose: The chair ensures that the board of directors fulfills its responsibilities for the governance and fiscal oversight of the organization. The chair is a partner to the executive director, helping the executive director achieve the mission. The chair optimizes the relationship between the board and the executive director.

Term: One year

Responsibilities:

◆ Lead the board and its individual members to provide governance and oversight as required by the organization's bylaws and any applicable laws.

◆ Facilitate meetings of the board of directors and work with the executive director to develop the agenda.

◆ Chair the executive committee and ensure the committee fulfills its duties and responsibilities.

◆ Ensure that the board of directors and its individual members function effectively, interact with staff optimally, and fulfill their respective duties.

◆ Help guide and mediate board actions with respect to organizational priorities and governance concerns.

◆ Serve as the primary board liaison for the executive director.

◆ Oversee an annual performance evaluation of the executive director.

◆ Encourage the board's role in strategic planning.

◆ Recommend, in partnership with the executive director, committee chairpersons and composition of board committees.

◆ Serve as ex officio member of committees and attend their meetings when possible.

◆ Ensure that financial planning occurs and financial reports are prepared as required.

◆ Play a leading role in supporting fundraising activities and cultivating a culture of board giving and board engagement in fundraising.

◆ Evaluate annually the performance of the organization in achieving its mission.

◆ Work with the governance committee to conduct board development, improve board effectiveness, recruit board members, and develop board leadership.

◆ Ensure that all policies are up-to-date and adhered to by board, staff, and other stakeholders.

◆ Fulfill such other assignments as assigned by the board.

Job Description:	Vice-Chair of the Board of Directors
Title:	Vice-Chair
Purpose:	The vice-chair works with the chair to ensure that the board of directors fulfills its responsibilities for the governance and fiscal oversight of the organization.
Term:	One year
Responsibilities:	

- ◆ Facilitate board meetings in the absence of the chair.

- ◆ Assist the chair in carrying out assigned responsibilities.

- ◆ Participate in meetings of the executive committee and other committees as assigned.

- ◆ Fulfill such other assignments as assigned by the board.

- ◆ Assume the chair position in the event the chair is unable to complete term of office.

Job Description:	Secretary of the Board of Directors
Title:	Secretary
Purpose:	The secretary works with the chair and executive director to ensure that all actions of the board are properly documented and all required government and legal filings are submitted as required.
Term:	One year
Responsibilities:	

- ◆ Record minutes from each board meeting.

- ◆ Distribute minutes to the board of directors in a timely manner.

◆ Participate in meetings of the executive committee and other committees as assigned.

◆ Work with staff to submit all federal and state filings as required.

◆ Sign legal documents requiring the board secretary's endorsement.

◆ Fulfill such other assignments as assigned by the board.

Job Description: Treasurer of the Board of Directors

Title: Treasurer

Purpose: The treasurer leads the board's fiscal oversight efforts and monitors the financial status of the organization, reporting on both regularly to the board of directors.

Term: One year

Responsibilities:

◆ Provide a regular treasurer's report, including financial statements and an analysis of cash position, to the board of directors.

◆ Review financial statements monthly and offer comments to the executive director.

◆ Chair the finance committee and ensure the committee fulfills its duties and responsibilities.

◆ Work with the finance committee and executive director to select and engage an accounting firm to conduct the annual audit and preparation of the IRS Form 990. Submit the audit contract to the board for approval and execution.

◆ Monitor compliance with the organization's financial policies. Review policies and recommend changes to the board for approval.

◆ Work with the executive director and finance committee to draft the annual budget. With the executive director, present the annual budget to the board of directors.

◆ Participate in executive committee meetings.

◆ Ensure adherence to restrictions on contributed funds.

◆ Protect the organization's tax-exempt status.

◆ Fulfill such other assignments as assigned by the board.

Sample Individual Board Member Fundraising Plan

Copies of the completed form go to the relevant board member, staff-level development officer, and development and governance committee chairs.

ABC Organization
Individual Board Member Fundraising Plan

Board member's name:_____

As a board member, I commit to contribute my own financial resources and to secure financial and in-kind support from others. Below is my plan for reaching both of those goals.

Personal Pledge

I understand that board members are asked to make a contribution to ABC Organization that is significant and meaningful to each of us individually. I personally pledge $2,500 for fiscal year 2016.

I would prefer to make: (please check)

       ☒ one annual payment to be paid by: 3/31/2016

       ☐ quarterly payments

       ☐ monthly payments of $

       ☒ my company will match my gift

Fundraising Development Plan

In addition to my personal pledge of support indicated above, I will fundraise from others through events and direct solicitations.

Fundraising Activity	Date of Activity or Deadline	Personal Financial Goal	Prospective Donors	Comments
Annual Gala & Auction	April 20	$500 in ticket sales	Colleagues	I will also help secure items for the silent auction.
Individual Solicitations	I will host a house party by June 30.	$2,000	Friends, neighbors, family members	
Corporate Solicitations	September 30	$1,500	My employer (ABC Inc.), my spouse's employer (XYZ Corp), and a small business owned by a friend (PQR, LLC)	I will approach three corporations where I have contacts.
Solicitation of Religious Organizations	Application due November 15	$500	My church's Social Action Committee	
Other				
In-kind donations	December 31	$500	Smith Office Supply	Office supplies: paper, printer toner
Total Fundraising Activities		$5,000		

In total during this fiscal year I plan to raise $7,500 in funds through personal contributions and fundraising activities.

I agree to participate in other fundraising activities as needed. I accept this commitment as one of my responsibilities as a board member.

Board Member Signature_____ Date_____

Sample Conflict of Interest Policy

The conflict of interest policy is used for all board members, officers, and key staff. Any employee who negotiates contracts or business for the organization should sign this policy. All relevant parties complete and sign a new policy form annually. The sample below was developed using templates from Calvary Women's Services and the IRS. To view a sample document from the IRS, see irs.gov/instructions/i1023/ar03.html.

Note: This is a sample only. Ask an attorney to review your draft before finalizing it for use in your organization.

ABC Organization
Conflict of Interest Policy

Purpose

ABC organization is a nonprofit organization whose board members, officers, and employees are chosen to serve the public purpose to which this organization is dedicated. The purpose of this policy is to protect ABC Organization when the organization is contemplating entering into a transaction or arrangement that might benefit the private interest of a board member, officer, or key employee or might result in a possible excess benefit transaction. This policy is intended to supplement but not replace any applicable state and federal laws governing conflict of interest that are applicable to nonprofit and charitable organizations.

Definitions

1. *Interested person:* Any board member, officer, member of a committee with governing board-delegated powers, or key employee who has direct or indirect financial interest as defined below.

2. *Financial interest:* A person who has, directly or indirectly, through business, investment, or family one or more of the following:

◆ An ownership or investment interest in any entity with which ABC Organization has a transaction or arrangement,

◆ A compensation arrangement with ABC Organization or with any entity or individual with which the organization has a transaction or arrangement, or

◆ A potential ownership or investment interest in, or compensation arrangement with, any entity or individual with which ABC Organization is negotiating a transaction or arrangement.

Compensation includes direct and indirect remuneration as well as gifts or favors that are not insubstantial.

A financial interest is not necessarily a conflict of interest. A person who has a financial interest may have a conflict of interest only if the appropriate governing board or committee decides that a conflict of interest exists.

Disclosure & Procedures

1. *Duty to disclose.* In connection with any actual or possible conflict of interest, an interested person must disclose the existence of the financial interest and be given the opportunity to disclose all material facts to the directors and members of committees with governing board-delegated powers considering the proposed transaction or arrangement.

2. *Procedure.*

   ◆ No interested person may vote, be present at any vote, lobby on the matter, or be counted in determining the existence of a quorum at the meeting of the board of directors at which such matter is voted on.

   ◆ Any transaction in which an interested person has a financial or personal interest shall be duly approved by noninterested or connected members of the board as being in the best interests of the organization.

◆ Any payments or other benefits resulting to the interested board member, officer, or key employee shall be reasonable and shall not exceed fair market value.

Compensation & Loans

No members of the board, including its officers, shall receive compensation, directly or indirectly, from ABC Organization for their board service.

ABC Organization shall not make loans to its board members, officers, or key employees.

An interested person may make a loan to ABC Organization but the loan's terms and conditions must be reviewed and approved by the full board.

Violations of the Conflict of Interest Policy

If the governing board or committee has reasonable cause to believe an interested person has failed to disclose actual or possible conflicts of interest, it shall inform the member of the basis for such belief and afford the member an opportunity to explain the alleged failure to disclose.

If, after hearing the interested person's response and after making further investigation as warranted by the circumstances, the governing board or committee determines the member has failed to disclose an actual or possible conflict of interest, it shall take appropriate disciplinary and corrective action.

Records of Proceedings

The minutes of the governing board and all committees with board-delegated powers shall contain:

◆ The names of the persons who disclosed or otherwise were found to have a financial interest in connection with an actual or possible conflict of interest, the nature of the financial interest, any action taken to determine whether a conflict of interest was present, and the governing board's or committee's decision as to whether a conflict of interest in fact existed.

◆ The names of the persons who were present for discussions and votes relating to the transaction or arrangement, the content of the discussion, including any alternatives to the proposed transaction or arrangement, and a record of any votes taken in connection with the proceedings.

Attestation and Disclosures

I affirm that I:

◆ Have received a copy of the conflict of interest policy,

◆ Have read and understand the policy,

◆ Agree to comply with the policy,

◆ Will submit a listing of all corporations, partnerships, associations, or other organizations for which I am an officer, director, trustee, partner, or employee, and I will describe my affiliation with such entities,

◆ Will submit a list of any proposed, existing, and/or past business dealings between ABC Organization and myself, my family members, and/or the above entities,

◆ Will submit a list of any other relationships, arrangements, transactions, or matters that could create a conflict of interest or the appearance of conflict,

◆ Understand that ABC Organization is a tax-exempt, charitable organization and in order to maintain its federal tax exemption, it must engage primarily in activities that accomplish one or more of its tax-exempt purposes.

Print Name:_____

Signature:_____

Title/Position with ABC Organization:_____

Date:_____

Sample Document Management, Retention, and Destruction Policy

The information contained here is not comprehensive; it may list documents unrelated to your organization or it may not include documents or records that are relevant to your nonprofit. This sample provides a starting point for items that are typically included in this policy and their suggested retention periods. Seek legal advice before your board reviews and approves such a policy.

When implementing this policy, list the location where each document can be found. If stored electronically, cite where each file may be accessed on a computer drive or in cloud storage. It's also useful to include a column that shows the next review date for a document or record; this makes the policy an effective tool to track compliance and review of key documents.

ABC Organization
Document Management, Retention, and Destruction Policy

Purpose

This policy outlines guidelines for the management, retention, and destruction of ABC Organization records and documents. It identifies how long to retain records and documents and when they are to be destroyed. The policy is designed to prevent the accidental or unintentional destruction of documents and to ensure that the organization remains compliant with all federal and state laws.

Document Management and Retention Timeline

The amount of time that documents must be retained is outlined in the table below. Documents not listed but that are similar to ones listed must be retained for like periods of time.

Document (includes electronic documents)	Retention Period	Location (file cabinet or computer drive/folder)	Next Review or Renewal Date
Incorporation and Other Legal Documents			
Annual reports to secretary of state/ attorney general	Permanently		
Articles of incorporation	Permanently		
Board meeting and board committee minutes	Permanently		
Board policies/resolutions	Permanently		
By-laws	Permanently		
Contracts and leases still in effect	Permanently		
Contracts, mortgages, notes, and leases (expired)	Ten years		
Correspondence (general, includes customers and vendors)	Ten years		
Correspondence (legal and important matters)	Permanently		
Fixed asset records (includes deeds, mortgages, and bills of sale)	Permanently		
IRS application for tax-exempt status (Form 1023)	Permanently		
IRS determination letter	Permanently		
State sales tax exemption letter	Permanently		

Document (includes electronic documents)	Retention Period	Location (file cabinet or computer drive/folder)	Next Review or Renewal Date
Accounting Payroll and Corporate Tax Records			
Annual audits	Permanently		
Bank statements and reconciliations	Ten years		
Cash books	Ten years		
Checks (canceled)	Ten years		
Checks (for important payments, e.g., taxes, purchase of property, special contracts, etc.)	Permanently		
Credit card receipts	Three years		
Depreciation schedules	Permanently		
Duplicate deposit slips	Ten years		
Payroll records and summaries (including payments to pensioners)	Ten years		
Electronic fund transfer documents	Seven years		
Expense analyses/expense distribution schedules	Ten years		
Financial statements (end of year)	Permanently		
Garnishment records	Seven years		

Document (includes electronic documents)	Retention Period	Location (file cabinet or computer drive/folder)	Next Review or Renewal Date
General ledgers and end of year statements	Permanently		
Insurance policies (expired)	Permanently		
Insurance records, current accident reports, claims, policies	Permanently		
Internal audit reports	Three years		
Inventories of products, materials, and supplies	Ten years		
Invoices from customers and vendors	Ten years		
IRS Form 1099s	Seven years		
IRS 990 tax returns	Permanently		
Journal entries	Ten years		
Subsidiary ledgers	Ten years		
Payroll registers	Permanently		
Payroll tax returns	Seven years		
Petty cash vouchers	Three years		
Sales records (e.g., box office, concessions, gift shop)	Ten years		
State unemployment tax records	Permanently		
W-2 statements	Seven years		

Document (includes electronic documents)	Retention Period	Location (file cabinet or computer drive/folder)	Next Review or Renewal Date
Employee Records			
Accident reports and workers' compensation records	Five years		
Employment and termination letters	Permanently		
Employment applications	Three years		
I-9 forms (after termination)	Seven years		
Records relating to promotion, demotion, or discharge (after termination)	Seven years		
Retirement and pension plan documents	Permanently		
Time sheets/cards	Seven years		
Volunteer records	Three years		
Donations and Fundraising			
Donation records of endowment funds and of significant restricted funds	Permanently		
Donor records and acknowledgement letters	Ten years		
Grant applications and contracts (after completion)	Five years		
Legal, Insurance, and Safety Records			
Appraisals	Permanently		

Document (includes electronic documents)	Retention Period	Location (file cabinet or computer drive/folder)	Next Review or Renewal Date
Capital stock and bond records	Permanently		
Contracts and leases still in effect	Permanently		
Contracts, mortgages, notes, and leases (expired)	Ten Years		
Environmental studies	Permanently		
Insurance policies	Permanently		
Real estate documents	Permanently		
Trademark registrations, patents, and copyrights	Permanently		
Client Information			
Client files and intake forms	Five years		

Document and Record Storage and Back-up

The organization's paper records will be stored in a safe, secure, and accessible manner. Electronic documents and information will be backed up and stored in a secure off-site location such as a web-based storage site. Backup and recovery methods must be tested on a regular basis.

Document Destruction

The executive director is responsible for identifying documents and records that have met the required retention period and overseeing their destruction. All paper documents to be destroyed must be shredded.

The executive director will provide the board of directors a listing of all destroyed documents.

In the event of an official investigation or potential lawsuit, all document destruction must cease immediately. Routine destruction shall not be resumed without the written approval of legal counsel or the board of directors.

Compliance

Failure on the part of board members, employees, or contract staff to follow this policy may result in civil and criminal sanctions against ABC Organization and possible disciplinary action against responsible individuals.

The secretary will annually review these procedures with legal counsel or the organization's accountant to ensure that they are in compliance with new or revised laws and regulations. The secretary will work with the executive director to keep the document retention table updated.

Modifications and Amendments

Any modifications or amendments to this policy must be approved by a majority vote of the board of directors.

Sample Whistleblower Protection Policy

This sample policy was developed from the one used by Calvary Women's Services. This policy should be signed by all board members and employees.

Before final board review and approval, ask an attorney to review your policy draft.

ABC Organization
Whistleblower Protection Policy

ABC Organization requires its board members, officers, and employees to observe high standards of business and personal ethics in the conduct of their duties and responsibilities. Board members, officers, and employees of ABC Organization must practice honesty and integrity in fulfilling responsibilities and legal requirements, operating in a manner that supports the organization's tax-exempt status and reputation.

Reporting Violations

It is the responsibility of all board members, officers, and employees to maintain the highest ethical standards and immediately report suspected or actual illegal or improper activity.

ABC Organization's board chair, unless suspected of illegal or improper activity, has specific and exclusive responsibility to investigate all reported violations.

An employee who has a reasonable belief that another employee, board officer, board member, or volunteer has engaged in any illegal or unethical activity, is expected to immediately report such information to the executive director. The executive director must report the issue immediately to the board chair. If the executive director is suspected of illegal or unethical activity, the employee must report the information directly to the board chair.

Board members should bring issues regarding violations and/or suspected illegal or improper activity to the attention of the board chair. If the board chair is involved in such an issue, it should be brought to the attention of the vice-chair or the governance committee chair.

No Retaliation

No board member, officer, or employee who in good faith reports an activity they believe to be illegal or improper shall suffer harassment, retaliation, or adverse employment consequence. An employee who retaliates against someone who has reported a violation in good faith is subject to discipline up to and including termination of employment. This Whistleblower Protection Policy is intended to encourage and enable employees, board members, and officers to raise serious concerns within ABC Organization prior to seeking resolution outside the organization.

Accounting and Auditing Matters

The executive committee of the board of directors shall address all reported concerns or complaints regarding accounting practices, internal controls, or auditing. The board chair shall immediately notify the executive committee of any such complaint and work with the committee until the matter is resolved.

Acting in Good Faith

Anyone filing a complaint concerning a violation or suspected illegal or improper activity must be acting in good faith and have reasonable grounds for believing the information disclosed is illegal or improper. Any allegations that prove not to be substantiated and which prove to have been made maliciously or knowingly to be false will be viewed as a serious disciplinary offense.

Confidentiality

Violations or suspected violations may be submitted on a confidential basis by the complainant or may be submitted anonymously. Reports of violations or suspected violations will be kept confidential to the extent possible, consistent with the need to conduct an adequate investigation.

Handling of Reported Violations

The board chair will notify the sender and acknowledge receipt of the reported violation or suspected illegal or improper activity within five business days. All reports will be promptly investigated and appropriate corrective action will be taken if warranted by the investigation.

My signature below indicates my receipt and understanding of this policy. I also verify that I have been provided with an opportunity to ask questions about the policy.

_____

Signature   Printed Name, Title, and Date

Sample Executive Director Evaluation Template

This is a suggested template to use to evaluate the executive director. Ideally, the evaluation form is divided into sections that rate the ED using a variety of criteria. The best evaluation form combines rating scales with opportunities to comment. The sections and specific criteria that your organization uses will most likely vary from what is presented below; this example is designed as a starting point. The evaluation form should combine standard elements with criteria or even sections that pertain to specific issues, challenges, or activities for a given year. For example, if the organization is in the midst of a capital campaign, the fundraising section will include criteria to evaluate the ED's role in the campaign. The form can both assess progress made toward any goals set the previous year and establish goals for the next twelve months.

ABC Organization
Executive Director Evaluation Template

Organization Performance and Impact	Strongly Agree	Agree	Disagree	Strongly Disagree	Don't Know
a. Works effectively with the board and staff to develop annual strategies and goals to achieve the organization's mission					
b. Works with the board and staff to develop a fundraising plan to achieve financial viability and sustainability					
c. Works with the board and staff to achieve annual organizational goals					

Organization Performance and Impact	Strongly Agree	Agree	Disagree	Strongly Disagree	Don't Know
d. Maintains a working knowledge of significant trends and developments in the organization's field					
e. Works with the board and staff to develop and revise a core set of metrics to measure organizational impact					
f. Provides leadership and guidance to optimize organizational impact					
g. Maintains official records and documents and ensures compliance with all federal, state, and local regulations as required					
h. Ensures that all policies are followed as required					
i. Maintains all organizational insurance policies					
General comments on organizational performance and impact:					

Communication	Strongly Agree	Agree	Disagree	Strongly Disagree	Don't Know
a. Establishes sound working relationships and collaborative agreements with community groups and organizations					

	Strongly Agree	Agree	Disagree	Strongly Disagree	Don't Know
b. Generates awareness and interest in the organization from diverse constituencies such as government agencies, foundations, individuals, corporations, houses of worship, and civic groups					
c. Ensures that the board is kept fully informed on the condition of the organization and all important factors influencing it					

General comments on communication:

Staff Management	Strongly Agree	Agree	Disagree	Strongly Disagree	Don't Know
a. Recruits and leads an effective management team and staff					
b. Ensures that job descriptions are current and regular performance evaluations are conducted for all employees					
c. Ensures compliance with workplace and employment laws as well as organizational personnel policies					
d. Ensures all employees are credentialed or licensed as required					
e. Encourages professional development for all staff					

General comments on staff management:

Fundraising	Strongly Agree	Agree	Disagree	Strongly Disagree	Don't Know
a. Works with the board and staff to annually establish a realistic fundraising plan and goals that adequately support the organization's programs and services					
b. Develops relationships with stakeholders and other constituencies to help ensure financial viability					
c. Makes significant progress toward fundraising goals which results in sufficient funding and support					
d. Effectively manages the board's involvement in fundraising					
General comments on fundraising:					

Finance	Strongly Agree	Agree	Disagree	Strongly Disagree	Don't Know
a. Ensures that financial policies are followed and the organization has sound financial operations					
b. Provides the board with accurate financial information as required and requested					
c. Monitors budget to ensure revenue and expense targets are achieved; communicates to board when issues arise					

d. Works with staff and the board finance committee to draft an annual budget for board review and approval				

General comments on finance:

Board	Strongly Agree	Agree	Disagree	Strongly Disagree	Don't Know
a. Provides effective and appropriate leadership to the board					
b. Partners with the board chair to create agendas and provide leadership to the board					
c. Provides the board with adequate information it needs to perform oversight responsibilities					
d. Works with the board to recruit new members who have skills needed by the organization and board					
e. Ensures all committees are supported by a staff liaison					

General comments on board:

Goals	
a. Achieved goals established during last year's evaluation	[Recommend listing goals from last year in this section. One option is to have the executive committee complete this section, assessing goal progress or achievement, and reporting results to the full board.]

Goals
General comments on goals:
General comments on the executive director's leadership:
Suggested areas for professional development:
Other comments you would like to share about the executive director's performance that were not discussed above:
Goals for the next twelve months: 1. 2. 3. 4. 5.

Signed:

_____

[Insert Name of Board Chair]   Date

Reviewed and Received:

_____

[Insert Name of Executive Director]   Date

Sample Succession Planning Elements

This list of elements is designed to be a framework that you can use to create a customized succession plan for your organization. There are some excellent templates for full plans on the Internet. Look for those from reputable umbrella or consulting organizations, or check with your state nonprofit association for samples to get you started. Succession plans can vary tremendously.

Short-term Absence

This type of absence typically lasts less than three months. Relevant planning items may vary if the absence is just three weeks versus a full three months. Consider including these sections in your plan:

Implementation

Will the entire board, the executive committee, or an ad hoc committee be responsible for implementing the plan as approved by the board?

Personnel

Who on the staff or board will assume the role of interim executive director? If the length of the absence is closer to three months, it might be necessary (if financially realistic) to hire an external person to fill the role. If your organization has a deputy director or another senior staffer, one of them might be the most logical choice.

Salary

If a staff person will fulfill the ED's duties, will pay be increased by a certain percentage or will the individual receive a bonus? If a board member steps into the ED's shoes temporarily, will that person receive any compensation?

Job description

The ED's job description should be outlined in the plan to ensure that all major duties are covered during the absence.

Inventory

Where are key physical and electronic documents located? Where is information kept on these key items: bank and investment account numbers, organizational passwords, safe combinations, and contacts such as bank officers, investment advisors, and even contact information for major grants or government contracts?

Parameters

Are there any restrictions placed on the acting ED's authority? Maybe the board prefers to exclude the acting ED from opening or closing bank accounts, taking out loans on the organization's behalf, or firing or hiring staff without board approval.

Communicate

If the ED is only going on a three-week vacation, no need to communicate the absence widely. In the case of an unplanned absence such as surgery with a long recovery time, outline what you will communicate, how you will communicate it, and to whom.

Oversight

Will the executive committee, board chair, or an ad hoc committee supervise the acting ED?

End date

As part of the implementation process, the board or committee should have a date by which the ED will return to work.

Long-Term Absence

Long-term absences generally last more than three months. The planning is similar to that above, with some nuances. For example, it may not be possible for another staff person to assume the ED role during an absence of say, nine months, and perform their other duties as well.

Finally, for a permanent departure—ED resigns, retires, or is fired—the hiring process can take three to six months. Many of the steps outlined above will apply in this situation, with one main difference: the board will need to begin the process of hiring a new executive director.

Index

Just Released from For the GENIUS Press:

Parenting for the GENIUS is for parents who would rather spend time with their families than read this book. It offers a no-nonsense approach to parenting that presents values you can proudly parent and live by in an accessible and enjoyable way. ***Parenting for the GENIUS*** is a guide for parents of children of all ages. It's a how-to book that supports parents in creating clear and realistic strategies based on reflective practice.

Thomas Edison famously said that "genius is 1 percent inspiration, 99 percent perspiration." Reading ***Fundraising for the GENIUS*** shows that you have the inspiration to master the art and science of fundraising for your nonprofit organization or institution, while the author helps you with the perspiration part by showing you how to dramatically increase your fundraising results. She employs tried-and-true methods used by the most successful nonprofits and institutions, and shows you to develop an integrated fundraising program that allows you to leverage your human and financial resources to create a strong organization.

Just Released from For the GENIUS Press:

Caregiving is a universal concern today. Sooner or later, you will be called to care for a loved one. An aging parent. An ill spouse, partner, friend, or child. And ultimately, you, too, will need additional care. Are you prepared to provide care? To receive care? These are important questions to consider before the caregiving crisis lands on your front porch. *Caregiving for the GENIUS* offers you the motivation, inspiration, and education necessary to be proactive instead of reactive when it comes to caregiving. Prepare to care—pure genius!

In *Retiring for the GENIUS,* we explore YOUR retirement, on YOUR terms. You'll gain a better understanding about what you've accumulated so that you can decide how to use those resources effectively throughout your retirement years. After all, if you don't know how every piece in your financial puzzle fits into your life, how can you build confidence about your financial future?

http://ForTheGENIUS.com

Just Released from For the GENIUS Press:

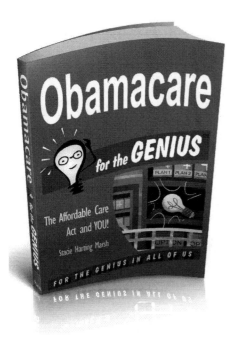

Wondering how Obamacare—the Patient Protection and Affordable Care Act—fits in with your retirement plans? In a nonpartisan approach, the author explores the topic in the full context that gave rise to the Affordable Care Act and how it's transforming the health care landscape. **Obamacare for the GENIUS** will provide a fuller appreciation for how *you* will be impacted, and you will learn key strategies to make the right decisions that impact the health care you and your loved ones receive.

Need to take the next step in your recovery from abuse or an alcoholic family? Ready to try sound, research-based alternative techniques? In **Alternative Healing Beyond Recovery for the Genius** you will find the answers you need!

66 *Let's end abuse! This book moves the cause to fast forward. Read and reap the tremendous insights.* 99

—Mark Victor Hanson, coauthor of *Chicken Soup for the Soul*

http://ForTheGENIUS.com

Made in the USA
Middletown, DE
06 February 2020